ANSELMIAN EXPLORATIONS

Anselmian Explorations

Essays in Philosophical Theology

THOMAS V. MORRIS

UNIVERSITY OF NOTRE DAME PRESS
NOTRE DAME, INDIANA

Copyright © 1987 by
University of Notre Dame Press
Notre Dame, Indiana 46556
All Rights Reserved

Paperback edition 1989
ISBN 0-268-00621-0

Library of Congress Cataloging in Publication Data

Morris, Thomas V.
 Anselmian explorations.

 Bibliography: p.
 1. Philosophical theology. 2. Anselm, Saint,
Archbishop of Canterbury, 1033-1109. I. Title.
BT40.M67   1987   211   86-40239
ISBN 0-268-00616-4

Manufactured in the United States of America

For my parents
HUGH THOMAS MORRIS
THELMA FRANCES MORRIS

In deep gratitude for their
love, support, and encouragement
throughout the years

Contents

Introduction

THESE ARE EXCITING TIMES for philosophical theology. Little more than a decade or two ago the number of professional philosophers actively working and publishing on theological topics was relatively small. The number of such topics commanding their attention was very small indeed. In just the last few years, however, all this has changed dramatically. It is hardly an exaggeration to say that we are in the midst of an explosion of activity in philosophical theology. The concerns of the medievals have been rediscovered and have been connected up with recent developments in logic, metaphysics, and epistemology in surprisingly fruitful ways. Even philosophers with no personal interest in religion have come to appreciate the purely metaphysical and epistemological benefits to be reaped by considering in some detail the claims of traditional theism.

The result of all this renewed interest has been to issue in an exciting period of fertile, creative chaos in contemporary thought about God. The journals now present us with a kaleidoscope of viewpoints on theological questions — theistic, atheistic, agnostic, Boethian, Anselmian, Thomistic, Scotistic, Ockhamistic, Humean, Kantian, Hegelian, Whiteheadian, empiricist, rationalist — practically any of the standard philosophical labels that come to mind can be used to categorize one or another perspective recently brought to bear on some issue or other in philosophical theology. The essays I have brought together in this book represent some of my own first attempts over the past couple of years to enter into this fascinating, manifold contemporary conversation. In them I have addressed, in an exploratory manner, a variety of issues raised by the

1

philosophically rich tradition of Judeo-Christian theology. Neither severally nor jointly do they pretend to any sort of completeness or comprehensiveness with respect to the philosophical domain of that tradition. What they do offer is a variously interconnected set of arguments arising in different ways out of a unified perspective which can, somewhat loosely but appropriately, in two different senses be characterized as Anselmian.

My perspective is Anselmian first of all in the sense of beginning with, and employing at every point, the metaphysically exalted, basic conception of deity articulated with such succinctness and clarity by Anselm. I think of God as a greatest possible, or absolutely perfect, being. It is this side of Anselm's thought which is best known to contemporary philosophers. He was the father of perfect-being theology. He is even said sometimes by overzealous philosophical admirers to have given the world a purely rational way of thinking about God, a way of doing theology completely free of the vagaries and uncertainties of claims to revelation. In this vein, for example, J. L. Tomkinson in a recent article entitled "Divine Sempiternity and A-temporality" purports to apply this side of the Anselmian perspective to the question of whether God should be thought of as a temporal individual. He arrives at a view which he takes to stand in a problematic, and even logically discordant, relation to the biblical portrayal of God, and yet goes on to defend the view against any biblically based objections by simply characterizing biblical data as "irrelevant to philosophical questions."[1] Later on in the article he explains his assumption that:

> The problem . . . of reconciling the results of philosophical theology with the claims of some revelation must always, insofar as philosophical theology is concerned, lie with the advocates of the revelation in question. It is hardly incumbent upon the philospher to demonstrate the compatibility of his findings with whatever may be advanced as the fruit of some revelation. This is an important methodological point. If an analysis of the received concept of God, i.e. as supreme being, leads to a conclusion which seems at odds with those of revelation, the former may claim the

credentials of reason, the analysis being open to inspection by all concerned. If and insofar as the supporting reasoning seems cogent it has a claim on us logically prior to that of the interpretation of some special experience.[2]

Whatever its merits as a piece of rhetoric, this passage presents us with false alternatives — purely rational philosophical theology versus claims to divine revelation or illumination arising out of (presumably from Tomkinson's point of view) idiosyncratic "special experiences." This is not an Anselmian perspective, but more like a very distorted misrepresentation of one half of an Anselmian perspective. Anselm was not just a "perfect-being theologian." He was a *Christian* theologian. One of the central sources of, and controls on, his thinking about God was the general conception of God as a greatest conceivable being. But it was not the only source of and control on his theology. As a Christian theologian, Anselm accepted the documents of the Bible and the traditions of the church as providing vitally important and inviolable standards for theological reflection. This is the other side of Anselm, not quite so widely appreciated in recent times. In the essays of this book I attempt to be Anselmian in this sense as well. Like so many other medieval theologians, Anselm brought a concern for both rational adequacy and biblical integrity to his own theological work. It is thus in this two-fold sense that the exploratory essays of this volume are Anselmian in spirit, or perspective. Unlike many contemporary theologians and numerous contemporary philosophers, I am convinced that such a two-fold perspective is not only possible, but even necessary for arriving at fully adequate results in philosophical theology.

I offer some argument for this reconciliation and mutual interpenetration of perspectives in essay number one, "The God of Abraham, Isaac, and Anselm." There I defend perfect-being theology against various philosophical objections, and present it as being such that it can be fully consistent with a biblical way of thinking about God. I contend that it is rational to think that the God of Anselm *is* the God of Abraham, Isaac, and Jacob, contrary to what many critics have alleged.

Essays two through five treat a related set of problems which arise for the Anselmian theist, as well as for most traditional theists, concerning some important aspects of divine perfection. Many theists hold that God is necessarily good, such that it is impossible that he do evil. Often they also hold that divine goodness can be understood in terms of moral goodness, and yet in other contexts, incline to endorse a libertarian conception of moral agency, a conception which appears to require the possibility of doing evil as well as that of doing good as a condition of being a moral agent at all. The logical problem that arises from this set of views is discussed in "Duty and Divine Goodness," and a new way of understanding the goodness of God is proposed.

But of course the problem of essay two arises only if God is held to be necessarily good in one particular, and nowadays controversial, sense. In "The Necessity of God's Goodness" I clarify what this sense is and examine a number of arguments for and against the claim that, in this problematic sense, God is necessarily good, such that it is metaphysically impossible that any individual who is divine ever do what is evil. A ground for rationally holding this view is then isolated and defended. I suggest that it can be a set of related intuitions operating in an Anselmian framework which can warrant this modal commitment concerning divine goodness.

Essay four, "Perfection and Power," is a short note on the widely alleged conflict between the conception of God as all powerful and the conception of him as unable to sin, a problem discussed briefly in the previous essay. Here I offer a slight new twist to the discussion by making what I think to be an elementary point of great importance surprisingly missed by most critics.

In essays two through four, I defend the view that God is necessarily good in such a way that it can be rational for a theist with certain intuitions to hold the view. But my defense allows that it can be rational for other theists to refrain from adopting this modally exalted conception of divine goodness. For theists who do so refrain, what can be thought about the constancy of the divine character? In essay five, "Properties, Modalities, and God," I develop some widely neglected modalities of property exemplification which can be applied to answering this question. Codifying and explicating at length some modal categories and arguments already alluded to and drawn upon in various ways in essays two, three, and four, I here lay out in detail the modalities of property stability which can be used to understand the dependability of the divine character as well as to provide a strong conception of divine immutability in general which is free of philosophical problems attending the most extreme conceptions of that second-order divine attribute.

Essay six, "On God and Mann: A View of Divine Simplicity," looks at one of the most interesting recent attempts to reformulate the medieval claim that God is utterly simple from a metaphysical point of view, devoid of any sort of ontological complexity or composition whatsoever. In this paper I concentrate on the work of William Mann. I find the notion of divine simplicity as developed by most defenders problematic, and in particular judge Mann's views, interesting as they are, to be unsatisfactory as he has formulated them, and unconvincing even as sympathetically reconstructed. While not rendering an absolute negative judgment on the doctrine of divine simplicity, I suggest that all the assurances about the nature of God it was meant to secure can be had otherwise by carefully delineating the modal features of deity, using the modal notions developed in "Properties, Modalities, and God."

Some interesting claims of contemporary process thought are discussed in "God and the World: A Look at Process Theology." I credit process thinkers with having some genuine insights, but also criticize them for falling into easily avoidable heterodoxy. This essay abstracts from the many details of contemporary process theology some main ideas of significant general import for philosophical theology. First, the neo-classical rejection of the classical conception of God as absolutely immutable, a-temporal, and utterly simple is discussed. Problems are raised which are not mentioned in the other essays that touch on immutability and simplicity. The concerns of process thinkers over these points are appreciated. Then I go on to treat in a much more critical way some well known process views concerning God's creation of the world and the future God has in store for his creatures.

Essay eight picks up the theme of creation and considers the question of whether it can be rational to believe the universe to have been brought into existence *ex nihilo* by God. Far from being anything like a comprehensive look at the idea of creation *ex nihilo*, this little paper serves only to raise a couple of interesting issues any traditional believer in creation *ex nihilo* can find himself confronting.

The scope of the doctrine of creation is viewed in its broadest possible form in essay nine, "Absolute Creation." This paper, originally co-authored with Christopher Menzel, considers the question of whether an ontology inclusive of such necessarily existent abstract objects as properties and propositions can be consonant with the traditional Judeo-Christian outlook, according to which God is the absolute creator of everything which exists distinct from himself. We suggest that a thoroughly theistic ontology is possible which sees even the realm of necessarily existing abstract objects as dependent on God. The picture we adumbrate is a modally updated version of an ancient Augustinian view.

Essay ten, "Necessary Beings," applies the perspective of "Absolute Creation" to a defense of that fascinating form of theistic argument bequeathed to the world by Anselm, the ontological argument for the existence of God. A very intriguing attack on the argument was recently launched by R. Kane in a paper entitled "The Modal Ontological Argument." He claimed that the only sort of defense which can be mounted for a crucial and controversial premise of the argument is such that it leads the Anselmian theist into holding an inconsistent ontology. To show how Kane is wrong I employ the views of "Absolute Creation" and discuss at some length the surprisingly neglected issue of the epistemic status of metaphysical intuitions, so often appealed to in discussion by philosophers, but so seldom examined with any degree of critical scrutiny. I thus pick up and extend the consideration of Anselmian intuitions begun in essay three.

Essays eleven and twelve signal a further broadening of concern from the metaphysical to the epistemological. In "Pascalian Wagering" I look at the notoriously controversial argument for religious belief formulated by the great seventeenth-century French scientist and mathematician Blaise Pascal in his rightly famous *Pensées*. I present it as an argument not for theism *simpliciter*, but for a distinctively Christian theism. It is formulated in such a way as to be completely immune to numerous, otherwise apparently decisive, contemporary objections.

In the last essay, "Rationality and the Christian Revelation," I tackle head on what may be the single greatest philosophical problem for a distinctively Christian theism: explicating and defending the central doctrine of the Incarnation. I focus on the question of whether it can ever be rational to believe the human individual Jesus of Nazareth to have been God Incarnate. I answer in the affirmative, reviewing a number of metaphysical and epistemological concerns along the way, and suggesting that the doctrine is compatible with even the most exalted conception of deity.

Thus, from first to last, these essays are Anselmian in the two-fold sense of seeking to develop an exalted conception of God and striving to attain results altogether consonant with distinctively Christian commitments. This collection is then neither a book about Anselm nor is it a systematic treatise in philosophical theology. It is rather a series of interconnected exploratory efforts, in the spirit of Anselm, to gain a bit of clarity here and there concerning some important theological issues.

I thank all the people who encouraged me to make these essays available together. They were written on a number of different occasions and have been published in earlier versions in a wide variety of places. It has been only in the process of choosing a group for this collection that I have come to a full realization of the nature of the philosophical and theological perspective which unifies them.

I am very grateful to the Department of Philosophy at the University of Notre Dame and its Center for the Philosophy of Religion for providing an Anselmian "best of all possible environments" for my work in philosophical theology. When I received my doctoral degree in December of 1980, I had only the vaguest idea about these subjects — my training lay elsewhere. It is my position at Notre Dame which has allowed me to develop the interests evinced in these essays and to launch the work they represent.

A hearty expression of thanks is due to the National Endowment for the Humanities for their award of a Fellowship for Independent Study and Research, which provided valuable leave time during which this book was completed, and many other projects were begun. I thank also a number of colleagues here and around the country who have read earlier drafts of these papers and whose comments have helped me improve their content (though perhaps they will say, "Not nearly enough"). I should mention in gratitude the names of a few in particular whose occasional comments and criticisms in person or by correspondence have helped me to begin to launch my own thinking about these issues: Frederick Crosson, Thomas P. Flint, Alfred J. Freddoso, Theodore Guleserian, Norman Kretzmann, William Mann, Richard McClelland, Alvin Plantinga, Philip Quinn, Eleonore Stump, Charles Taliaferro, and Allen Wood. And I should single out one colleague for a special word of thanks, a nearly Anselmian co-author of the original version of essay nine and perspicacious critic of almost all the rest, Christopher Menzel.

Lastly, I thank the editors who first published these papers for allowing me to present them again here. The present versions have been altered only in a few respects, so that I might refine some of my arguments and highlight their interconnectedness. The history of the essays is as follows: Essay one first appeared in *Faith and Philosophy* 1 (1984), 177–187, and served as a section of chapter four in my recent book on the doctrine of the Incarnation, *The Logic of God Incarnate* (Ithaca: Cornell University Press, 1986); Essay two was published in the *American Philosophical Quarterly* 21 (1984), 261–268; Essay three has appeared in the *New Scholasticism* 59 (1985), and has been used in chapter five of *The Logic of God Incarnate*. Essay four is previously unpublished; Essay five appeared in the *Philosophical Review* 93 (1984), 35–55; Essay six was published in *Religious Studies* 21 (1985), 299–318; Essay seven was commissioned for a project on process theology, and contains some prose which found its way into chapter nine of *The Logic of God Incarnate*; Essay eight first saw the light of day in the pages of the *International Journal for the Philosophy of Religion* 14 (1983), 233–239; Essay nine is scheduled to appear in the *American Philosophical Quarterly*; Essay ten was published in *Mind* 94 (1985), 263–292. Essay eleven is slated for publication in the *Canadian Journal of Philosophy*, and Essay twelve, which contains material from the Incarnation book, was produced for a conference on Christian Theology in a Post-Christian World, held at Wheaton College in March, 1985. It is due to be published in a volume deriving from that conference.

1

The God of Abraham,
Isaac, and Anselm

WITHIN THE CREATIVE CHAOS of contemporary thought about
God, there is at least one great divide. On one side are those
who work in the a priorist, Anselmian tradition which begins
with a purportedly self-evident conception of God as the greatest possible being. This exalted yet simple conception of deity
is taken to entail all the divine attributes and acts as the single
most important control on philosophical theology. On the other
side of the divide are those who are committed to an a posteriori, empirical, or experiential mode of developing our idea
of God. These theologians most commonly take as their starting point and touchstone for truth the data of religious experience and biblical revelation. Variations on these two very
different procedures for conceptualizing the divine have re-
sulted in a bewildering multiplicity of portrayals of God, ranging from the relatively naive and anthropomorphic to the utterly abstruse and mysterious.

Many philosophers who travel the high road of a priorism
are a bit perplexed by their biblicist colleagues and find the
God of the two testaments something of an embarrassment.
Those who draw their sustenance from the pages of scripture
and the day to day realities of religious experience are for their
part apt to contrast starkly the God of faith with the God of
reason, the God of history with the God of the academy, the
God of Abraham, Isaac, and Jacob with the God of the philosophers, even going so far as to denounce the latter as an
abstract theoretical construct bearing no interesting relation

10

to the true object of religious devotion. One respected Christian theologian, for example, not too long ago proclaimed with great flourish and finality that *"Deus philosophorum* is not the God and Father of our Lord Jesus Christ."[1]

There is a growing number of religious philosophers, however, who are attracted to the Anselmian a priorist conception of God and yet who also take seriously the empirical phenomena of religion. Many of us who find ourselves in this position have in effect internalized the dichotomy and are quite unsure how exactly to relate these two very different ways of thinking about God. Does, for example, one of them deserve our primary allegiance, the other properly serving an ancillary role? Or should one be chosen to the exclusion of the other?

In this essay I want to address the question of whether this deep divide in theology, or perhaps meta-theology, can be bridged. It seems to me that it can be and should be. In particular, I think an interesting *prima facie* case can be made that the God of Anselm *is* the God of the patriarchs. At least this is what I want to suggest. More precisely, I shall argue that under two simple conditions, the very different ways of thinking about God can rationally be held to converge. I hope to show that if the object of worship in the Judeo-Christian tradition is indeed intended to be God—the ultimate reality responsible for the existence and activity of all else—and if the Anselmian conception is coherent, then it can be quite reasonable to hold that the God of Anselm is one and the same as the God of Abraham, Isaac, and Jacob, the God and Father of Jesus the Christ.

I believe that my argument will have some interesting implications for the general question of method in philosophical theology. Within the broad categories of a priori and a posteriori approaches, there are indefinitely many specific methods possible for constructing a conception of God. One of the most neglected and important questions in philosophical theology may be the question of whether there is a way of rationally selecting any one of these possible methods as a method which ought to organize and structure our thinking about God. Some of my conclusions will imply that a broadly Anselmian approach may provide such a method. We shall see that, as it is standardly developed, the Anselmian way of thinking about God is such that if its resultant conception is coherent, or even possibly exemplified, it is guaranteed to be right. That is to say, it will follow both that such a being exists (that the concept *is* exemplified) and that the being is God. Even such a conditional guarantee as this will be sufficient, I think, to recommend the Anselmian method as one we ought to pursue. Yet we shall also see that it cannot be pursued properly in isolation from a posteriori sources such as the data of purported revelations and the deliverances of religious experience.

If I am right, then it very well may be that the only adequate and fully responsible way of developing either of the major competing traditions of theological thinking, the a priori tradition and the a posteriori tradition, is by drawing on the other. Philosophers can no longer discount the data of religious experience. Theologians can no longer ignore all distinctively philosophical arguments about God. And those of us who have been caught in the middle can begin to map out some order amidst the disarray which has characterized recent talk about God.

The Anselmian conception of God is that of a greatest possible, or maximally perfect, being. On this conception, God is thought of as exemplifying necessarily a maximally perfect set of compossible great-making properties. To put it simply, a great-making property is understood to be a property it is intrinsically better to have than to lack. If, for instance, the exemplification of a state of knowledge is of greater intrinsic value than a lack of its exemplification, it will follow that one of the divine attributes is that of being in a state of knowledge. Likewise, if it is better to be omniscient than to be deficient in knowledge, God will be thought of as omniscient, and so forth. Traditionally, the Anselmian description has been understood to entail that God is, among other things, omnipotent, immutable, eternal, and impeccable as well as omniscient.

There are significant advantages to this conception of deity.

For one thing, it can generate an ontological argument for the existence of God. It also appears to be a conception of great simplicity and power. All the divine attributes are unified under the single notion of maximal perfection. And in addition to these obvious benefits, there are less obvious ones as well. Consider for example the doctrine of creation *ex nihilo*, the belief that the entire contingent universe is created by God from nothing. The core of this doctrine is the claim that all things are ontologically dependent on God, that he relies on nothing existing independently of his creative power for the generation of the universe he has brought into being. What is the warrant for this doctrine? Biblical documents are not wholly unambiguous on this issue. There is significant scholarly dispute over whether it is even a biblical doctrine at all. Nor is there anything about religious experience which would clearly warrant this position. But it is entailed by the Anselmian conception of God, as standardly explicated. More precisely, it will follow from the Anselmian conception that if any contingent being, or universe of such beings, exists, it must stand in the relation of being created *ex nihilo*. For the Anselmian God is understood to be omnipotent or almighty. And it is a conceptual truth that an omnipotent or almighty being cannot rely on any independent source for its power or its products. In short, the Anselmian conception of God has the powerful effect of logically integrating a good deal of traditional theology as well as of providing a completely a priori argument for its truth.

Because of its rational appeal and the many benefits it offers, the Anselmian formula has recently experienced a resurgence of popularity among philosophers. But a number of objections can be raised against the claim that it is a correct conception of God. Let us consider a few.

It might be suggested that the property of efficiency is surely the sort of property it is better to have than to lack. A maximally perfect being then will be perfectly efficient in whatever he does. But if any version of the story of evolution is true, the development of organized systems up to the point of the emergence of intelligent and rational life has been as inefficient a process as can be imagined. The story of evolution appears to many to be a tale of the grossest inefficiency on a colossal cosmic scale. The conclusion thus would seem to be forced on us that if the Anselmian conception of God were correct, there would be no maximally efficient being in charge of things, and thus no God. Conversely, it would follow that if there is a God, the Anselmian conception cannot be right. Since theists are committed to there being a deity, they must reject the a priorist account of what God is like.

An argument such as this can at first appear quite reasonable, and even compelling. It may even capture one way in which many people feel that the theory of evolution is incompatible with religious belief. But the flaws of the argument should be evident on even a moment's reflection. First of all, efficiency is always relative to a goal or set of intentions. Before you can know whether a person is efficient in what he is doing, you must know what it is he intends to be doing, what his goals and values are governing the activity he is engaged in. In order to be able to derive from the story of evolution the conclusion that if there is a God in charge of the world, he is grossly inefficient, one would have to know of all the divine goals and values which would be operative in the creation and governance of a world such as ours. Otherwise, it could well be that given what God's intentions are, he has been perfectly efficient in his control over our universe.

Suppose, for example, that in bringing about the existence of a physical universe it was one of God's ultimate goals to bring into being a complexly structured physical system containing an enormous variety of subsystems, including finite, embodied rational agents capable of moral development and spiritual communion with him, and to accomplish all this through the workings of wholly natural mechanisms. It could be argued that to assess the efficiency of God's creative actions in this regard by contemplating the profligacy of evolution alone is misdirected. Many physicists tell us of the astounding unity and simplicity of nature at its most fundamental levels, and this may be enough to launch a profound defense of divine efficiency. What could be more efficient than using the simplest of basic materials to bring about a result of extraordinary complexity?

But even if such a defense should not succeed, the Anselmian view of God could turn back this sort of objection with ease. The argument directed against Anselmianism takes as its major premise an assumption eminently worthy of questioning, the claim that efficiency is a great-making property. What reason do we have to hold that efficiency is a great-making property at all? It is a property which it is *intrinsically* better to have than to lack? What is the property of being efficient, anyway? An efficient person is a person who husbands his energy and time, achieving his goals with as little energy and time as possible. Efficiency is a good property to have if one has limited power or limited time, or both. But apart from such limitations, it is not clear at all that efficiency is the sort of property it is better to have than to lack. On the Anselmian concept of God, he is both omnipotent and eternal, suffering limitations with respect to neither power nor time. So it looks as if there is no good reason to think that efficiency is the sort of property an Anselmian being would have to exemplify. This argument against the Anselmian conception thus does not succeed.

A more important and quite common worry about Anselmianism goes as follows. It is argued that the notion of a greatest possible being makes sense only if there is some single, all encompassing objective scale of value on which every being, actual and possible, can be ranked, with God at the top. But surely, it is insisted, not all things are commensurable with respect to value. It just makes no sense to ask which is of greater intrinsic value, an aardvark or an escalator. The conclusion is then drawn that since there seems to be no such comprehensive scale of value, the Anselmian formula is meaningless.

This objection is well known. And just as well known is the Anselmian rejoinder that the characterization of God as the greatest possible being does not require universal value-commensurability. It does require that every object be value-commensurable with God, but not that every object be so commensurable with every other object. In fact, the Anselmian will often have the same intuitions about this latter claim as his critic. So the Anselmian will characteristically, and most plausibly, hold that God is greater than any other being, and that many other beings are incommensurable with each other.

There is an argument, however, by means of which the critic might be tempted to reject this common response and insist that the Anselmian is logically committed to universal commensurability. The Anselmian is attempting to defend his position by allowing that for some x and some y, God is greater than x, God is greater than y, and x and y are pair-wise incommensurable. Letting the sign '>' represent the predicate 'is greater than' and the sign '$\geq\leq$' stand for 'is greater than, or less than, or equal to', the Anselmian is trying to acknowledge that:

(A): $(\exists x)\,(\exists y)\,((G>x)\ \&\ (G>y)\ \&\ (-(x \geq\leq y)))$

where 'G' denotes God. But for any values of x and y, the following argument can be constructed to show that the first two conjuncts of (A) entail the denial of its third conjunct (letting 'a' and 'b' denote any two individual entities distinct from God):

(1) $G>a$	Assumption
(2) $G>b$	Assumption
(3) $(G>a) \rightarrow (G \geq\leq a)$	1 Addition, def. of '$\geq\leq$'
(4) $(G>b) \rightarrow (G \geq\leq b)$	2 Addition, def. of '$\geq\leq$'
(5) $G \geq\leq a$	1,3 Modus Ponens
(6) $G \geq\leq b$	2,4 Modus Ponens
(7) $a \geq\leq G$	5 Symmetry of '$\geq\leq$'
(8) $a \geq\leq b$	7,6 Transitivity for '$\geq\leq$'

If this argument is cogent, the Anselmian cannot consistently hold that God is greater than every other being, but that many beings are value-incommensurable with each other.

Is the argument sound? It certainly can appear to be. The

inference rules it employs are all standard and truth preserving. The relation of being greater than, less than, or equal to is clearly symmetric. And unlike the relation of being greater than or less than, it can seem to be transitive as well. The relation of being greater than or less than ('> <') can be seen not to be transitive very simply. Obviously, it is symmetric. If a > < b, then b > < a. So if it were transitive, it would be reflexive as well, which it clearly is not. No object is greater or less than itself in intrinsic value. But the relation denoted by '>_<' clearly is reflexive. So it is not on that ground ruled out from being transitive as well as symmetric. But is it after all a transitive relation?

The critic of Anselmianism has taken the original relation under discussion, that of being greater than—a transitive, a-symmetric, and irreflexive relation—and performed a simple operation on it to attain additively a relation composed of it, its converse, and identity, a relation intended to be transitive, symmetric, and reflexive. However, a general proof can be given to show that this operation cannot be relied upon to succeed in producing relations with the desired properties of transitivity as well as symmetry, properties necessary for the critic's argument to go through.

Consider for example a case from set theory. Let '⊃' denote the relation of being a superset of (the converse of the subset relation) and '⊃⊂' denote the transform produced by our critic's general operation, the relation of being a superset of, a subset of, or the same set as. Now consider an argument strictly parallel to the one offered against Anselmianism (where 'G', 'a', and 'b' here denote sets of objects):[2]

(1)	$G \supset a$	Assumption
(2)	$G \supset b$	Assumption
(3)	$(G \supset a) \rightarrow (G \supset\subset a)$	1 Addition, def. of '⊃⊂'
(4)	$(G \supset b) \rightarrow (G \supset\subset b)$	2 Addition, def. of '⊃⊂'
(5)	$G \supset\subset a$	1,3 Modus Ponens
(6)	$G \supset\subset b$	2,4 Modus Ponens
(7)	$a \supset\subset G$	5 Symmetry of '⊃⊂'
(8)	$a \supset\subset b$	7,5 Transitivity for '⊃⊂'

The conclusion in this second argument can be shown diagrammatically not to follow from its assumptions:

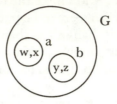

In what is represented by this diagram, it is true that:

(B): $(G \supset a) \ \& \ (G \supset b) \ \& \ (-(a \supseteq\subseteq b))$

which is precisely parallel to what the Anselmian envisions to be the case with respect to certain value rankings concerning God and his creatures, as expressed in (A).

The Anselmian can thus consistently affirm (A), because he can deny that the relation of being greater than, less than, or equal to—the relation of being value-commensurable with—is transitive. In particular, he can ground this denial with a claim that relations of intrinsic value comparison have a property akin to that ascribed to the identity relation of Geach and others. For want of a better name, let us speak of the Value Relativity Thesis, the thesis that for any objects x and y, x is greater than, or less than, or the same in value as y only if there is some feature with respect to which the comparison holds, and some scale on which the ranking can be made. Retaining our previous assignments, and letting the lower case letters 'f', 'g', and 'h' stand in for features or value scales with respect to which a relation of value comparison holds ('f' and 'g' acting as constants, 'h' as a variable), the Anselmian can consistently hold that:

(C): $(G \underset{f}{>} a) \ \& \ (G \underset{g}{>} b) \ \& \ -(\exists h) (a \underset{h}{>\!\!\!<} b)$

The argument against the standard Anselmian position on value commensurability is thus a failure. The Anselmian can quite consistently concur with the common intuition that not all objects are value-commensurable. The Anselmian conception of God thus does not require at this point a position which is clearly false.

There are a number of worries one might have about the notion of intrinsic value being employed here, and about our epistemic access to the value rankings requisite for the Anselmian conception. but I can think of no other *arguments* by means of which this conception of God can be impugned along these lines. So let us then turn our attention in another direction.

There is a simple yet forceful thought experiment which can appear to show the Anselmian description not to capture the properly religious concept of God at all. This is the last of the major objections to Anselmianism I shall consider at any length, because it is the only remaining line of reasoning which I think could be perceived as counting decisively against the a priori view.

Suppose we somehow discovered that a less than Anselmian being, an individual who was very powerful but not strictly omnipotent, very knowledgeable but not literally omniscient, and very dependable but not altogether immutable, etc., had created our universe and was responsible for the existence of intelligent life on earth. Suppose we found that he had been the one to call Abraham out of Ur, to speak to Moses, and to send the prophets. Suppose he had somehow become incarnate in the man Jesus, and that he will be the one responsible for giving eternal bliss to all who are properly related to him. Let him even sustain directly the very existence of the universe moment to moment. Would we rightly on a priori grounds refuse to call him 'God', just because he did not satisfy St. Anselm's precise requirements?

The most common response to this question is to say of course not—it would be absurd to refuse to call such a being 'God'. If he is the being the Bible is about, then Jews and Christians would just be committed to acknowledging him as God, regardless of the requirements of a priorism. Few if any people would doubt whether the Anselmian formula specifies a sufficient condition for deity. But many would deny that it presents a necessary one. And this is what our brief thought experiment could be taken to show. Surely, it might seem, we have here a set of circumstances in which a being would rightly be characterized as God without his satisfying the Anselmian description. I think this would be a common judgment, and that it is on the basis of some such consideration as this that many people reject the a priorist tradition. Our thought experiment can appear to show that Anselm's concept of God just is not the Judeo-Christian concept.

This, however, would be a hasty conclusion to draw. For consider an important feature of the Anselmian conception. As standardly understood, it entails that among the properties of a maximally perfect being is that of being necessarily existent, or existent in every possible world. If the Anselmian conception as a whole is coherent, or more exactly, if maximal perfection is possibly exemplified, then it is necessarily exemplified as well. With this in mind, let us return to our story. Call the less than Anselmian being 'El' and the world in which he accomplishes all those prodigious feats W. If Anselmianism is coherent, the theist who follows Anselm in his way of thinking about God can plausibly hold that an Anselmian being exists in some possible world.[3] But by virtue of being necessary, he exists in every other world as well, including W. Now if in W there is a being who is omnipotent, omniscient, and all the rest, surely El is *not* God, but rather, at best, the vicegerent or deputy of God, a sort of demiurge. If El is less than omnipotent, and there is an omnipotent, omniscient individual, then clearly anything El accomplishes is done only at the good pleasure, or according to the wishes, of the Anselmian being. El would not be the ultimate reality. He would not be God. I think this conclusion is fully in accord with the properly religious usage of 'God' in Judeo-Christian orthodoxy, and in fact that it is a conclusion forced on us by that usage. If the object of worship in the western tradition of theology is intended to be the ultimate reality, and if the Anselmian conception of God is coherent, if maximal perfection is possibly exemplified, then the God of religious devotion is the God of the philosophers.

A number of problems could be raised for what has just been argued. Suppose for example that El was less than Anselmian not by lacking all the maximal perfections but rather by lacking just one or two. He could be fully omnipotent and completely omniscient, but less than wholly immutable, or somewhat short of perfectly just. In that case, he need not be dependent on any other being, even a fully Anselmian one, for his power and deeds. In light of this apparent possibility, my response to the thought experiment might be considered incorrect.

However, this second supposition, unlike our first, could rationally and quite plausibly be judged not to portray a real possibility at all. For it is a commitment of many Anselmians that the divine perfections are all necessarily co-exemplified. Further, I think it is also implicitly held by many that the exemplification of any perfection entails the exemplification of some maximally perfect set of great-making properties. This might even be taken to be the clearly intelligible core of the doctrine of divine simplicity. Note that is not claimed that all great-making properties are necessarily co-exemplified—an obviously false proposition—only that all the divine perfections are. Great-making properties fall into various categories. First, there are those that are degreed and those that are not. Likewise, among degreed properties such as that of being powerful, there are those that have logical maxima, or highest possible degrees, and those that admit of infinite increase.[4] A property which is constituted by the logical maximum of an upwardly bounded, degreed great-making property is a perfection. Clear examples of perfections would be omnipotence and omniscience. If the divine perfections are all necessarily co-exemplified, then the supposition that a being could have some without others conveys an impossibility, and thus can raise no genuine difficulties for the position that the Anselmian description expresses a necessary condition for deity.

It should be noted that the claim that the divine perfections are necessarily co-exemplified is an ontological position which does not entail the epistemological claim that we can deduce the various perfections from each other. Claims to

display entailment relations between conceptually distinct
divine attributes, such as R. G. Swinburne's recent attempts
to deduce God's goodness from his omnipotent freedom and
omniscience, tend to be less than fully convincing.[5] The Anselmian need not hold that this second supposition is *demonstrably* inconsistent, only that what it supposes is in a broadly
logical sense impossible. The existence of an omnipotent and
omniscient, but less than maximally perfect, being may then
be in some sense *conceivable*, but it is not, in a metaphysical
or broadly logical sense, *possible*. So if the Anselmian conception, so understood, is coherent, and is possibly exemplified,
then no less than Anselmian being is God.

However, at this point, an epistemological query could be
raised. Can we not imagine a set of circumstances in which
(1) we have found no logical or metaphysical flaw in the Anselmian conception, and thus on these grounds have good reason
to believe it coherent, but (2) we have a body of strong evidence
that a being, El, exists who created the world, spoke to Moses,
etc. and is not Anselmian, and (3) on all the available and
relevant evidence, we are justified in believing that El is the
ultimate reality in the actual world, and thus is God? In such
circumstances, would not (2) and (3) block any warrant for the
conviction we might otherwise hold in the context of (1), the
conviction that the Anselmian description is both possibly and
actually exemplified, and thus that an Anselmian being is God?

Of course, if we had a strong *proof* that the Anselmian
description is possibly exemplified, then (3) would not be true,
we would not be justified in believing that any less than Anselmian being is is actually the ultimate reality. But short of such
a proof, (2) and (3) could both be true, and thus the most obvious and perhaps otherwise justified conviction the Anselmian
theist would hold in the context of (1) would be overturned.

These are some of the dynamics of the situation. There are
two ways of blocking the Anselmian claim. One would be to
show that conditions (2) and (3) obtain. We would then have
good evidence that maximal perfection is not actually exemplified, and thus good indirect evidence that it is not possibly

exemplified, however coherent the conception might seem, and however plausible the possibility claim might otherwise appear. Unfortunately for non-Anselmians, conditions (2) and (3) clearly do not obtain in our present circumstances. At worst, we could be thought to lack sufficient evidence that maximality is possibly exemplified. And lacking good evidence that there is an Anselmian ultimate reality is quite different from having good evidence that there is a non-Anselmian ultimate. So Anselmianism cannot be circumvented in this way.

The second way to dispose of the a priorist claim would be to show directly an incoherence or inconsistency in the Anselmian conception of deity. This could be done in either of two ways. First, it could be argued that the notion of maximal perfection entails individual properties which are self-contradictory, or not possibly exemplified. This has been tried quite recently, for example, by Morris Lazerowitz.[6] Lazerowitz argues that a perfect being is understood to have infinite properties, and that no such properties can be had. The paradox of omnipotence could also be taken to have the same force: maximal greatness requires omnipotence, and there can be no omnipotent being.

The second strategy would consist in arguing that some two or more properties entailed by maximal perfection are logically incompatible with each other, and so not compossibly exemplified by any single being. This is a common sort of move used against traditional theism. It has been argued in recent years that there is a logical incompatibility between immutability and omniscience, necessary omnipotence and essential goodness, incorporeality and agency, and omniscience and omnipotence, to name a few. If the Anselmian conception could be shown to entail two such incompatible properties, it would be shown not to be a coherent conception.

If this were accomplished, what would follow? That there is no God? No, only that there is no Anselmian being. I have argued that the Anselmian formula provides a necessary condition of deity only if it is coherent and possibly exemplified. That is the condition under which, and under which alone, the ultimate reality will be Anselmian. Otherwise, it could be that there is a less than Anselmian being, such as El, who is the ultimate reality and is a proper object of religious devotion. Or it could be that there is no such being at all.

Is the Anselmian right in thinking there is no incoherence in his specification that God is the greatest possible being? I think it would be extraordinarily difficult, much more difficult than most critics realize, to show Anselmianism to be incoherent. One obvious flaw in most incoherence arguments is that they deal with explications of the divine attributes which some Anselmians may hold but which are not necessary for the Anselmian to espouse. A critic will, for example, present a faulty definition of omnipotence and then go on to show to almost no one's surprise that there cannot be an individual with the property defined. Detractors such as Lazerowitz then hastily conclude that they have shown the conception of a perfect being to be incoherent. And it must be admitted that many theists encourage this sort of thing. Many Anselmians act as if the formula of maximal perfection self-evidently entails all the divine attributes, and even gives us a precise understanding of each of those properties God must have. And surely this is not the case at all.

It is well known that the classical divine attributes are seriously under-determined by the data of religious experience and biblical revelation. What is not as widely recognized, or at least acknowledged, is that there is under-determination in the a priorist tradition as well, such that the core elements of the Anselmian tradition do not yield self-evidently a determinate array of precisely defined attributes. When a certain understanding of omniscience is shown to be incompatible with a particular interpretation of immutability, as Kretzmann once attempted, or with an explication of omnipotence as Blumenfeld has argued, the Anselmian can thank the critic for his help and conclude that those precise versions of the divine attributes are not the ones a maximally perfect being must exemplify.[7] The specific properties an Anselmian God must have are under-determined by the Anselmian formula and by the basic intuitions by means of which it is applied (e.g. in identifying great-making properties).

Of course, Anselmians could not with any legitimacy endlessly exploit this fact. If every attempt to explicate the perfections was an obvious failure, the Anselmian could not responsibly appeal again and again to the "open texture" of his conception of God to evade the obvious conclusion that it is incoherent. But it has been argued by a number of philosophers in recent years that the traditional divine attributes can be seen to be coherent after all—in spite of the many attacks which have been launched against them. I believe this is correct, that there exists at least a strong *prima facie* case for the coherence of the elements of classical theism, and so for the coherence of an a priori conception of deity understood as entailing these elements.[8] If this is right, then there can be a strong *prima facie* case for the God of Abraham, Isaac, and Jacob, if indeed he is God, being the God of Anselm, a maximally perfect being.

There must be controls over philosophical theology, if it is to be anything more than just creative speculation. We can have good reason to believe that one of the controls must be the Anselmian formula. But in light of the open texture of even Anselmianism, it seems that the data of religious experience and purported revelation must function as a control as well. A Christian, for example, need not and in fact should not follow any Anselmian construction of an idea of deity which disallows the possibility of a divine incarnation—the central doctrine of the Christian faith. Such fundamental beliefs as this can rightly act as a control over the specification of what God is like. A priori and a posteriori elements can thus both enter into an articulation of the nature of deity. And neither should be ignored.

2

Duty and Divine Goodness

THROUGHOUT THE HISTORY of western theology, divine goodness has been explicated in a number of different ways. Central
among these is the important religious claim that God is morally good. This form of divine goodness usually is thought to
consist in God's acting always in accordance with universal moral
principles, satisfying without fail moral duties such as truth-
telling and promise-keeping, and engaging in acts of gracious
supererogation. Divine moral goodness is understood basically on the model of human moral goodness. Let us refer to
the part of this conception having to do with duty as 'the duty
model' of divine goodness. According to the common employment of this model, God like us has moral duties, but unlike
us satisfies those duties perfectly.

Now of course, on any reasonable construal of the duty
model, God is not thought to have all and only those moral
duties also had by human beings. We, for example, have a
duty to worship God and be thankful for his benefits. Presumably, he has no such duty. Conversely, in virtue of his exalted role *vis a vis* the entire universe, God may well have duties
shared by no one else, and even of which we have no conception. So divine and human duties presumably diverge. But
it is a widespread and fundamental religious belief that they
must also overlap. If God deigns to communicate with us, he
will speak the truth, in accordance with a universal duty. Likewise, if he makes a promise, he will keep it, consistent with
another general duty. This area of overlap between human and
divine obligation is vital to religious faith. In our ability to
know moral principles which bind human conduct, we have

the ability to anticipate important features of divine activity. The belief that such duties as truth-telling and promise-keeping govern divine conduct grounds the trust the religious believer has in God.

Yet two other common, and also quite important, traditional theistic commitments seem to create a serious logical problem for the duty model of divine goodness. I shall indicate what this problem is, comment on some unsatisfactory attempts to avoid it, and then propose an adequate solution which involves a new account of the way in which the notion of a moral duty can be used to characterize divine action.

I

A great many theists favor a libertarian (agent-causation) analysis of free action. Nearly all are committed to a libertarian account of divine action. At the same time, it is a standard theistic belief that God is necessarily good, that goodness is an essential property of the individual who in fact, and of necessity, is God. If God is necessarily good, and part of what that goodness involves is given by the duty model, then it follows that God necessarily acts in accordance with moral principles. But if this is so, a quite modest libertarian principle will entail that God does not exemplify the kind of freedom requisite for being a moral agent with any duties at all. On this principle it will be logically impossible for any individual to have moral duties he necessarily satisfies. In short, there can be no necessarily good moral agent. It is this entailment which will generate our problem. The logical problem then is one of compatibility among three common theistic commitments: (1) the duty model of divine goodness, (2) a libertarian account of moral freedom, and 3) the claim that God is necessarily good.

Most accounts of free action include a condition to the effect that an act is performed freely only if its agent in some sense *could have done otherwise*. The libertarian characteristically insists on a strong, categorical construal of this condition. It is exceedingly difficult to state an unproblematic formulation of this requirement, but it is clear that it must contain *at least* the relatively modest principle that an agent S performs an act A at a time t freely only if no conditions exist prior to t which render it necessary, or unavoidable, in a broadly logical sense, and by doing so in fact bring it about, that S performs A.[1] Let us refer to this condition as the Principle of Avoidance (PA). The libertarian will insist on conditions a good deal more stringent than PA as well, but at least all forms of the libertarian account of freedom will incorporate this requirement, and it is all that is needed to produce our problem. According to the libertarian, it is only acts satisfying this minimal condition which are free acts. And only free acts are morally characterizable as the satisfaction or violation of duties.

PA is to be understood as specifying that whenever there are *any* conditions prior to the time of an act (other than any immediately efficacious decision or intention of the agent to perform that act) which render it in a broadly logical sense unavoidable, it is not a morally characterizable act. Such an act will be judged not to exemplify the sort of freedom necessary for its being morally assessable. Likewise, any *feature* of an act which is such that it can not be avoided by the agent is not such that the agent is morally responsible for it. And this in particular is relevant to the case of God.

Suppose God promises to bless Abraham. If God necessarily acts in accordance with moral principles, it seems that once the promise is made he is logically bound, bound in such a way as to deprive him of the freedom the libertarian analysis requires of a morally characterizable act. Suppose the promise is made at t to bless Abraham at $t + n$. At that later time is God free to bless and free to refrain from blessing Abraham, all relevant prior conditions remaining the same? If he is free to refrain, he is free to break a promise. But God can be free to break a promise only if there is a possible world in which he does so. And if he is necessarily good, there is no such world. Jonathan Edwards once put this point strongly by saying:

God's absolute promise of any things makes the things promised
necessary, and their failing to take place impossible . . .[2]

There is no possible world containing both a promise of God's
and the everlasting lack of that promise's fulfillment. So when
God blesses Abraham, his act of blessing fails to satisfy PA.
Conditions prior to the time of his act render it necessary, or
unavoidable, in a broadly logical sense that he perform that
act. Thus, on the libertarian analysis, it is not morally
characterizable, and so cannot count as the fulfillment of a
duty. And surely this result of PA will be entirely general. From
the necessity of God's acting in accordance with moral principles, it will follow, for example, that no divine act can possibly
constitute in a moral sense the keeping of a promise, and so
it will follow that God cannot make any promises at all. Likewise, analogous reasoning will show that God cannot act in
such a way as to *morally* satisfy *any* duty, and thus cannot be
such as to have any moral duties at all.[3]

It should be pointed out at this stage that libertarian principles do not entail that God is not in any sense free. Nor do
they entail that by making a promise he would deprive himself
of all freedom with respect to the act promised. God always
has a range of free choice, but the argument is that it is not
such as to ground moral characterization with respect to duty.
For example, if God were to promise to give Abraham a son,
he could not then do otherwise. But suppose that in keeping
his promise he gives Abraham Isaac. The exact way in which
he keeps the promise is such that the could have done otherwise. He could have given Abraham another son. It was in no
sense necessary or unavoidable that he give Abraham Isaac.
There is always this sort of "open texture" to promises and
promise-keeping. This sort of freedom God does have. And
of course God is presumably free with regard to whether he
will ever make such a promise in the first place. So God is free
both to promise and not to promise. Likewise he is free in exactly how he keeps the promise. He lacks freedom only with
respect to whatever feature of a state of affairs or event will
render his actualization of it the keeping of his promise. He

is not free to refrain from bringing it about that something have that particular feature. Given prior conditions, it is necessary or unavoidable in the broadly logical sense that he bring that about. So on the libertarian analysis he is not free in his bringing it about that that feature obtain.

The case of truth-telling may serve to highlight these distinctions. Suppose God chooses to reveal some proposition P at time t. If he is necessarily good, then anything he asserts must be true. He cannot lie. Now according to PA, why can't we count God's telling the truth in uttering P at t as the satisfaction of a moral duty not to lie? Is God free to assert P at t and free to refrain from asserting P at t? Surely circumstances are easily conceivable in which this is so, in which God's revealing P satisfies the Principle of Avoidance. He could have revealed some other true proposition Q instead, or just have chosen not to communicate anything at t. His act of revelation is thus in this sense a free act. But the libertarian principle generates the following argument: At t God freely tells a truth. But there is a sense in which he could not have done otherwise. He could not have asserted intentionally a falsehood at t. This is the morally significant alternative from which he is debarred by his character. And his having such a character is a condition which obtains, and obtains of necessity, prior to t. If he chooses to communicate, God cannot refrain from bringing about that feature of an assertion which alone would render its utterance the satisfaction of a duty not a lie. If he decides to speak, his goodness logically necessitates his telling the truth. So on the libertarian analysis, since he is not free to utter a falsehood knowingly, he does not have the sort of freedom requisite for his uttering a true statement to count as morally characterizable, and thus as the satisfaction of any duty.

This can be put in another way. Those states of affairs which God can actualize fall into two categories—those in which he communicates and those in which he refrains from communicating. It is a simple necessary truth that if he does not communicate, he does not lie. And if he essentially acts in accordance with moral principles, it follows that, necessarily, if he does communicate, he does not lie. Thus it is impossible that God actualize a state of affairs in which he refrains from not lying. Being such that in it God does not lie is the feature of any state of affairs which would render God's actualization of it the satisfaction of a moral duty not to lie. But it is not a feature which God is, in the sense of PA, both free to actualize and free to refrain from actualizing. Thus, at no time does God's not lying satisfying PA.

Again, the libertarian Principle of Avoidance does not impugn the divine freedom in any wholesale way. It just precludes God's having the sort of freedom which is necessary condition of his having moral duties. It seems therefore that a libertarian theist must deny that a necessarily good moral agent is possible, and thus deny that God is necessarily good—where his goodness is at least partially explicated by the duty model—or else reject the duty model of divine goodness.

II

Faced with such a choice, the theist committed both to the position that God is necessarily good and to the duty model of divine goodness might consider re-thinking his account of freedom and moral responsibility. He might consider adopting a general account of moral freedom which will not give rise to this dilemma. However, this way out of our problem is unattractive initially for at least three reasons. First, it is not altogether obvious that even the most lenient compatibilism of any merit will allow an act to count as free and morally significant if at its performance, given the conditions prior to its performance, it is *logically impossible* (in the broadly logical sense) that its agent refrain from doing it. And this is what we have in the case of God's acting in accordance with moral principles. Secondly, even if such an account of freedom is available, it may not be consistent with other standard doctrines of traditional theism concerning human sin, divine pun-

ishment, and the compatibility of God's goodness with the
evil in the world. And finally, with all the data of common
sense and theological backing which can be marshalled in favor
of a libertarian position, the traditional theist will probably
find this resolution of the problem no more attractive than
either horn of the dilemma which otherwise faces him.

In light of this, it can be tempting for the theist to jettison
the duty model altogether. There are other traditional explications of divine goodness available. There is for example in
patristic and medieval theology what we might call 'the plenitude of being model' of divine goodness. According to this
tradition, to attribute goodness to God is to hold that he is
in some sense the fullness of being and the ground of all value.
He is said to have necessarily the maximally perfect set of compossible, ontological great-making properties, construed along
Anselmian lines. Such affirmations clearly constitute a metaphysical rather than a moral explication of God's goodness.

Another understanding of divine goodness may be referred to as 'the benevolence model'. On this model, to say that
God is good is to say that he freely actualizes moral value he
is not obligated to bring about. The goodness of God is thought
of as consisting in divine grace, kindness, mercy, and other
dispositions to something like supererogation. Some philosophers may find this explication alone quite satisfying. It can
seem to circumvent altogether the difficult issue of whether
God has moral duties, and it avoids the sort of metaphysical
assumptions involved in talk about plenitude of being which
nowadays are so dubious to many philosophers and theologians.
So it might appear easy for the libertarian theist to give up
the duty model in order to attain consistency within his overall
position. Either, or both, of these other models may seem to
give him all he needs for a satisfactory explication of divine
goodness.

However, I am afraid that to substitute either or both of
these other models for the duty model would be religiously
unacceptable within any remotely orthodox variant of the
Judeo-Christian tradition. In the biblical tradition, God has

been experienced as one who makes and keeps promises, who enters into covenant relations, and who does not lie. Repeatedly, the biblical authors affirm not only that God is concerned with moral behavior on the part of his people, but also that he himself will surely do justice for them as well. He is presented as engaging in just the sort of behavior to be expected of a perfectly good moral agent. The duty model thus captures an important element in the biblical experience and portrayal of God. As such it seems indispensible to any orthodox account of his character and activity.

If the theist wishes to retain both a libertarian account of moral freedom and the duty model of divine goodness, it can look as if the only way to avoid our logical problem is to abandon the claim that God is good of logical necessity. This can even seem at first to be a relatively attractive way out, since the thesis that God is necessarily good can appear to be in some sense the most remotely theoretical of our three conflicting commitments, the one least supported by the data of experience and reflective common sense. In a recent book,[4] Bruce Reichenbach has argued that the sort of problem I have articulated forces us to conclude that being morally perfect is not one of God's essential properties. Recognizing a distinction between the moral and the metaphysical goodness of God, he holds that the claim that God is good expresses a necessity *de dicto* with respect to both forms of goodness but a necessity *de re* only in the case of metaphysical goodness. It is a necessary condition of deity that an individual be both morally and metaphysically good. It may even be required that he have metaphysical goodness as one of his necessary, or essential, properties. But because of logical incompatibility with PA and the duty model, it cannot be a requisite of deity that an individual be morally good of necessity, or essentially. And of course on the same ground Reichenbach holds that the individual who in fact is God just cannot himself be necessarily good in a moral sense. The conclusion Reichenbach draws then is that the libertarian who holds God to be a moral agent must allow that he is in fact morally good only contingently.

Of course, Reichenbach is not the first philosopher to think that the theist is forced by some logical problem to hold that God's moral goodness is only contingent. In a well known article,[5] Nelson Pike has drawn the same conclusion from a different problem, one allegedly arising between omnipotence and necessary goodness. I have suggested elsewhere that Pike's argument in no way forces the theist to give up the traditional claim that God's moral goodness has the modal status of *de re* necessity.[6] And I think it is even easier to see that the abandonment of necessary goodness is not called for to solve our problem here — primarily because this move will not itself circumvent the problem at all unless other quite radical and unacceptable alterations are made to the traditional concept of God as well.

Reichenbach assumes that if the individual who is God, say, Yahweh, is morally good only contingently, it follows that it is at least possible, in a broadly logical sense, for him to cease being good at any time, by contravening at that time some moral duty. It is only if this entailment holds that Yahweh's being good only contingently would guarantee that his acting in accordance with moral principles could satisfy PA and thus qualify as his moral fulfillment of duties. But, unfortunately, the entailment does not hold. From the fact that a property is contingent for an individual, such that the individual could have existed without ever having it at all, it does not follow that the individual, once he has it, can ever possibly *cease* to have it. God, for example, has now the property of having once spoken to Abraham. He has this property contingently. But even though it is among God's contingent properties, it is not the sort of property he could ever cease to exemplify. This should be clear. And the same will be true for a number of different kinds of contingent properties.[7] It is perfectly compatible with a property's being exemplified contingently that its full mode of exemplification be such that the individual having it cannot cease to have it. So even if God were morally good only contingently, it would not follow straightforwardly that he could ever act in such a way as to cease being perfectly good.

In fact, in the case of God, it can be strictly demonstrated from other divine attributes that if he is ever morally good at any time, even contingently, he can never thereafter cease to be good. As I have advanced proofs of this elsewhere at some length, I shall not rehearse the arguments here.[8] However, I should at least indicate their direction. If God is necessarily omnipotent, and essentially omniscient, it will follow that he cannot possibly cease to be good in a moral sense. The goodness of his character will have a strong stability. So to circumvent our logical problem in Reichenbach's manner, the theist will have to abandon a good deal more than merely the necessity *de re* of God's moral goodness. He will have to relinquish the *de re* necessity of his power and knowledge as well. But even this will not be enough. For even if God's omniscience and omnipotence are among his contingent properties, it is implied by even a modest form of the doctrine of divine immutability that they are not such that the individual who is God could ever cease to have them. And if this is the mode of their contingent exemplification, it also follows that God can never cease to be good. So in order to take Reichenbach's way out, the theist would have to alter the traditional concept of God a great deal more than he might initially expect. He would have to deny the stability of divine power and knowledge in order to arrive at a conception of deity according to which God's acting in concurrence with moral principles could satisfy the libertarian principle PA, and thus count as morally good. I think any theist of remotely orthodox inclinations will find this prospect quite unsatisfactory. So this way out of our problem has little to recommend it, as little as either of the other obvious avenues of escape.

III

I would like to suggest that there is a way of applying the duty model to God which avoids completely the logical problem which otherwise arises between the libertarian account of freedom, the claim that God is necessarily good, and the use of that model as at least a partial explication of what religious people mean to convey when they ascribe goodness to God. Should it be judged successful, there will be no need to give up any of the three commitments which have seemed to form an inconsistent triad. If what I have to suggest is right, employing the duty model as at least a partial explication of divine goodness need not commit one to holding that God actually has any duties at all. A fairly simple distinction will render intelligible this admittedly paradoxical claim.

For a number of years, philosophers have drawn a distinction between following a rule and merely acting in accordance with a rule. Behavior which results from obeying a rule can be distinguished logically from behavior which otherwise accords with that rule, even though the two may be empirically indistinguishable to an observer. Although we cannot appropriate this precise distinction to solve our problem, the application of this sort of distinction to our employment of the duty model of divine goodness is relatively simple and will give us exactly what we need. We can hold that those moral principles which function as either deontically prescriptive or proscriptive for human conduct stand in some other relation to divine conduct. We could even go so far as to claim that they are merely descriptive of the shape of divine activity. But the important difference is as follows. We human beings exist in a state of being *bound* by moral duty. In this state we act under obligation, either satisfying or contravening our duties. Because of his distinctive nature, God does not share our ontological status. Specifically, he does not share our relation to moral principles — that of being bound by some of these principles as duties. Nevertheless, God acts *in accordance with* those principles which would express duties for a moral agent in his relevant circumstances. And he does so necessarily. So although God does not literally have any duties on this construal of the duty model, we still can have well grounded expectations concerning divine conduct by knowing those moral principles which would govern the conduct of a perfect, duty bound moral agent who acted as God in fact does. We understand and anticipate God's activity by analogy with the behavior of a completely good moral agent. And this is an application of analogy in our understanding of God which in no way impedes that understanding. On this application of the duty model, just as much as on its literal employment, we know that if God says that he will do A, then he will do A. We can depend on it. Likewise, if he communicates any proposition, we can be assured that it will be a true one. When we use the duty model in this way, we retain all that is religiously important about it while avoiding the problem a literal application would generate.

A couple of objections to this application of the duty model easily come to mind. First, it might be pointed out that on this interpretation, God can never actually make any promises, since promising generates literal duties. And this surely seems counter-intuitive. Don't traditional theists often talk of "the promises of God"?

There is no substance to this objection. R. L. Franklin has characterized the purpose of promising as "that of committing a man reliably to future acts."[9] God can certainly declare his intention to bless Abraham, thereby committing himself reliably to do so (where 'commiting himself' amounts to intentionally generating justified expectations in his hearers). The libertarian can hold that in making this sort of declaration God is doing something for his creatures with an effect analogous to that of promising, or even that in an analogical sense he is making a promise. In holding that God cannot literally make promises, the libertarian would only be acknowledging in a particular type of case that the relation holding between God and moral principles is different from that holding between us and those moral principles. And so long as God necessarily acts in the way a perfectly good moral agent would act, nothing of religious importance is lost in this difference.

A more substantial objection would go as follows. If God does not actually have any moral duties he satisfies, we have no basis on which to praise him. Praise, according to this line of thought, is appropriate only for acts which satisfy moral duties, and only for agents in so far as they perform such acts. On this understanding of praise, a theology which claims that God can have no duties thereby debars God from ever being praiseworthy.

This objection is based on a very common and mistaken assumption about moral praise. It is the position that fulfillment of duty, and that alone, merits praise. I would argue, on the contrary, that praise is never strictly appropriate for duty satisfactions. The proper response of one moral agent to another when the lattter has done his duty, and when none other than moral considerations obtain, is something weaker than, and distinct from, praise. One who does his duty ought to be morally acknowledged, accepted, or commended by his fellows, not praised. Admittedly, in this world of ours, where duty fulfillment under difficult conditions is somewhat rare, there can be significant social utility in praising such accomplishment. But strictly speaking, praise is morally proper only for acts of supererogation.

God's lacking duties, then, will not amount to his being unworthy of praise. In so far as he actualizes great value he is not bound to bring about, he is worthy of praise. For example, when God "makes a promise," do we praise him for being so good as to keep it? I think not. When he speaks to his people, is he praised for restraining himself from lying? Clearly not. What we praise him for is for condescending to make us promises or communicate with us at all, for deigning to involve himself at all in our small lives. And these are acts of supererogation, not fulfillments of duty.

Are there any costs incurred by employing the duty model in this new analogical manner? It might seem that at least we lose any answer for such questions as "Why does God keep his promises?" or "Why does God do what is morally right?" We can no longer say "Because he ought to." But actually nothing is lost. It can be maintained that as a maximally perfect being, God necessarily acts in accordance with those principles which lesser beings ought to comply with. This is his nature.

And as his activity and nature is, in a less than Cartesian sense, the ground of all possibility, it is impossible that he not so act. We would have a troubling unanswered question about his activity only if it were a contingent fact that his conduct accords perfectly with moral principles. But of course, the traditional theist denies that this is a contingent matter.

IV

One final question remains. In applying the duty model in an analogical manner, are we any longer giving an account of God's *goodness*? Can divine goodness even partially consist in God's acting in accordance with moral principles if none of those principles provides him with moral duties? The most obvious answer to this may seem to be — no. Human action in accord with moral principles can count as the moral satisfaction of duties, because of the nature of the human condition. Our ontological status and our freedom is such that we have duties we can morally fulfill and thereby count as good agents. With the analogical deployment of the duty model, the theist could say that it is not strictly true that God's goodness partly consists in his acting in accordance with moral principles. With this model, we are just explicating part of what religious people usually *mean to convey* when they say that God is good. Strictly speaking, God's non-metaphysical goodness consists only in his disposition to, and effectuation of, supererogatory activity.

But this answer is not forced on the theist. It seems at least possible to argue without absurdity, and with a significant measure of plausibility, that some conditions for goodness vary with the ontological status of the agent concerned. I have referred to both moral and metaphysical goodness in the case of God. It is possible to treat both these sorts of goodness as species of a broader category of what we might call 'axiological goodness'. To be an agent, such as a human being, who gladly engages in deeds of supererogation and freely acts in accordance with moral principles, satisfying moral duties, is to be in a state of axiological goodness. To be an agent such as God who freely engages in acts of grace, or supererogation, but necessarily acts in accordance with moral principles, is to be in the greatest possible state of axiological goodness. It may be held that for human beings, axiological goodness and moral goodness coincide. For God, however, one form of moral goodness (supererogation) is a component of his axiological goodness; whereas another aspect of his axiological goodness is his necessarily acting in accordance with moral principles — not literally a form of moral goodness at all on the libertarian analysis, but on this view a contributing element or aspect of divine axiological goodness.

On this possible view, God's intentionally acting in accordance with what for us are moral principles specifying duties would be sufficient, given his nature and ontological status, for that conduct counting as good, not morally but axiologically. Axiological agency need not be thought of as logically incompatible, on every ontological level, with all forms of necessitation. Brand Blanshard once argued that being determined by the moral law is, unlike being causally determined by prior states of the physical universe, a condition of the highest (i.e. most valuable) sort of freedom.[10] Of course, because of PA the libertarian cannot hold this to be true of moral freedom. But it could be reasonable for the libertarian theist to hold that a form of moral necessitation is compatible with, indeed a condition of, God's being a perfectly good axiological agent, a greater than which is not possible.

With these distinctions in hand, the theist could say that an analogical employment of the duty model is indeed a partial explication of divine goodness. Part of God's goodness does consist in his acting in perfect accord with those principles which would provide duties for a lesser being. This use of the model would be an explication not of God's moral goodness, but of his axiological goodness. When religious people claim that God is morally good, meaning that he acts in accord with moral principles, they are merely using that axiological conception with which they are most familiar, moral goodness, to describe or model an aspect of divinity functionally isomorphic with, though ontologically different from, human goodness. The point of importance here is that either answer to our question could be defended, whichever is preferred. And neither is obviously inimical to traditional theology.

It seems then that a traditional theist can hold to (1) a libertarian analysis of free action, (2) the position that God is necessarily good, and (3) the duty model of divine goodness without incurring any logical inconsistency among these commitments just by employing the duty model in a carefully controlled analogical manner. The resolution of the problem we have examined seems to be attended by no peculiar difficulties of its own, and seems to be perfectly consistent with any broadly orthodox theology in the Judeo-Christian tradition. And as the same problem of logical consistency may arise on any plausible analysis of free action, this new understanding of the duty model of divine goodness may be of importance to any traditional theist, whatever reasonable position he adopts concerning the conditions of moral freedom.

3

The Necessity of God's Goodness

I. The Traditional View

MANY THEISTS, especially those with Anselmian convictions, affirm that God is necessarily good. To be more precise, they hold that the proposition

(1) God is good

expresses *de re* as well as *de dicto* a necessity. It is necessary *de dicto* in virtue of specifying a condition of deity. Goodness is a requisite for holding the divine office, or for having the ontological status of being God. It is also held to express a necessity *de re* because goodness is believed to be an essential property of the individual who in fact, and of necessity, is God. Indeed, the proposition

(2) God is necessarily good

is held by many to express *de dicto* a necessary condition of deity. In order for an individual to be God, it is not enough that he be as a matter of fact good—he must be good *essentially*.

The proposition that goodness is a requirement of deity—as deity is understood in at least the Judeo-Christian tradition—is a relatively uncontroversial conceptual claim. This is due, I think, to the intimate connections which have been forged between the concepts of divinity and worship-worthiness, and the obvious containment of the notion of goodness in the latter. But the stronger traditional claims about necessary goodness are far from uncontroversial. Among the tenets of classical theism are the beliefs that the individual who is God is a necessarily existing entity who exemplifies all of the attributes constitutive of deity as essential properties. He is thus, for example, believed to be necessarily omnipotent, necessarily omniscient, and necessarily good. In recent years, however, a number of philosophers, including some otherwise quite traditional theists, have come to believe that this exalted conception of God goes a bit too far, and thereby falls into logical difficulty. Most locate the problem in the claim that God's goodness is among his essential properties and appear to hold that if only this one modal claim is given up, otherwise intractable problems for theism vanish, leaving the concept of God intact, at least with respect to its modal elements. Many such philosophers are content to allow other divine attributes to be viewed as properties essential to the individual who is God. In this, they often seem to acknowledge the deep religious conviction that nothing could possibly thwart God's power or escape his knowledge. They disavow the *de re* necessity only of God's goodness.

Traditionally, the goodness of God has been understood in two distinct ways. First, there is a conception of what often has been referred to as 'metaphysical goodness'. On this understanding, God's goodness involves his having, in some important and axiologically relevant sense, ontological completeness. He is held to exemplify a maximally perfect set of compossible, ontological great-making properties, construed along Anselmian lines. On the other hand, there is a very different and quite important religious belief that God is good in much the same way as an ideal human moral agent would be. On this view, it is held that God acts in perfect accord with all moral principles relevant to his actions. Along these lines, religious believers often speak of the 'moral goodness' of God.

To my knowledge, no one has found any special problems with the claim that God is necessarily good in the distinctively metaphysical sense. It is only with respect to the other sort of divine goodness, that having to do with agency and moral principles, that significant modal controversy has arisen. In fact, some philosophers who make it a point to assert that God is necessarily good in the metaphysical sense explicitly deny the *de re* necessity of his goodness as an agent.[1]

In order to gain some perspective on this controversy, and to arrive at some sort of assessment of the dispute, let us begin by asking what sorts of considerations can seem to raise special problems for the view that any divine being necessarily acts in perfect accord with all moral principles relevant to his conduct.

II. *Challenges to the Tradition*

For convenience, and in accord with somewhat standard usage, we can refer to the view that any individual who is God exists necessarily (in every possible world) and necessarily exemplifies each of the properties constitutive of deity (such properties as omnipotence, omniscience, and perfect goodness) as 'Anselmianism', or 'the Anselmian conception of God'. A number of well known arguments have been constructed to show that anyone who holds God to be necessarily good will become entangled in logical incoherence if he embraces the other elements of the Anselmian conception as well. More than a decade ago, for example, Lawrence Resnick argued as follows: An Anselmian God would create or allow to exist only a best of all possible worlds. There can be such a world only if there are a number of possible worlds differing in overall value, some worse than others. But a world is possible only if it could be actual. And if God is necessarily good, as well as existent in and responsible for all possible worlds, no less-than-optimal world could be actual. That is to say, given Anselmianism, there are no less-than-optimal possible worlds. But if possible worlds cannot differ in this way in overall value, the notion of a best of all possible worlds loses its sense. And since the existence of such a world is entailed by the Anselmian conception of God, that conception itself is thereby shown to be incoherent.[2]

It is notorious that arguments such as this are, in all epistemic propriety, reversible. The Anselmian could thus begin to counter Resnick's charge by reasoning that precisely because of the evident problem in combining his conception of God with a notion of a best possible world, Anselmianism does not entail that God would create or allow to exist only a best possible world. In fact, many traditional theists have argued on completely independent grounds that the idea of a best possible world is no more coherent than that of a greatest possible integer.[3] And even if on some construal the notion could be made coherent, the assumption that any Anselmian being necessarily would be a universal maximizer of value is itself far from uncontroversial.[4] So Resnick's argument can be said to employ premises a good deal more dubious than any element of the traditional view he means to impugn.

On the basis of such moves, the Anselmian could respond to Resnick that it is entailed by his conception of deity only that God will create a good world. But of course, this is not enough as a response, for the Resnick ploy can be re-introduced here: The notion even of a good possible world depends for its sense on there being a number of possible worlds differing in overall value, some worse than others. But a world is possible only if it could be actual. And if God is *necessarily* good, as well as existent in and responsible for all possible worlds, no less-than-good world could be actual. That is, given Anselmianism, there are no less-than-good possible worlds. But there is an important sense in which 'good' is just as much a comparative concept as 'best', depending for its meaning on possible contrast. So if possible worlds cannot differ in this way in overall value, the notion of even a good possible world loses its sense. And since the Anselmian conception of God entails the existence of such a world, it is thereby shown to be itself an incoherent conception.

Here we have the argument of Resnick considerably strengthened. But the traditional theist has a simple and decisive reply at hand. Given the existence of an Anselmian God, there are no less-than-good worlds which are genuinely possible, in the broadly logical sense. But such worlds are, in an important sense, at least partially *conceivable*. That is, worlds are (at least partially) conceivable which if, *per impossible*, the Anselmian God did not exist, would be possible.[5] A number of these are worlds in which, in the final analysis, the overall condition of God's creatures is less-than-good. The excellence of the actual world, its ultimate overall goodness, is highlighted in its contrast to these *conceivable* worlds. It is in this context that the claim that God will create or allow only a good world has its sense. With these distinctions, which I shall develop a bit more presently, the Anselmian who holds God to be necessarily good can turn back the force of Resnick's argument completely. In this light, his reasoning can be seen to be totally ineffectual as an attack on any careful version of traditional theism.

Far better known than Resnick's argument is Nelson Pike's contention that necessary goodness is incompatible with omnipotence, and so should not be ascribed to God.[6] The sort of reasoning offered by Pike is basically quite simple. Surely, many states of affairs are conceivable which it would be wrong for any rational agent intentionally to bring about. If God were necessarily good, logically unable to violate any moral principle, he would be unable to bring about any such state of affairs. But then, surely this would constitute a limitation on God's power incompatible with his being omnipotent. Further, we might add in suppport of Pike, God would seem thereby to lack a sort of creative power had by many of his creatures. And in that case, it would be absurd to call him omnipotent.

As initially plausible as Pike's argument might seem, it has been as well rebutted as any in the literature. First of all, even if we were convinced that there is an ineliminable logical incompatibility between the properties of omnipotence and necessary goodness, it would not be altogether obvious which one should be relinquished as a divine attribute. This is shown clearly by the case of Peter Geach, who believes there to be such an incompatibility, yet unlike Pike chooses to give up the traditional claim that God is omnipotent, adverting instead to a notion of what he calls 'almightiness' to explicate the nature and extent of divine power in a way obviously compatible with God's being necessarily good.[7]

But what is more important is that Pike's argument fails to provide us with any good reason to think that there is such an incompatibility in the first place. Some criticize him for relying on too simplistic and inadequate an understanding of what the property of omnipotence involves. And it is true that he operates with a very unrefined conception. But the real problem with his argument is that he makes too quick a transition from the claim that a certain sort of state of affairs is (in some sense) conceivable to the stronger assumption that it represents a genuine, broadly logical, possibility. As we have seen, no state of affairs incompatible with the goodness of the Anselmian God will represent, from the theistic point of view, a genuine possibility. In a less than Cartesian sense, the God who is perfectly good is to the Anselmian the ground of all possibility. This is certainly important, for on any standard traditional account of omnipotence, this maximal extent of power is supposed to range over only what is possible. The Anselmian will remind Pike that many impossibilities are consistently describable *to a point*, and in this sense conceivable. Thus, for reasons having nothing to do with theism, we must always carefully distinguish between conceivability and possibility, or at least between partial conceivability and genuine possibility. Something is genuinely possible in the broadly logical sense, and, we might say, in the fullest sense conceivable, only if its actuality would be compatible with all the necessary features of reality, including for example the laws of mathematics. Among those necessary features of reality, the Anselmian will hold the nature of God to be the most important of constraints on what is possible.

So the Anselmian reply to Pike goes as follows.[8] No state of affairs whose actualization would be prohibited to just any moral agent, which would be such that God would be blameworthy in intentionally bringing it about or allowing it, represents a genuine possibility. Thus, on any careful definition of omnipotence, God's inability to actualize such a state of affairs no more detracts from his omnipotence than does his inability to create spherical cubes or objects which are green yet uncolored.[9] And none of God's creatures has the power to trespass beyond the bounds set by the necessities of the divine nature.

In both the argument of Resnick and this response to Pike, we find an important corollary of the Anselmian conception of God brought to light. Such a God is a delimiter of possibilities. If there is a being who exists necessarily, and is necessarily omnipotent, omniscient, and good, than many states of affairs which otherwise would represent genuine possibilities, and which by all non-theistic tests of logic and semantics do represent possibilities, are strictly impossible in the strongest sense. In particular, worlds containing certain sorts or amounts of disvalue or evil are metaphysically ruled out by the nature of God, divinely precluded from the realm of real possibility.

In a recent article entitled "God and Possible Worlds: The Modal Problem of Evil," Theodore Guleserian takes issue with this entailment of Anselmianism.[10] Guleserian points out that there are common modal intuitions, intuitions concerning what is possible, which conflict with Anselmian strictures on possibility. And certainly, this much is undeniable. But Guleserian goes on to argue that when forced to choose between our theistically untutored intuitions and the dictates of Anselmianism, it is more reasonable to follow those intuitions and reject the conception of God with whose implications they conflict. If successfully made out, this contention would undermine the Anselmian solution to Pike's problem, although that is not exactly Guleserian's particular intention. He offers his argument as a general case for jettisoning at least one of the modal attributes ascribed to God by classical theists, and suggests that it is necessary goodness which most obviously should go.

He asks us to engage in a thought experiment. We can easily imagine, he suggests, a single rabbit living in a desert environment, leading a thoroughly wretched, miserable, pain-racked existence. The existence of such a creature is surely conceivable.

And our modal intuitions assure us that, so far, we are dealing with the conception of a genuine possibility. But certainly, if the existence of one such poor creature is possible, so is the existence of a second, and of a third, and so on. Nothing in the conception of one miserable rabbit logically precludes the existence of two or more, or for that matter of any number, however great. The additive expansion of our conception seems on modally solid ground. And as the existence of one wretched rabbit will not logically preclude the sufferings of a horde, there is nothing in the conception of a multitude of such creatures which entails the existence of any other contingent sentient beings not sharing their plight. Guleserian thus concludes that it is possible that a world exist whose only contingent denizens are those myriads of thoroughly miserable creatures. Such a world would contain any amount you like, however great, of disvalue or evil whose existence contributed to no greater or justifying good. If God exists necessarily and, by virtue of his necessary omnipotence and omniscience, would thus be responsible for the features of any possible world which was actual, it follows that he is not necessarily good. For any being who intentionally brought it about or unnecessarily allowed it to be the case that the only other individuals who existed were creatures totally immersed in pain to no good purpose would surely be evil. It is possible for such a world to exist. So it is possible for the individual who is God to be evil. His goodness thus is not among his essential attributes.

Strictly speaking, as Guleserian acknowledges, this argument alone could show at best only that there is a possible world in which God either fails to exist or else lacks at least one of the properties of omnipotence, omniscience, or goodness. It gives us no special reason to pick out goodness as what would be lacking. But Guleserian feels that there is good reason to see necessary goodness as the modal attribute which must be given up. Before I comment on that reason, I should focus on what is particularly interesting in Guleserian's contribution, which otherwise can be seen on close inspection to differ very little in fundamental structure from Pike's reasoning. The dis-

tinctiveness of his argument lies in his emphasis on modal intuitions and how they come into play in the assessment of
Anselmianism.

As we have seen clearly by now, the Anselmian will argue
that if the existence of such a rabbit-world as Guleserian depicts
would in fact be inconsistent with the reality of the Anselmian
God, its conception does not represent a genuine possibility.
It is one of Guleserian's main objectives to counter this sort
of move. He maintains that to rule out the possibility of there
being a wretched rabbit-world on the basis of a belief that
there is a necessary individual who would not allow it is on an
epistemic par with ruling out the possibility of there being any
pink and purple moons by holding there to exist "a necessary
being that would prevent, in every world, the actuality of a
pink and purple moon." He goes on to say that this sort of
thinking would lead "to the bancruptcy [*sic*] of our knowledge
claims about nonactual possibilities."[11] The point seems to be
that any such modal proscription of what our theistically untutored intuitions deem to be possible would be arbitrary, or
otherwise ill-grounded.

But of course the Anselmian restrictions on the realm of real
possibility are far from arbitrary. They are grounded in an utterly simple, unified conception of the nature of the ultimate
Source of reality. It is the strongest of intuitions for the traditional theist that God is a greatest possible, or maximally
perfect, being. Informing this conception are value intuitions
regarding what properties are, objectively, perfections. That
goodness is one of those properties is about as strong a value
intuition as there can be, whose content borders on analytic-
ity. There is, of course, absolutely no parallel in the view that
a necessary being exists who essentially prevents pink and purple
moons, which is as arbitrary a claim as one could imagine. To
allow any more than the mere (partial) conceivability of such
beings would indeed signal "the bankruptcy of knowledge
claims about nonactual possibilities." But Anselmianism does
not have this effect.

Now of course the Anselmian's judgments about what conceivable worlds do or do not represent real possibilities will be no stronger than his judgments concerning what the moral principles are in accordance with which God necessarily acts. But these moral intuitions are at least as strong as any modal intuitions with which their deliverances might conflict. To see this let us consider that there are at least three different sorts of modal intuitions. First, there are modal intuitions about what is or is not logically possible, in a narrow sense. These intuitions will have to do with what the laws of logic are and when a proposition or set of propositions contains a violation of these laws. They will also have to do with what entails what, by virtue of logical form alone. We can call these 'logical intuitions'. Secondly, there are modal intuitions concerning semantic matters. These intuitions will have to do with the concepts in language, with matters concerning the intensions and extensions of predicates, with such things as conceptual truths. Call these 'semantic intuitions'. A third sort of modal intuition we apparently must recognize, one which draws the battle line between philosophers such as Guleserian and their Anselmian opponents, is an intuition concerning the status of logical and semantic intuitions. Are logical and semantic intuitions the only legitimate guides to nonactual modal reality, or not? Guleserian's intuitions lead him to say yes; the Anselmian disagrees.

With these distinctions drawn, we can see clearly something important which Guleserian seems to fail to appreciate sufficiently. The Anselmian can follow him in his logical intuitions concerning the conception of the rabbit-world — there is no strictly logical flaw in the idea of a terminally miserable rabbit, or in the conception of any number of such creatures. The Anselmain also can accept Guleserian's semantic intuitions that nothing in the ideas and stipulations involved is conceptually amiss, given only the concepts employed. So if the Anselmian rejects the genuine possibility of such a world, it is not because he is resisting any relevant logical or semantic modal intuitions. He is differing with Guleserian only with respect to what we might call his apparent 'meta-modal intuition', the intuition that genuine, broadly logical or metaphysical possibility always is established by the consultation of logical and semantic intuitions alone. For the theist, Anselmian intuitions may rule out what logical and semantic intuitions alone do not.

The Anselmian would be in a dubious position if he were committed to resisting left and right common logical and semantic intuitions. For such intuitions have nearly as strong an epistemic status as one could like. We are, after all, inveterate language users. We have basis in our lives for having logical and semantic intuitions. They are grounded in our successful activity as speakers and thinkers. But what is the epistemic status of the meta-modal intuition which Guleserian affirms and the Anselmian denies? What is its strength? How is it grounded? Whatever we say in answer to these questions, I think that we must recognize that Guleserian's restrictive meta-modal intuition is at a significant epistemic remove from his logical and semantic intuitions. It is certainly rationally deniable. There is nothing particularly dubious or suspect about the Anselmian registering disagreement at this point. The value intuitions which inform his conception of God and provide a context for a contrary meta-model judgment, as firmly grounded as they are in his activity and judgment as a moral agent, combine to provide the theist with a position having at least as strong an epistemic status as Guleserian's. No amount of logical or semantic intuitions, no cumulative effect of their plausibility, can throw into question the Anselmian's judgment that a world in which God would be blameworthy does not represent a genuine possibility. So I think Guleserian has done nothing to undermine the corollary of Anselmianism that God is a delimiter of possible worlds.

To be as fair to Guleserian as possible, nothing he says strictly rules out his accepting, on intuitive grounds or otherwise, some *de re* essentialist strictures on what is genuinely possible, apart from the deliverances of logical and semantic intuitions alone. But if he does accept some such strictures on possibility, then it is clear that his argument turns on a meta-modal intuition very closely related to the one I have already identified, and just as vulnerable to Anselmian resistance. For he provides no justification whatsoever for being selectively essentialist in such a way as to rule out Anselmian delimitations of possibility as distinctively groundless, unacceptable, or even suspect.

In the last section I shall have a bit more to say on the epistemic status of modal, moral, and metaphysical intuitions as they relate to our central concern — the traditional claim that God is necessarily good. But now I should focus briefly on an argument which Guleserian merely mentions at the end of his article. It is the real basis on which he picks the necessity of God's *goodness* as the modal attribute which should be rejected when counter-intuitive results or logical difficulties arise out of the fully developed Anselmian conception of God. But it also can be seen as providing an entirely independent, logically distinct reason for holding that God's goodness must be contingent rather than necessary. In this capacity, Pike sketches it out in one paragraph of the article whose central claims we already have considered. It is the main argument on the basis of which such otherwise traditional theists as Bruce Reichenbach and Stephen Davis recently have given up the *de re* necessity of divine goodness in the sense which is our concern.[12] So it deserves at least some attention in its own right.

The claim is made by all these philosophers that God's goodness could not consist, even in part, in his acting in accordance with moral principles unless he had a certain sort of freedom — the freedom to act or to refrain from acting in the way these principles determine. As a perfectly good agent, God must be free to do evil; otherwise, his continually refraining to do so would not be worthy of praise. The argument seems to be that perfect goodness *as an agent* requires that one have moral duties which one satisfies without fail; moral principles do not provide moral duties for any individual who cannot possibly act contrary to their leading; and so, if God is a perfectly good agent, it must be possible for him to act contrary to moral principles — i.e. there must be possible worlds in which God lies, breaks promises, tortures innocent beings for no good reason, and so forth. For this reason, the notion of a necessarily good agent is something of a self-contradiction. If God is perfectly good, his goodness must be one of his contingent properties.

Suppose for example that God tells Moses at some time t that at a later time $t+1$ he will be given divine assistance in carrying out some important mission. At $t+1$ the required aid is forthcoming and the mission succeeds. On the view under consideration, what has happened is relevant to God's goodness only if at some point in the story God stood under, or incurred, a moral duty, which his actions then satisfied. In this particular instance, only if we have a case of moral truth-telling or promise-keeping, the satisfaction of a duty not to lie or not to break promises, do we have on God's part a good act. God's communication at t can count as the making of a promise only if it generates, at least *prima facie*, a duty. But God can be such as to have duties only if he has full moral freedom. Specifically, he can have a duty to give Moses aid at $t+1$ only if he is genuinely free to give or withhold that aid when the time comes. But if God necessarily acts in accordance with moral principles, then once he has committed himself at t to giving the future assistance, he is not subsequently free in the manner required by these philosophers for his actions to count as the moral satisfaction of any duty. If, given the stipulated history of his dealings up to $t+1$, it is not then possible that he not help Moses, his granting aid is not a morally relevant act and so not worthy of any sort of praise. It neither contributes to, nor exemplifies, divine goodness.

This sort of argument has seemed quite plausible, and even convincing, to many philosophers, but it faces a number of serious problems. As I have discussed the cluster of issues it involves at much greater length elsewhere,[13] I shall here make only the briefest of comments on it. First, it should be pointed out that if it were a compelling argument, selectively giving up the necessity of God's goodness would alone do nothing toward solving the problem of moral freedom it poses. It seems that the assumption made by philosophers like Reichenbach and Davis is that if God's goodness as an agent has the modal status *de re* of contingency, it follows that at the time of any of his acts he is able to do morally otherwise than he does. But if God exemplifies all the other attributes constitutive of deity with either the modal status of necessity, or even just immutability, it can be strictly demonstrated that from God's being contingently good at any one time it follows that he cannot cease to be good at any subsequent time.[14] Thus, if such a God is good at t, he will not have the sort of freedom at $t+1$ these philosophers require. The problem they raise is solved on its own terms only if both the *de re* necessity *and* even the immutability of other important defining attributes of deity are given up as well. And this results in such an extreme emaciation of the traditional conception of God as to be wholly unsatisfactory to most theists, being contrary to some deep religious convictions.

But this says nothing about the argument itself. The whole line of reasoning is based on a failure to appreciate a perfectly reasonable way in which the traditional religious convictions about God's goodness as an agent can be explicated. The religious belief is fundamentally that God acts in perfect accord with principles which for human moral agents express moral duties, for instance the principle that it is good to deal truthfully and honestly with others. It is in no way necessary to this religious belief to hold that these principles actually bind God himself with moral duties. In fact, some theists would find such a claim to border on the blasphemous. The relevance of God's acting in perfect accord with moral principles to his goodness need not depend on his standing in exactly the same ontological and axiological relations to these principles as we do. His goodness need not encompass his having and satisfying any literal duties at all. I only indicate here the view I have attempted to develop elsewhere[15] that God's axiological goodness as an agent consists in his necessarily acting in accordance with moral principles as well as his freely engaging in acts of gracious supererogation. The perfect goodness of any created moral agent would be ontologically different from, although in principle functionally isomorphic with, the goodness of God as an agent. Divine goodness is distinct from, though appropriately modeled by, moral goodness. And in each one of God's necessarily good acts which benefit us, there is an element of supererogation of grace sufficient for grounding our gratitude and praise. The main point is that so long as God's goodness as an agent is not held to be in *every* respect like the goodness of his creatures, this argument against the necessity of divine goodness cannot even get off the ground. And as the ontological status of God is in other respects so different from that of his creatures, it is eminently reasonable for the theist to articulate his view in this way. So from this point of view, I think the argument can be judged a failure as an attempt to show that God's goodness as an agent cannot be among his essential properties.

The developed arguments of Resnick, Pike, and Gulesarian, as well as this particular line of thought, basically exhaust the major contemporary challenges to the belief that God is necessarily good. I think it is safe to say that none of them is a clear success. At least, on the basis of what we have seen, I think we can give a sympathetic hearing to some arguments in favor of God's goodness being among his essential properties. Even if there is no decisive reason to give up this traditional tenet of theism, we still need to see whether there is any good reason for the theist to affirm it.

III. *Arguments for the Tradition*

It has been urged by some philosophers, quite recently by Richard Swinburne and Keith Ward, that from God's power and freedom together with his omniscience we can deduce his goodness.[16] If this sort of argument could be made out in a fully convincing way, it obviously could be used by anyone who held God to be necessarily omnipotent and necessarily omniscient to establish that he is necessarily good as well. However, the versions of this argument to have appeared in the literature depend on a highly controversial assumption con-

cerning the inability of an omnipotent and omniscient being
to act on occasion without regard to anything like moral reasons. This assumption has not been made to look sufficiently
plausible to render it likely that such an argument can succeed. So I shall not discuss here the versions due to either Swinburne or Ward. However, there is a distinct form of argument
from necessary omnipotence and necessary omniscience to necessary goodness which does not share the form or assumptions
of the Swinburne-Ward arguments. I think it does merit our
attention. A faulty version of this argument recently was advanced by W. R. Carter in an article entitled "Omnipotence
and Sin."[17] Although I have explored various forms of this sort
of argument elsewhere,[18] I should lay out one version here,
as its results will be important in another context later on.

Carter thinks that a certain kind of *reductio* argument can
be used to show that the traditional theist must hold God to
be necessarily good. Formulated rigorously, the sort of argument he has in mind can be presented like this: Suppose there
is an individual, call him 'Yahweh', who is necessarily omnipotent and necessarily omniscient. Suppose further for *reductio*
that there is a possible world W in which Yahweh is, as a matter
of contingent fact, perfectly good and thus blameless, let us
say 'sinless,' up until some time t, at which time he performs
an evil deed, sinking into sin and thus ceasing to be perfectly
good. Now, at some time just prior to t, say $t-1$, either Yahweh
intends to sin at t, or he does not so intend. If he does, then
in having such an intention he sins at $t-1$, and is not then
blameless, contrary to our assumptions. For given that intentions to sin are just as much worthy of blame as the act or acts
intended, an intention to sin is itself a sin. If on the contrary,
Yahweh does not intend at $t-1$ to sin at t, it is either because
he intends at $t-1$ not to sin at t, or because he has at $t-1$ no
intention at all concerning whether he will sin at t. If the former
is true, then by stipulation of W his intention is thwarted and
so he is not omnipotent, contrary to our assumptions. No being will count as omnipotent who cannot see to it that his intentions are carried out concerning his own conduct. At $t-1$,

Yahweh in this case would lack an important power—the power to see to it that his present intentions are enacted at t. If on the other hand, Yahweh at $t-1$ has no intention at all concerning whether he will sin at t, then at that prior time he fails either to be sinless, or to be omniscient, or both. In the case of an omnipotent and omniscient individual such as Yahweh is stipulated to be, being perfectly good or sinless, even contingently, entails intending never to sin. Thus, in order to be sinless at $t-1$, Yahweh would have to intend then never to sin, and thus not to sin at t. His lacking any such intention would entail his not being sinless at $t-1$, contrary to our assumptions. In addition, it can be argued that if Yahweh were omniscient at $t-1$, then he would know at that time that he was about to sin at t. None of the even remotely plausible arguments that omniscience does not entail foreknowledge of some sort or other would block this modest inference. But Yahweh could not know he was about to act in a certain way without intending so to act. This follows from the freedom which is an essential component of necessary omnipotence and omniscience. So if Yahweh did not intend at $t-1$ to sin at t, it would follow that he did not know at that earlier time that he was about to commit such an act. But in that case, he would not be omniscient at $t-1$, again contrary to our assumptions. And at this point, our *reductio* is complete.

Carter believes that this sort of argument establishes that Yahweh cannot cease to be good, and so is good necessarily. I think it does show, quite successfully, that if God is essentially omnipotent, essentially omniscient, and good at some time, then he can never thereafter cease being good.[19] But this can be true even if God is good only contingently, such that he could have existed without ever being good at all. From the fact that an individual *can* cease to have a property without thereby ceasing to exist, it follows that the property in question is not among that individual's essential properties. But from the fact that a being *cannot* cease to have a certain property so long as he continues to exist, it does not follow that it is one of his essential properties. Carter, for example, has the property of apparently having believed otherwise, a property which, unfortunately, he can never cease to have while continuing to exist. Yet, obviously, it is not one of his essential properties. There are possible worlds in which he avoids this modal mistake altogether. So the sort of argument which he thinks can be used to prove that the necessity of God's goodness is entailed by that of some of his other attributes does not succeed at its appointed task.

It is a bit surprising that, given the strength with which many theists will insist on the necessity of God's goodness, there are so few arguments which have been advanced for this view. There is a well known, and rather rhetorical contention that since God is omnipotent, sin can have no power over him. But by simply distinguishing between moral weakness and the sort of weakness conceptually incompatible with omnipotence — weakness in creative power — Pike has neutralized this sort of appeal.[20] And then there is the well known claim that it is not possible that God do evil since whatever God does is by definition good. But, notoriously, the problem with this sort of reasoning is that it evacuates the belief in God's goodness of any determinate and stable content. The theist traditionally holds that God necessarily acts in accordance with a certain invariable set of principles, a set inclusive of principles which express moral duties for his creatures. Theists do not standardly hold that set to be malleable to divine whim. No such view is implied by even any reasonable version of a divine command theory of ethics. So this line of thought fails to provide the kind of support needed for the tradition.

It could be argued that it is a firm religious requirement that the believer trust God absolutely and obey him unconditionally, and that this sort of trust and obedience would be morally unwarranted and improper unless God was held to be necessarily good. This would be an argument that for religious and moral consistency, the believer must hold God's goodness to be among his essential properties. I think it is an argument that a number of theists would give to support their holding of this belief. However, it too seems to be a failure.

For in light of the sort of argument to which Carter has drawn our attention, the religious believer who is convinced that God is good now, or even that he has been good at some time in the past, and who holds God's other attributes to be at least immutably exemplified, can be absolutely assured that God's goodness will continue unfailingly into the future. Even if his goodness is contingent, God cannot cease to be good, and so rightly is worthy of the strongest trust and obedience. Thus, again, we have no line of reasoning which establishes either the necessity of divine goodness or even the religious need to affirm it.

To my knowledge, the arguments just mentioned and briefly discussed come close to exhausting the basic forms of ratiocinative support which recently have been marshalled by traditional theists for the view that God is necessarily good. There is, however, one other argument which could be developed for this view, an argument which appeals to a striking metaphysical principle favored by a number of great philosophers, and proceeds by means of the argument that a being such as God could never cease being good, once he is good at some time. It may be interesting for us to consider.

The principle which launches this new argument is the ancient Principle of Plenitude, the thesis that, given infinite space or infinite time, all possibilities are actualized. It is a thesis espoused in one form or another by philosophers from at least Aristotle to Russell. And certainly, there are interpretations under which it would be embraced by numerous philosophers of the present day. Our argument then begins with an assumption of the Principle of Plenitude, an assumption that God is temporally everlasting, existent through infinitely many moments of time, and for *reductio* the assumption that God is good, but is so only contingently, from which it follows that it is possible, in a broadly logically sense, that God sin. These assumptions together entail that there is some time at which God sins. But, as we have seen earlier, it is provable that if God is necessarily omnipotent and necessarily omniscient, or even if he has these properties in a contingent yet immutable manner, and he is perfectly good at some time, it follows that he never can subsequently sink into sin, regardless of whether his goodness is contingent.

From this we can conclude rigorously that there can be no time of perfect divine goodness before the time of a divine sin. Thus, either there was a single divine sin which occurred infinitely long ago and was preceeded by no prior moments, which is strictly impossible, or it is the case that at every moment God sins. But if the latter is true, God would not be contingently perfectly good, as was assumed. So if God is good at all, he is good *necessarily*. Our argument is complete.

As interesting at this argument is, I believe it cannot be used by the traditional theist to support his position. Persuasive though it might appear at first glance, it too is a failure. For consider more carefully the principle on which it is constructed, the principle that given infinite space or time, there are no unactualized possibilities. The modal element of this principle can be given either of two interpretations. First, there is the logical interpretation: In infinite space or time, anything which is logically possible will come about at some time. Since Aristotle's attempt to define the alethic modalities extensionally, some philosophers have held to the Principle of Plenitude under this interpretation. But a traditional theist is theologically committed to judging the thesis under this construal to be false. For it is then incompatible with the central religious belief that God is a free creator, free to bring contingent things into existence and free to refrain from ever so doing. If the logical reading of the principle were true, God would not have this freedom. Everything whose existence was logically possible would come into being, regardless of God's desires.

But more is wrong with the principle so understood than just its incompatibility with the traditional doctrine of creation. For one thing, in order to be acceptable at all, the principle as it stands would have to be qualified in various ways. For example, it is logically possible that I sit at some time t and equally possible that I not sit at t. But it is clearly impossible that both these possibilities be actualized. The principle must therefore be qualified so as not to apply to temporally indexed properties. But the very point of carefully introducing such qualifications so as to provide a principle immune from obvious counter-example would itself have to be questioned. For under the logical interpretation, there seems to be absolutely no good reason to accept any such principle in the first place. It seems utterly gratuitous. Aristotle's definitions of necessity and possibility just do not capture the logical conception of these modalities. ⌜Necessarily p⌝ can be argued to entail ⌜p at every time⌝ , but the converse entailment cannot plausibly be thought to hold. Likewise, ⌜p at some time⌝ does entail ⌜Possibly p⌝ , but the converse entailment, the one expressed in the Principle of Plenitude, does not obviously, or even plausibly, hold at all.

In an article entitled "Nature, Plenitude, and Sufficient Reason," R. H. Kane has argued that the Principle of Plenitude follows from the Principle of Sufficient Reason.[21] And in that case, it would seem that many traditional theists who value a cosmological argument for God's existence would find themselves committed to its truth, inconsistently with their doctrine of creation. But no such quandary actually arises, as the precise version of the Principle of Sufficient Reason required for the entailment is a version which few, if any, philosophers would view as having much plausibility at all, and which is not required for the construction of any standard cosmological argument. So I think it is safe to conclude that the logical version of the principle has problems, seems totally unwarranted even if it can be formulated in such a way as to circumvent obvious counter-examples, and could not be accepted with theological consistency by any traditional theist anyway.

The other interpretation of the principle, one on which it is accepted by a great number of philosophers nowadays, is a physical interpretation: Given infinite space or time, anything physically possible will become actual. Again, it seems that there are plenty of cases in which it would be physically possible for me to sit at some time t and physically possible for me not to sit at t, so the principle would have to be qualified accordingly, unless a view of complete determinism is embraced. But I suspect that many who hold the principle on this reading do accept its deterministic implications in unrestricted form.

The warrant for this interpretation of the principle is fairly simple to state. If to say that something is physically possible is to say or imply that, given relevant prior physical conditions and natural laws, it has a positive finite probability, however small, the truth of the principle arguably follows on one other assumption. Consider some event E understood in this way to be physically possible. Assign E a probability of 1/1 trillion. Given an infinite succession of times, or an infinite spatial continuum, containing unlimitedly many events, sufficiently many events will occur that if the probability assignment is right, E will come to obtain.

This argument itself would admit of a good deal of critical analysis and comment, but for our purpose, such a discussion would be useless. Even if the Principle of Plenitude is true on the physical interpretation, and we are justified in accepting it, suitably qualified, it is on this construal completely irrelevant to the case of God and unusable in the argument for the necessity of divine goodness. For, from the assumption that God is good only contingently, it follows only that it is *logically* possible, not that it is *physically* possible, that God do wrong. Physical possibility just has no relevant connection to our question about the modal status of divine goodness.

So we can conclude that, of the two basic interpretations of the Principle of Plenitude, the one that is necessary for the argument is wholly ungrounded, apparently false, and unusable for any traditional theist. The one which can be said to have any significant plausibility at all is, unfortunately, inapplicable to the argument. So once again we see the failure of an argument purporting to support the belief in the necessity of God's goodness.

IV. The Anselmian Appeal

We have considered a number of arguments for and against the belief that God is necessarily good. I judge them all failures. I have no closure principle by which to establish that these are the only lines of deductive argument which might be used with

any significant appearance of plausibility to assess this important religious belief, so I do not pretend to have established
that no such argument for or against this belief can succeed.
But I do think that at this point it can be reasonable to hold
that no well known argument has in fact settled the issue. And
further, it seems also reasonable to conjecture that no such proof
will be forthcoming. We are left then with an important question. Is the belief that God is necessarily good one which it
is rational for any theist to hold? And, connected to this: If
there is a ground on which the theist can affirm reasonably
the necessity of divine goodness, what is it?

In section II, while discussing the arguments of Guleserian,
I suggested that the traditional theist, especially of the Anselmian stripe, develops his conception of God from, among other
sources, a set of intuitions. There is first of all the core intuition that God is a maximally perfect, or greatest possible, being. This is the religious intuition which is most central to the
Anselmian. And then there are all the value intuitions about
what properties are perfections which allow the Anselmian to
fill out this conception of deity. I would like to suggest that
this may be an ultimate ground of the belief that God is necessarily good. It can be a function of traditional religious and
value intuitions. It is intuitively held that the property of being good as an agent is a great-making property. And it may
be a further deliverance of the Anselmian's intuitions that necessary goodness as an agent is a perfection as well. Both properties can in this way be judged to be of the sort it is intrinsically better to have than to lack. I want to contend that a case
can be made to show that the Anselmian can be reasonable
in believing such deliverances of intuition to be reliable.

First I should do something to indicate, at least briefly, the
variety of intuitions which may serve to ground the belief that
God is necessarily good. I think that many religious people
hold intuitively that God is as firmly entrenched in goodness,
or alternately, that goodness is as firmly entrenched in God,
as it is possible to be. Most who have this sort of intuition would
go on to insist that it is not possible for God to do evil. It seems

then that a further conviction is had, presumably also intuitively, that it is possible that God be necessarily good as an agent. And of course the implication of these two views is that God's goodness is among his essential properties.

A slightly different grounding for the modal belief about God we are examining may arise from an application of an axiological principle once discussed by J. N. Findlay.[22] Findlay allows that theists with Anselmian inclinations may hold intuitively that goodness is a perfection, and thereby ascribe it to God. But then it is claimed that believers go on to hold that God is *necessarily* good only by applying to that intuitive starting point a principle which Findlay finds dubious. The principle as reported by Findlay is that if to have any property F is good, then to have F necessarily is better. If the belief that God is necessarily good were derived from an application of the principle as stated by Findlay, it would be on shakey ground. For that formulation is critically flawed. To see this, consider a property G, a property of performing freely some supererogatory good act. Surely, to exemplify G is good. But just as surely, it cannot be the case that it is better to have G necessarily. For it is not even coherent to suppose that G could be exemplified necessarily by any individual who has it. So the principle as stated leads to incoherence. But of course it can be qualified to apply only to cases of properties capable of essential exemplification. And, so qualified, I can see nothing at all wrong with the principle. Findlay might find the restricted version dubious as well, and it surely is such that it can be doubted, but it seems to me not to be such that it is clearly more reasonable for just any rational person to doubt it than to accept it. In particular, if an Anselmian theist finds it intuitively plausible, I see no reason why he cannot be fully justified in applying it to his other relevant intuitions and thereby justifiably arriving at the view that God is necessarily good.

Each of the intuitive groundings just mentioned has involved a cluster of intuitions and an inference to the proposition that God is necessarily good. I think it is important to point out that it may be the case for many theists that the necessity of God's goodness is a direct deliverance of intuition, not merely inferred from, though perhaps also suppported by, the other sorts of intuitions just discussed. Rooting such a modal belief directly in intuition, however, may worry and even irritate many philosophers, goading them to question the epistemic status of any such moves as those I have just briefly surveyed. For even if there are such intuitions, the critic may say, they provide at best no more than *prima facie* and tentative support to the proposition believed. But further, it might be asked, why in the first place should we endow such otherwise unsupported proclivities to assert the necessity of divine goodness with the honorific title of 'intuitions', allowing them to count as even *prima facie* warrant, however slight, for the claim?

First, the least difficult point. All apparent deliverances of intuition may be defeasible. What is held intuitively as true at one time may at a later time be rejected as false because of some countervailing argument whose soundness appears even more obvious. In this sense, it may be agreed that the warrant provided by intuition is only *prima facie*. Intuitively held beliefs must withstand the fire of criticism. But after examining the arguments which can be given against the necessity of God's goodness, I think it is safe to say that the *prima facie* support any intuitions may have provided this belief need not be judged defeated. Further, I do not think that to agree that the defeasibility of intuitive support renders that support *prima facie* is to concede that there is any likelihood that it will be defeated, rendering it tentative at best. So the claim of intuitive support for the belief that God is necessarily good as an agent should not be thought of as a minimalist claim with little epistemic significance.

But why ascribe it any such support at all? First, I should say something about intuitions in general. I think of a belief as intuitively held by a person just in case: (1) it is held by the person, and (2) it is not the case that it is held only because of some inferential relations it stands in to other beliefs. An intuitive belief is something like a basic belief or a natural belief. Accordingly, an appeal to intuitions to justify a belief is an acknowledgement that the proposition believed strikes one naturally as being true.

Kripke once responded to philosophers who depreciate appeals to intuition by countering that he takes a deliverance of intuition to be "very heavy evidence in favor of anything," going on to say that he does not know of "what more conclusive evidence one can have about anything, ultimately speaking."[23] I have to admit to not being quite so sanguine about this apparent noetic faculty. In fact, I think we have to distinguish carefully between sorts of intuitions we are justified in taking to be reliable and sorts of intuitions we have no good reason to trust. Bluntly, I think we have no good reason to trust many intuitions about relatively abstruse metaphysical matters. Unfortunately, it is often in disputes about such matters that we find intuition prominently appealed to. As I have indicated earlier, I think it is our successful activity as speakers and thinkers which grounds our logical and linguistic intuitions. And it is our moral activity which grounds at least some of our value intuitions. There are things about our lives which give us some reason to think that our intuitions about such matters as these deserve a strong measure of trust. But what in the world could account for any alleged intuitions on most matters of metaphysical esoterica, I have no idea.

Against this backdrop of general doubt about the status of many metaphysical intuitions, however, I believe the Anselmian theist to be justified in marking out some few intuitions about metaphysical matters as trustworthy. Included among these will be intuitions relevant to the existence and basic nature of God. The Anselmian's intuitions about God, or more broadly, all those intuitions which together yield the Anselmian conception of God, generate without intentional contrivance an overall belief-set in which it makes sense that there should be such intuitions and that they should be, at least a core of them, reliable.[24] For if an Anselmian God exists, and creates rational beings whose end is to know him, it makes good sense that they should be able to come to know *something* of his existence and attributes without the need of highly technical arguments, accessible to only a few. It makes sense that there be reliable intuitions such as those which yield the Anselmian conception of God. So, it is my suggestion that within a framework which they themselves contribute to providing, the Anselmian intuitions on which the doctrine of necessary goodness rests have a firm grounding as at least *prima facie* reliable indicators of religious truth.

I am not making the empirical claim that all theists intuit that God must be necessarily good. For of course, not all even believe this. But it does seem to be the case that theists fail to hold this belief only if they either never have reflected on such modal matters at all or else have become convinced by apparently plausible arguments such as those discussed in section II that God's goodness cannot be among his essential properties. In cases such as the latter, it may be that initial intuitions have been had, which then have been thought to be defeated by contrary considerations. So there are ready explanations as to why some otherwise traditional theists do not hold the belief in question. After all, whatever intuition is, it is such that it must be brought into play by contact with the appropriate context, and when it is, or at least appears to be brought into play, its apparent deliverances are not incorrigible or indefeasible. In addition, the Anselmian can even have plausible explanations distinct from these to account for the lack of general acknowledgement of such intuitions in the population at large. By these means, the argument that from an Anselmian God's existence, we would be led to expect to find such intuitions amongst his rational creatures need not founder on any empirical data, or allow from such data an argument actually disconfirming theism.

A point which will bear repeating is that it is not the case that on this view of Anselmian intuitions, the Anselmian will have an incorrigible, priviledged access to truth in the form of intuition, whose apparent deliverances he would always be justified in accepting uncritically. Nothing of the sort follows from what I have suggested at all. In fact, as I have indicated elsewhere, the apparent deliverances of intuition concerning the nature of God need to be checked by a number of *a posteriori* controls derived from general experience, religious experience, the data of purported revelation, and critical argument.[25]

So with respect to the Anselmian belief that God is necessarily good, I think the following can be said: Traditional theists who hold this belief intuitively, or infer it from more general beliefs or principles they hold intuitively, can be justified in taking such intuitions to be reliable and in maintaining there not to exist any defeaters of those intuitions. Even without the sort of deductive support from other theistic beliefs which philosophers have sought, I think the Anselmian is justified fully in holding to the high modal status of God's goodness, both as a fact about the individual who is God and as an element in his concept of God.

4

Perfection and Power

THE TRADITIONAL THEISTIC conception of God, captured well by St. Anselm, is that of a greatest possible or maximally perfect being. God is thought of as necessarily exemplifying a maximally compossible collection of great-making properties, properties that, roughly, it is intrinsically better to have than to lack. On a standard explication of this conception of deity, an explication informed by value intuitions concerning what properties are great-making properties, God is said to be, of necessity, omnipotent, omniscient, omnipresent, and incorporeal. Among other things, he is also said to be impeccable, or essentially good—such that it is not possible that he sin or do evil. In a recent paper entitled "Impeccability Revisited," W. R. Carter has criticized this conception of deity, saying in particular of any being who is essentially sinless that:

> Such a being not only does not but *cannot* do many things (murder, rape) that ordinary humans can do! Such a being has no claim at all to being judged omnipotent.[1]

It is Carter's conclusion that the traditional conception of God which presents as requisites of deity both omnipotence and impeccability is logically inconsistent on that account. A being who cannot sin cannot do many things we ordinary humans can do, and so cannot possibly be characterized properly as omnipotent.

But of course if there is such a problem in the concept of God relating to omnipotence, it is not one exclusively raised by impeccability. For we ordinary humans can go to previously existing places we have never been before. But then it seems that we can do something God cannot do, for if God is necessarily omnipresent, he cannot possibly go somewhere he has never been before. Likewise, any normal human being can think of something he has never thought of before. But if God is necessarily omniscient, it can be argued that he cannot possibly think of something he has never thought of before. And even that notorious weakling of philosophic lore, Mr. McEar, who is capable of scratching his own left ear but essentially incapable of performing any other task (not entailed or required by the capacity to scratch), would seem to have a capacity or ability not had by an essentially incorporeal being such as God. In his distinctively divine state of existence, God cannot scratch his own left ear. Such a being as God is said to be not only does not but cannot do many things that ordinary humans can do. How then can a being who is necessarily omnipresent, omniscient, incorporeal, and necessarily sinless also be said in any reasonable sense to be omnipotent? Of course, an answer to this question will turn on our understanding of what the theist means to ascribe to God when characterizing him as 'omnipotent'.

The concept of God is the concept of a maximally powerful perfect being, a being who, among other impressive attributes, has the maximal degree of power it is possible (in a broadly logical or metaphysical sense) to exemplify. God is thus a perfect being who is perfectly powerful. To specify this further, the traditional theist typically makes three claims. First, there are and can be no independent, externally determined constraints on divine power. Secondly, the internally determined structure and scope of God's abilities to act (those parameters on divine action set by his own nature and activity) are not, and cannot be, such that he lacks any possible ability or power it is intrinsically better to have than to lack. And finally, God is the sole source and continuous support of all the power there is or could be. Thus, no individual can possibly exemplify or exercise any ability, capacity, or power whose existence does not ultimately derive from God.

This small bit of clarification concerning the scope of power

ascribed to deity on the traditional conception of God can serve
to provide us with a better perspective on the sort of problem
Carter claims to find with theism. The theist with a clear view
of omnipotence will just deny that the impossibility of God's
going somewhere he has never been before, thinking of something for the first time, scratching his own left ear, or doing
evil entails or in any way signals God's lacking some ability
or power it is intrinsically better to have than to lack. Moreover, in each of these cases, and in particular, in the case of
impeccability, there is no good reason at all to think that the
impossibility we must recognize indicates any sort of lack in
divine power whatsoever. For consider the following three
propositions:

(1) God cannot sin.
(2) It is impossible that God sin.
(3) God lacks the power to sin.

Carter and many others seem to understand (1), which is a
commitment of traditional theism, to be equivalent in meaning to (3), which seems clearly to indicate that God lacks some
power ordinary human beings in fact have. But (3) is not an
accurate paraphrase of (1), nor is it even entailed by (1). As
is now well known, the little word 'can' can serve many different functions, and so, accordingly, 'cannot' cannot always
be taken to mean the same thing. Often, when we say something of the form ⌜S cannot do A⌝ , we do mean to say of
some individual that it lacks some power. But nothing of the
sort is meant when the theist utters (1). (1) is intended only
to convey (2), not (3).

Let us focus for a moment on the phrase 'the power to sin'.
Critics of theism such as Carter often talk as if there is a discrete
power of sinning, a power had by us but lacked by God. But
that there is no such discrete power can be seen, I think, quite
easily by reflection upon a simple type of thought experiment:
We can construct any number of pairs of stories of the following form — Some individual S exercises casual powers P_1–P_n in
performing actions A_1–A_n in order to achieve G. In story I
the circumstances are such that achieving G by A_1–A_n is evil,

or a sin; in story II the circumstances are such that achieving G by A_1–A_n is morally permissable. For example, suppose Smith, a policeman, raises a 38 calibre hand gun in his right hand, aims it at Jones, whom he correctly believes to be an innocent person, and for no good reason squeezes the trigger with the aim of killing Jones, which is thereby achieved. Surely Smith has thereby sinned, or done evil. Suppose now for a parallel story that Smith, a policeman, raises the 38, aims it at Jones, whom he correctly believes to be a mass murderer about to commit his next heinous act which otherwise cannot be stopped, and squeezes the trigger with the aim of killing Jones, which is thereby achieved. In this second story we can suppose that what Smith does is, in the circumstances, morally permissable however regrettable. Thus, in the first story he sins, in the second he does not. In the first story does Smith exercise a power which he does not exercise in the second story, a distinct power to sin? By supposition, he does not. The causal powers exercised remain, by hypothesis, invariant between the two stories.

So what of the phrase 'the power to sin'? There are powers, and degrees of powers, *necessary* for sinning or doing evil. More exactly, different powers or abilities are required for engaging in different sorts of sin. As we age, certain ways of getting into trouble become unavailable to us. But there is no discrete power of sinning, no distinct power to sin, no power the exercise of which is, in itself, *sufficient* for doing evil or sinning. And only if there were would (3), the proposition that God lacks the power to sin, follow from (1), the proposition that God cannot sin.

But, I can imagine an objector saying, what of the power to rape, the power to lie, the power to steal, the power to murder? Surely each of these is a power any exercise of which *in itself* sufficiently qualifies as evil. The response to this is that it is precisely the point of our thought experiment to show that there are no such distinct causal powers. We cannot allow a common *façon de parler* to be canonized so easily as a philosophical commitment.

As Anselm puts it in *De Casu Diaboli*, "Lots of things are

improperly expressed in ordinary speech, but when it is necessary to get to the heart of the truth, we must get rid of the
bothersome impropriety so far as is advisable and possible."[2]
In *Cur Deus Homo*, he at one point remarks that when we
say of a man in battle that he is able to be overcome, we attribute a power not to him but to others; so likewise if we were
to say that he is not able to be overcome, we would attribute
a lack of power not to him but to his adversaries. The surface
grammar of ability talk can be misleading with respect to where
powers or the lack of powers are being located. Perhaps ability locutions always entail something about power or the lack
of power. If so, Anselm might reject the proposition

(4) God is able to sin,

not because it attributes a power to God which he does not
have, but rather because it would imply that temptation or
evil has a power over God which it does not have. Likewise,
he might endorse

(5) God is unable to sin,

not because it correctly specifies a power God does not have,
but rather because it indicates that temptation, sin, or evil lacks
a power over God.

However, if what we are concerned with are *causal* powers,
the sort of powers relevant to considerations of omnipotence,
it seems to me that both (4) and (5) can be highly misleading.
Neither seem to me to be legitimately understood as having
to do with causal powers. As (1) is true only if understood as
equivalent in meaning to (2), (5) would be true only on the
same condition. But perhaps if there is a conceptual tie between ability talk and causal power, (5) is much more misleading than (1), which is merely ambiguous between (2) and
(3). When it is necessary to get to the heart of the truth, the
theist may be best off insisting that both (1) and (5) are misleading and offer an explanation of (2), the claim that it is
impossible that God sin.

On the traditional concept of God, it is necessarily the case that the individual who actually and of necessity is God does not do evil. Yet he does not lack, or necessarily lack, a power to sin. It is rather necessarily the case that he never *uses* his perfect power to order to sin. As a perfect being, there is no possible world in which he wills to do evil. Theists maintain that

(6) God cannot do evil because he cannot intend to do evil,

whose truth follows from God's necessary goodness and freedom, the latter of which implies that God does nothing he does not intend to do. But most theists take a very different attitude toward.

(7) God could not do evil even if he intended to,

which would indicate a lack of power rather than a fixity or firmness of will on the part of God being responsible for his necessary sinlessness. Now, of course, this is in itself of some philosophical interest, for (7) can most naturally be understood as a subjunctive conditional about God with a necessarily false antecedent which, on a standard construal of such statements, should come out true. In so far as theists are committed to judging it false, they are committed to rejecting the standard semantics which assigns it the contrary truth value. And this is the traditional theistic commitment. But that is a story for another time.

The point which Carter's paper has made clear that it is vital for us to grasp if we are to understand traditional theism is that the various logical impossibilities concerning divine activity, just like his omnipotence, all flow from his perfection, or from properties his instantiation of which follows from his exercise of the powers which flow from his perfection. The consistency of the concept of God thus consists in the integrity of the concept of perfection.

5

Properties, Modalities, and God

A MAJOR SUBJECT MATTER of philosophical theology concerns the divine attributes, that set of properties such as omnipotence, omniscience, a-seity, and perfect goodness which traditional theists ascribe to God. In recent years, philosophers have rediscovered the importance of gaining as clear an understanding as possible of what each of these properties amounts to, and of how they relate to one another. It has been widely recognized that a part of this task involves ascertaining the modalities of God's exemplification of these various properties. Most theistic philosophers hold, for example, that God is necessarily omniscient, but only contingently the God of Abraham, Isaac, and Jacob. He is thought to be contingently creator of this world, or for that matter of any physical world at all, although it is held that necessarily he is the creator of any contingent being, and of any such world, that exists.

There are often interesting logical connections which hold between the modalities of different properties' exemplifications. For example, in light of the contingency of his being a creator, a problem could arise as to whether God has the property of omnipresence necessarily or just contingently. If omnipresence is a relational property holding between God and all spatially located objects, as it patently appears to be (regardless of whether we explicate omnipresence as God's location at each and every point in space, or as his knowledge of and power over every entity with spatial location), then it might seem that the contingency of creation would entail the contingency of divine omnipresence. However, if omnipresence were understood as holding just in case there is no place from which God is absent, that property could be exemplified even if there were no spatial universe, and thus no places from which to be absent. So far as I know this has not been discussed in the literature. But other problems concerning the modalities of God's properties have been discussed at length, such as the question of whether God can be both necessarily omnipotent and essentially sinless.

Yet the range of modalities recently examined by philosophers of religion has been small. Indeed I think it safe to say that few have gone beyond asking whether this or that property of God's is necessary or contingent, essential or accidental for him. In this paper I want to suggest that there are other modalities of property exemplification whose examination can throw some light on theistic claims about the nature of God. First I shall delineate a few of these neglected modalities, and then indicate a couple of ways in which their recognition can be of significant interest in philosophical theology.

I. Property Stability: Some Definitions

It often happens that an individual begins to have a property, exemplifies it for a while, and then ceases to have it. Let us call any such property exemplification the having of a *temporary* property. Of course not all properties are temporary properties. That is to say, not all property exemplifications are temporary. It may happen, for example, that an individual has a property which it cannot cease to have. Let us refer to such a case as one of an *enduring* property. Likewise, it is conceivable that an object have a property which it cannot have begun to have. We shall call this an *immemorial* property. Finally a property which is both enduring and immemorial will be characterized as *immutable*. An immutable property is such that the individual having it cannot have begun to have it and cannot cease to have it. We can call any property which is immemorial or enduring or immutable a *stable* property. A property which is stable in more than one way is then, of course, immutable.

Notice the modalities in these definitions. The mere fact that an entity has a property which in fact it never began to have and never will cease to have is not enough for that property to count as immemorial or enduring by our definitions. The modal element in each definition should indicate that with the notion of a stable property we are concerned with something more than the mere *de facto* histories of property bearers. Notice also that each definition has been framed in such a way as to allow timeless or atemporal objects (if there are any) to have stable properties. Finally, each of these categorizations of property exemplification must be distinguished clearly from the more common classifications involving modality, those divisions of essential/accidental or necessary/contingent.[1] An individual has a property essentially just in case the individual has it and could not exist without it. Something has a property contingently if it in fact exemplifies the property, but could exist without it. As the definitions make clear, a property which is immemorial, or enduring, or immutable is not necessarily thereby essential for its bearer. This is because a property which is such that an individual in fact exemplifies it in a stable manner might be such that its bearer could have existed without ever having it at all. However, there is a sense in which a property which is essential for its bearer is thereby immutable, and thus both immemorial and enduring for that individual.

In order to clarify the sense in which this last remark is true, we need to specify a bit more precisely the categories of stability. One simple distinction must be drawn which obtains within each sort of stable exemplification. A property can be immemorial, enduring, or immutable in either a *weak* or a *strong* sense. A property is weakly enduring for an individual just in case that individual has the property, and there can be *no time during the individual's existence* when it will have ceased to have that property. It is strongly enduring just in case it is exemplified and there can be *no time* at which the individual ceases to have to. My house has the property of having been built in South Bend, Indiana. There can be no time during its existence when it will have ceased to exemplify this property.

In this sense, we can say of it that it cannot lose this property. Thus, having been built in South Bend is a weakly enduring property of my house. Its exemplification by my house is weakly enduring. However, given that my house can cease to exist, and given the not unreasonable position that an object cannot exemplify properties at any time after it has ceased to exist, my house has no strongly enduring properties. Every property it has it can cease to have at some time. What then would be an example of a strongly enduring property? A fairly straightforward example would be the number three's property of being prime.

A property is weakly immemorial for an individual just in case the individual has the property, and there can have been *no time during the individual's existence* after which it began to have that property. It is strongly immemorial just in case it is exemplified and there can have been *no time* at which its bearer began to exemplify it. My house's property of being built originally in South Bend is a weakly immemorial property. There can have been no time during that structure's existence after which it began to have this property. But given that it follows from a general truth about houses (an implicate of a more general truth about all artifacts) that my house began to exist when it was originally built, along with the reasonable assumption that no individual can exemplify any properties at any time before it exists, that structure has no strongly immemorial properties. Every property it has it in fact began to have at some time. For an example of a strongly immemorial property we can again consider the number three, which has many of its properties, including that of being prime, in this way.

A property is weakly immutable if and only if it is weakly enduring and weakly immemorial. It is strongly immutable just in case it is both strongly immemorial and strongly enduring. My house's property of being built or having been built originally in South Bend is weakly immutable. It has no strongly immutable properties. It should be remembered that from the fact that my house has this disjunctive property of origin in a weakly immutable manner, it does not follow that this is one of its essential properties. That very house could have been built in Bloomington, or better yet (if I in that possible world am one of its residents) in the Bahamas.

Unlike the properties of my house, many properties of the number three, for example that of being prime and that of being the square root of nine, are strongly immutable. There can have been no time when it began to exemplify these properties, and there can be no time when it ceases to have them. The properties just mentioned are among the essential properties of the number three, but again it should be emphasized that even from a property's being strongly immutable for an individual it does not follow that it is one of that individual's essential properties.

Again, let me point out that all these categories of stability have been specified in such a way as to allow any timeless entities to have, trivially, stable properties. So if for example the number three is an entity residing outside time, there can have been no time during its existence after which it began to have the property of being prime, and there can be no time during its existence when it will have ceased to have that property, because *there can be no time during its existence*. So it can have weakly immutable properties. Likewise, if three is timeless, there can have been no time when it began to be prime and there can be no time when it ceases to have that property because *there is no time at which it exists* at all. Thus, it can have strongly immutable properties.

I have said that there is a sense in which a property which is essential to its bearer is thereby immutable, and thus both immemorial and enduring. It can be made clear now the exact sense in which this is true. If we operate with a strict understanding of essentiality, according to which a property is essential to an object just in case it is impossible that the object both exist and lack that property, then all essential properties are weakly immutable for their bearers.

We have at least this link between essence and stability. Many properties are stable in virtue of being essential to their bearers. But not all are. Some properties are *intrinsically stable*, i.e. such that, necessarily, all their exemplifications are stable, regardless of whether they are essential to their bearers. Some kinds of temporally indexed properties, for example, fall into this category. And further, it seems that exemplifications of other properties can be *extrinsically stable*, such that they are endowed with stability by the effect of other properties had by their bearer or some other individual.[2] In section IV we shall examine what appears to be a significantly interesting example of this in the case of God. So although essentiality and stability are logically related, it must be kept in mind that they are distinct notions.

II. *Strong Stability: A Query*

Every object has weakly stable properties, since every object has essential properties. But not every object has strongly stable properties. Reflecting on this may lead us to wonder what an individual has to be like in order to be able to manifest strong as well as weak stability in any of its property exemplifications. This is especially important to get clear on since, as I hope to show, it is a fundamental conviction of traditional theists that God is an individual who has such properties. So let us turn for a moment to the question: What sort of individual can have strongly stable properties?

The simplest examples of objects with strongly stable properties, the examples which come to mind most easily, involve entities like numbers. And it is generally agreed by those who believe there are any such entities at all that they have necessary existence. So we might be led to think that necessary existence is a requisite for having strongly stable properties. But this is incorrect. Having necessary existence is sufficient for having strongly stable properties, but it is not necessary. It is sufficient for a quite simple reason. If an object is such that it necessarily exists, such that its non-existence is impossible, it is not such that it could come into or go out of existence. Its existence is strongly stable in more than one way. That is to say, necessary existence entails strongly stable existence. So existing necessarily is sufficient for having at least one strongly stable property—the property of strongly stable existence.[3]

But necessary existence is not a requisite for having strongly stable properties. For consider a being which (1) in fact exists, and either (2) could not have begun to exist, or (3) cannot cease to exist, but (4) could have failed to exist at all. Surely this seems possible. And some traditional theists are committed to its possibility, a commitment whose source I shall identify in a moment. Such a being would exist only contingently, because of (4), yet either without the possibility of a beginning or without the possibility of an end. Its existence would be strongly immemorial or strongly enduring. If it satisfied (2) and thus had strongly immemorial existence, it also could have other strongly immemorial properties. If it satisfied (3) and thus had strongly enduring existence, it could have other strongly enduring properties as well. The theists I mentioned are those committed to holding the latter possibility to be true of contingent, created human souls. Just in case an individual satisfied both conditions (2) and (3), it would have strongly immutable existence, and thus could have other strongly immutable properties—without existing necessarily.

It is important to realize that necessary existence is not required for strong stability. Because of this, non-theists and others who reject the claim that God's existence is necessary can still be receptive to theistic claims concerning the strong stability of some divine properties. The non-theist can agree that if there were a God, he would exist and manifest many of his properties in a strongly stable manner. Thus, as we shall see, some important claims concerning the concept of God can stand independent of the controversy over necessary existence.

In order for an individual to be able to have strongly stable properties it is necessary that it have non-temporary (timeless or temporally infinite) existence. An individual with strongly stable properties must exist in such a way that either it never in fact began to exist, or it never will cease to exist, or both.

This is necessary because (1) if an individual ever did cease to exist it would have had no strongly enduring properties (there would be a time when it ceased to have any of its properties whatsoever, namely the time when it ceased to exist), and (2) if an individual ever began to exist it would have no strongly immemorial properties (there would be a time when it began to have any of its properties, the earliest such time being the time when it came into existence). So in order to have strongly stable properties, an individual must have non-temporary existence. And on any conception of God adequate to the dominant western religious traditions, if there is such a being, he qualifies in this way for having strongly stable properties. Categorizing any entity which has a least one of its essential properties in a strongly stable manner as a strongly stable individual, we can say that God is traditionally conceived of as a strongly immutable individual. He is such that he never can have begun to exist and never can cease to exist. Thus he can exemplify both strongly immemorial and strongly enduring properties.

At this point enough has been said about the forms and conditions of stability to facilitate our grasp of these modalities of property exemplification. We turn now to apply these notions briefly to the case of God. We shall consider a couple of interesting issues concerning the divine attributes which the modalities of stable exemplification may serve to illuminate.

III. God and Stability

Among the divine attributes discussed by philosophers in recent years are omnipotence, omniscience, incorporeality, omnipresence, perfect goodness, and immutability. The last property in this short list, immutability, has been understood by a number of theists to be the property of being absolutely incapable of undergoing or engaging in any sort of real change whatsoever. This understanding of divine immutability has been held mainly by philosophers who subscribe to the doctrine of divine timelessness, the position that God is outside time, having no temporal properties and standing in no temporal relations. Some have mistakenly thought that divine changelessness entails divine timelessness, and thus have held the latter position on the basis of their desire to embrace the former. The converse entailment, however, does hold; so those who think they have independent grounds for ascribing timelessness to God must hold God to be incapable of real change, and so they tend to hold this absolutist conception of divine immutability.

So understood, the claim that God is immutable encounters a number of difficulties. It takes a great deal of ingenuity, for example, to reconcile this claim with the fundamental Judeo-Christian conviction that God is a moral agent who acts in history. No such attempts I know of seem altogether plausible. And if absolute changelessness is incompatible with divine agency, it is inconsistent with a fundamental presupposition of the doctrines of omnipotence and perfect goodness, as normally understood by theists. It is also well known of course that in the past, Norman Kretzmann and Anthony Kenny, among others, have argued that this sort of immutability is incompatible with omniscience. Given certain plausible assumptions about human freedom and the ontological status of the future, this case can be made much more strongly than it has been so far in the literature. And finally, all the more serious problems alleged against divine timelessness, although not all directly problems for this conception of immutability, do tend to impugn rather seriously the major ground usually appealed to for holding God to be absolutely incapable of real change.

I think these problems provide us with sufficient motivation to consider re-thinking the notion of divine immutability. Philosophers who hold the absolutist view seem to go too far in one direction, claiming too much, whereas many contemporary theologians who hold that divine immutability amounts to no more than God's reliable conduct of his affairs err in the other extreme and claim too little. I believe that the modalities of property exemplification explored in this paper can provide us with a way of explicating divine immutability which will avoid both extremes. It will be a position which in one possible variant happens to be logically consistent with the thesis of timelessness, but it is in no way dependent upon or motivated by that controversial view. On the contrary, it is motivated by the need to provide an adequate and precise account of the sort of substantive immutability ascribed to God by many theists who hold him to be a temporal individual who is unceasingly active, and thus not incapable of every sort of change.

Those properties exemplified by God which are dignified with the appellation 'divine attributes' are held by many theists to be properties constitutive of divinity. They are such that, necessarily, no individual could have the status of deity without exemplifying them, and any individual who does instantiate them is God. This marks them off in a most important way from all other properties had by the individual who is God. The predication of any divine attribute, for example the proposition 'God is omniscient', is thus *de dicto* a necessary truth following from the concept of God.

It is a deep theistic conviction that the divine attributes are not exemplified in a temporary manner by any individual who is God. It is unthinkable for theists that, say, Yahweh once began to be God, enjoyed that exalted status for a while, and then subsequently ceased to be God by, in turn, beginning to exemplify the divine attributes, having them for a time, and then ceasing to be characterized by them. The divine attributes are exemplified, if at all, necessarily in a non-temporary manner. And this is part of what theists in the Judeo-Christian tradition usually are expressing when they reflectively hold as a doctrine of theology that God does not change.

I think that, accordingly, a part of what divine immutability consists in can be spelled out by saying that the divine attributes are exemplified in a strongly immemorial and strongly enduring way. They are thus, in my technical sense developed above, strongly immutable for any individual who is God. It then follows that any being who is God exemplifies deity in a strongly immutable way. This is an important part of what reflective religious people are concerned to affirm when they assert that God is immutable.

But why not just say that the divine attributions, propositions like 'God is omnipotent', express necessary truths *de re* as well as *de dicto*? This is a position which many theists hold, and which, along with the common claim that any individual who is God exists necessarily, or in every possible world, entails that none of the divine attributes is exemplified temporarily. In other words, the question is whether we can't explicate divine immutability perfectly well with only the standard modal notions of necessity and contingency. Do we need the modalities of strong stability?

First, it is true that from the two premises

(1) The divine attributes are essential properties of any individual who is God

and

(2) Any individual who is God exists necessarily

it follows that

(3) No individual who is God can begin or cease to exemplify a divine attribute.

Both premises represent accurately tenets of traditional theism, and are, I believe, in fact true. Further, the proposition they entail, (3), is the thesis I am holding to be partially constitutive of the doctrine of divine immutability. But let us reflect on this argument a bit.

Propositions (1) and (2) entail something stronger than (3) as well, namely

(4) No individual who is God could fail to exemplify a divine attribute.

In another idiom, (4) states that there is no possible world in which an individual who is God in any world fails to exemplify one of the divine attributes, either by failing to exist, or by existing without having one of those properties. This proposition is important for a central form of classical theism but is, I believe, too strong to serve as an explication of any component of the particular doctrine of divine immutability. It is (3), which of course (4) entails, that serves this function. So I think we shall uncover what is necessary for explicating this aspect of immutability if we ask what propositions would entail (3) without also entailing (4).

Consider first of all the second premise. In order to obtain (3) from (1) all that is needed is the weaker

(2´) Any individual who is God exemplifies strongly immutable existence,

which is the claim that the changes of coming-to-be and passing-away can not occur with respect to divine beings. If (1) is true, then there can be no time during the existence of any being who at any time is God before he begins to exemplify any of the divine attributes or after he ceases to have one of them. Such a being can thus begin or cease to have a divine attribute only if he can begin or cease to exist. And this is precisely what is ruled out by (2´), thus producing (3).

Now let us consider the first premise. It tells us that in no possible world could any individual who is God in any possible world both exist and fail to have one of the divine attributes. Although many theistic philosophers would hold this to be true, I do not believe that on reflection they would consider it to express exactly even part of what they mean when they ascribe immutability to God. We might say, somewhat loosely but with a helpful degree of vividness, that in affirming immutability their concern is not so much with what God could or could not be like in some other possible world as it is with what he might or might not become in the actual world. The primary religious concern at this point is to deny that the individual who is God could *cease* being the way he is and become instead another sort of being. And in holding this I think most theists would be maintaining a view according to which neither could God have become divine after having been otherwise. This view, though entailed by (1), is expressed precisely by

(1′) The divine attributes are strongly immutable properties of any individual who is God.

And of course (1′) and (2′) entail the desired conclusion (3), which amounts to the claim that all the divine attributes are exemplified in a strongly immutable way by any individual who has them. The modalities of strong stability have thus been employed to explicate part of what reflective religious people attempt to express by the doctrine of divine immutability, a commitment which does not seem amenable to clear and precise expression in any other terms.

Again, I should stress that by suggesting the replacement of (1) and (2) above with (1′) and (2′) I do not intend to cast any shadow of doubt on the truth of the former propositions. I am suggesting only that those claims do not serve to explicate (although they do entail) that aspect of divine immutability having to do with the divine attributes. So although the *de re* necessity of the divine attributes may be held in some sense to account for or explain this element of divine immutability, the position that they are necessary *de re* does not constitute a part of the doctrine of immutability. As a result, someone can hold God to be in this sense immutable even if he does not accept the stronger theses (1) and (2) about the necessity of the divine attributes and existence.

But if the standard modal notions of necessity and contingency alone fail to provide a precise account of this aspect of divine immutability, they fail even more obviously to explicate what I think can be argued to be a second component of that doctrine. In addition to the thesis that the divine attributes are exemplified in a strongly immutable manner, I would like to suggest that there may be one other ingredient in any adequate conception of God's immutability. That is the claim that divine intentions are maintained in a strongly stable way. God's intentions or plans to act are not the mere result of, or capriciously subject to, sudden decisions or changes of mind. In a traditional terminology, they are eternal. But we must be careful about exactly how we spell this out. Some divine intentions can be held to be strongly immutable. For example, it can be argued that if God intends my salvation and beatitude, he always has and always will. And further, he could not have begun so to intend, and cannot cease having such an intention. If this is so, then that intention would be both strongly immemorial and strongly enduring; hence strongly immutable.

But, supposing God to be a temporal individual, not all divine intentions can be held to be strongly immutable. I shall explain this in a moment. But first we need to see that all divine intentions can be strongly immemorial. And arguments can be presented that this must be the case. For example, if God is omniscient he presumably knows what he would do under any conceivable future circumstances. If his omniscience is exemplified with strong immemoriality, such intentions of his to act must be strongly immemorial as well.

Admittedly, such an argument will be resisted by some philosophers on the ground that its conclusion does not square well with biblical portrayals of divine-human interaction. Richard Swinburne, for example, has said:

> If God had thus fixed his intentions 'from all eternity' he would be a very lifeless thing; not a person who reacts to men with sympathy or anger, pardon or chastening because he chooses to there and then.[4]

But this need not follow at all from the strong immemoriality of divine intentions. The position I am presenting is perfectly consistent with the divine intentions being indexed to, or conditional upon, contingencies arising in the created universe. Thus God can act often in response to human actions. As many biblical scholars have pointed out, and as the prophet Jonah discovered to his chargrin, divine warnings, announcements of God's intentions to punish, often if not always express conditional intentions. Why can't it always and immemorially have been the case that God intends to do A if B arises, or C if D comes about? This would be fully compatible with an informed reading of those passages which seem to portray God as changing his mind in response to human activity as situations develop.[5]

But a few words should be said about this compatibility. One must always exercise caution when operating at the interface of philosophical theology and biblical hermeneutics. It can be argued persuasively that no adequate conception of deity will characterize God as the sort of being who can literally repent of a decision or intention. And if this is so, a philosophical understanding of divine intention such as that being developed here need not be consistent with a literal reading of those Old Testament passages which describe God as repenting or changing his mind. However, from the point of view of someone who takes seriously the biblical documents as data for theological reflection, it is desirable to so characterize divine agency as to allow for God's acting in a way which might be described naturally by an ancient Hebraic writer, from his perspective, as repenting.[6]

If some strongly immemorial divine intentions are conditional in form, it may be true at one time that because of present conditions in Ninevah, God is going to punish the Ninevites, and then later when conditions change, no longer true that he is going to punish them. In the same way that we allow the sun to be described as rising and setting, we can understand how this change could be represented as a change on the side of God. In reality of course, there would be no change in God's intentions, just a change with regard to which of his immemorial intentions he would in fact enact. And this would be wholly due to their conditional form, not to any change of mind on God's part.

I should add that an even looser explication of the stability of divine intentions could conceive them as immemorially held in disjunctive clusters conditional upon contingent developments in the world. And such a conception clearly would be consistent with the view of Swinburne and others that God is the sort of agent who makes choices in response to, and at the time of, his creatures' activities. For example, God could intend immemorially to do A or B or C should D arise. Then in response to the actualization of D he might choose B. Even on this conception, the sense in which the divine intentions are strongly immemorial would be an important one. No development would take God by surprise and force him to improvise in his governance of the world. But it is not entirely evident that the sense in which God's intentions are strongly immemorial need be this loose one.

I have claimed that all the divine intentions can be strongly immemorial in one of these senses. But if God is a temporal individual, not all his intentions can be strongly immutable, because not all can be strongly enduring. As a matter of necessity, the only divine intentions which can be strongly enduring as well as strongly immemorial are intentions to effectuate states of affairs which are themselves strongly enduring and dependent for their persistence moment to moment on God's continuing activity. My eternal salvation would be a good example of this kind of state of affairs. Only concerning deeds which in this way never can be completed can God have strongly enduring intentions. For any task which is completable, God can intend to carry it out only so long as it is not completed. This follows from a general conceptual truth about temporal intention applied to the case of an omniscient being such as God. An intention to bring about some state of affairs S can be maintained only so long as the agent believes the bringing about of S not to have been accomplished. Since God can have no false beliefs, he can intend to bring about S only so long as the bringing about of S has not been accomplished. If all God's intentions were strongly enduring, and thus could never cease to obtain, it would follow that he could never accomplish any completable task — an obviously unacceptable conclusion for any form of traditional theism. If he ever completes tasks, God has intentions which are not strongly enduring. Yet all his intentions have a property akin to that of being strongly enduring. They cannot cease to obtain through change of mind or forgetfulness, only by being enacted. And this sort of cessation is due wholly to the logic of intention, not to any unworthy variableness in God.

So theists who both hold that God is in time and feel that part of God's immutability consists in the strong stability of his intentions cannot claim simply that all the divine intentions are strongly immutable. What can be claimed is that (1) all of them are strongly immemorial, (2) some of them are strongly enduring and thus also strongly immutable, and (3) those which are not strongly enduring have the analogous property of being such as never to cease to obtain unless the logic of intention so requires. In any case, every divine intention is maintained in a strongly stable manner.

It is important to realize that theists who hold the divine intentions to be strongly stable need not, and for the most part will not hold them to be necessary. Let us suppose that in fact God does intend my salvation and beatitude. It is not a necessary truth that he so intends. There are plenty of possible worlds in which I am not saved, at least those worlds in which I do not exist. And in at least those worlds, of course, God does not intend my salvation. It is only when we recognize and employ the modalities of strongly stable exemplification that we can explicate this position concerning the divine intentions.

I am suggesting that the doctrine of divine immutability may be understood as the position that both the divine attributes and the divine intentions are strongly stable for any individual who is God. Let us refer to God's attributes and intentions collectively as his *constitutive character*. The modalities of property exemplification we have examined allow us to explicate divine immutability as the strongly stable exemplification of God's constitutive character. I believe this conception is much more adequate and a good deal less problematic than rival conceptions propounded by many philosphers and most contemporary theologians. And it is a position which only the modalities of stability allow us to formulate.

IV. Divine Dependability

Suppose a theist gets himself into the following position. He holds omnipotence and omniscience, among other attributes, to be essential properties of the individual who is God. He views God as a moral agent and believes him to be in fact sinless, but is not convinced that sinlessness is an essential property of God's. He may have been persuaded to some extent by arguments such as that offered by Nelson Pike that necessary omnipotence is logically incompatible with essential sinlessness. Or he may just find sinlessness an unlikely candidate for the role of essential property. He may hold, for example, that any logically simple (e.g. non-disjunctive) property which is essential for any individual necessarily is essential for every individual which exemplifies it, and recognize that sinlessness does not meet this condition. Whatever the reason and whatever its cogency, a theist could get into such a position without obviously flouting any clear canons of rationality. And in this position, we might wonder how firm the theist's trust in God rationally could be. Can a deity who is heretofore blameless, but is not believed to be essentially so, be trusted to persevere in the straight and narrow way? Or might such a being suddenly and capriciously lapse into moral iniquity?

Let us pose the problem in a slightly different way. Suppose our imagined theist accepts the proposition 'God is sinless' as a necessary *de dicto* truth following from the concept of God. So he agrees that no individual can enjoy the status of deity without being sinless. But now he wonders whether the individual who in fact is God can cease to be God by ceasing to be good. Must he merely trust the assurances of Pike and others that Yahweh has a very firm and dependable character? Or can he have a stronger ground for depending on God?

There is a form of argument available to such a theist which proceeds from the premises that the individual who is God is essentially omnipotent, essentially omniscient, and in fact at some time sinless to the conclusion that this being can never cease to be sinless. In other words, an argument can be constructed from those premises to the conclusion that any such divine being exemplifies sinlessness in a strongly enduring manner. So even if he is not believed to be necessarily sinless, such a being is demonstrably dependable. The upshot of the argument is that God cannot lapse into sin, or cease to be God by ceasing to be good.

The form of argument I have in mind is *reductio ad absurdum*. I shall present two, slightly but interestingly different, versions of such an argument.[7] Both will proceed on the assumption that God is a temporal individual. On the contrary supposition, the desired conclusion would of course follow much more directly but much less interestingly.

Let us suppose for *reductio* that there is a possible world *Ws* in which an individual who in that world is God, say Yahweh, sins at some time *t* and thereby loses the status of deity which he has enjoyed up until *t*. We take it here as given that omnipotence, omniscience, and sinlessness are divine attributes or requisites for deity. Consider first Yahweh's omniscience, and his position in *Ws* at some time *t*–1, a moment just before *t*. At *t*–1 Yahweh must know that in *Ws* he will sin at *t*. None of the even remotely plausible arguments that omniscience does not entail foreknowledge of some kind or other would block this modest inference. And at that prior time, Yahweh either lacks or has the power to see to it that he does not sink into sin at *t*. This is merely the power to maintain an intention not to sin at *t* as well as the power to see to it that this intention is not thwarted. If he lacks the power, then Yahweh is not omnipotent and thus not God at *t*–1 contrary to our assumption. No adequate definition of divine omnipotence will allow a being to lack the power to maintain his own intentions and still qualify as maximally powerful. Nor will a being count as omnipotent who cannot see to it that his own intended acts are performed. If on the other hand Yahweh has the power, then by stipulation of *Ws* he chooses not to use it and so is not sinless, and thus not God, at *t*–1, again contrary to our assumption. God does nothing unintentionally. If he sins at *t* then he intends to sin at *t*. More precisely, if he sins at *t*, then he intends at *t* to sin at *t*. Further, God is never at a loss as to what he will do under any circumstances. It may follow from any adequate understanding of omniscience and may be, as I have suggested, a component of the doctrine of divine immutability, that for any of his conceivable future actions (indexed if need be to possible contingencies), God either intends to do it or intends not to do it. Certainly this will be so concerning possible actions in the next moment. So if at t–1 Yahweh does not choose not to intend at t to sin at t, that is, if he does not intend at t–1 not to intend at t to sin at t, then he intends at t–1 to intend at t to sin at t. But of course for God to intend to intend to $\varnothing$ is for him to intend to $\varnothing$. So at t–1 Yahweh intends to sin at t. Given that intentions to sin are just as much worthy of blame as the act or acts intended, an intention to sin is itself a sin. So at t–1 Yahweh sins and is thus not God, contrary to our assumption. And of course, strictly isomorphic arguments will apply to t–2 in reference to t–1, to t–3 in reference to t–2, and so on recursively to any prior t–n in reference to t–$n+1$. Thus no possible world is coherently describable in which a divine being is God for a while and then lapses into sin, thereby ceasing to be God.

Now consider a slightly different version of the same sort of argument. We assume once again for *reductio* that there is a possible world Ws in which some individual, Yahweh, satisfies the requisites for deity up until a time t, at which time he sins, thereby ceasing to be God. We assume again that deity requires omniscience as well as omnipotence and sinlessness. At some time t–1 just prior to t, either Yahweh intends to sin at t, or he does not so intend. If he does, then in having such an intention he sins at t–1 and is thus not then God, contrary to our assumption. If on the contrary, he does not intend at t–1 to sin at t, it is either because he intends at t–1 not to sin at t, or because he has at t–1 no intention concerning whether he will sin at t. If the former is true, then by stipulation of Ws his intention is thwarted and he is thus not omnipotent, and so not God, at t–1, contrary to our assumption. Of course the intention had at t–1 not to sin at t would be thwarted at t, and so it may seem that it is not until t that Yahweh thus lacks omnipotence. However, there would be a power he lacks at t–1 — the power to see to it that his present intention is enacted at t. If on the other hand Yahweh at $t-1$ has no intention at all concerning whether he will sin at t, then at that prior time he fails to exemplify at least one requisite of deity and so fails then to be God. Either he lacks sinlessness, or he lacks omniscience, or both. In at least the case of an individual such as God, being sinless entails intending never to sin.[8] Thus, in order to be sinless at $t-1$, Yahweh would have to intend then never to sin, and thus not to sin at t. His lacking any such intention would entail his not being sinless and so not God at $t-1$, contrary to our initial assumption. In addition, it can be argued that if Yahweh were omniscient at $t-1$, then he would know at that time that he was about to sin at t. But God cannot know he is about to act in a certain way without intending so to act. This follows from the divine freedom (an implicate of omnipotence and omniscience). So if Yahweh did not intend at $t-1$ to sin at t, it would follow that he did not know at $t-1$ that he was about to commit this act. But in that case, he would not be omniscient and so not God at $t-1$, again contrary to our assumption. Once more our *reductio* is complete.

What these two arguments show is that God, if he is essentially omnipotent and omniscient, and in fact sinless at some time, is sinless in a weakly enduring manner. He is not such that he could cease to be sinless while yet continuing to exist. Coupled with the belief that any individual who is God exists necessarily, or even exists in a strongly enduring manner, they yield the conclusion that God's sinlessness is strongly enduring as well. And either of these additional premises could be produced by an interestingly parallel argument from omnipotence and omniscience, as well as on independent grounds.

So even for the theist who is not convinced that God is essentially sinless, a divine dependability is demonstrable which amounts to the stability of God's moral character. This is surely an interesting result. And it shows again how the modalities of stable exemplification can throw light on a fundamental issue in philosophical theology.

A final word should be said about the stability of divine

sinlessness just demonstrated. It seems that we have here an instance of an extrinsically stable property. It is not obvious that sinlessness is stable for God in virtue of being essential to him. Nor is it an intrinsically stable property. Our arguments seem to indicate that it can be viewed as a property whose stability is conferred on it by the nature of its bearer, or by other properties exemplified by its bearer. Unlike intrinsically stable properties, sinlessness is not the sort of property stable for just any individual who exemplifies it. The case of Adam is enough to show that. It seems rather to be endowed with stability by the other properties with which it is co-exemplified in the case of God. And this is interesting indeed. It would also be interesting to ask whether God's sinlessness is provided with more than one mode of stability by those other properties, and thus with immutability. But space prevents such a discussion here.

I have attempted to develop and apply some modalities of property exemplification neglected in recent literature. I hope to have shown that they can serve some useful purpose in the philosophy of religion, specifically in exploring the elements of theism. They may have applications other than those adumbrated here, but at least in the cases I have discussed, their usefulness is evident.

6

On God and Mann:
A View of Divine Simplicity

ONE OF THE MOST difficult and perplexing tenets of classical theism is the doctrine of divine simplicity. Broadly put, this is generally understood to be the thesis that God is altogether without any proper parts, composition, or metaphysical complexity whatsoever. For a good deal more than a millennium, veritable armies of philosophical theologians—Jewish, Christian, and Islamic—proclaimed the truth and importance of divine simplicity. Yet in our own time, the doctrine has enjoyed no such support. Among many otherwise orthodox theists, those who do not just disregard it completely explicitly deny it. However, in a couple of recent articles, William E. Mann has attempted to expound the idea of divine simplicity anew and to defend it against a number of criticisms.[1] He even has gone so far as to hint at reaffirming its importance, suggesting that the doctrine may have a significant amount of explanatory power and other theoretical virtue as part of an overall account of the nature of God, by either entailing or in other ways providing for much else that traditional theists have wanted to say about God. In this paper, I want to take a close look at Mann's formulation of the doctrine and at a general supporting theory he adumbrates in his attempt to render more plausible, or at least more defensible, various of its elements and implications. As Mann has made what is arguably one of the best attempts to defend the doctrine in recent years, I think that such an examination is important and will repay our efforts.

I. Two Views of Simplicity

What exactly the doctrine of divine simplicity is is not easy to say. Clearly Parmenidean in pedigree, the claim that the Ultimate Reality is simple has been articulated within a Neo-platonist framework as well as in Aristotelian terms. To the extent that its expression in patristic and medieval texts is often terse and somewhat metaphorical, it is not always clear precisely what was being claimed. One noteworthy feature of the contemporary discussion of simplicity is that it has involved no extended effort to examine those original metaphysical contexts for all they might provide us in our attempt to explicate the doctrine.[2] Nevertheless, the main lines of various possible interpretations are fairly clear. In one well known formulation of the doctrine, the following claims are made: We customarily, and permissibly ascribe numerous predicates to God—We say, for example, that God is wise, good, and powerful. However, we are not thereby properly attributing a multiplicity of different properties to him. That is, we are not to be understood as holding that God stands in relations of exemplification or participation to a diversity of properties existing distinct from, and independent of, him. In the case of God, and of God alone, there is no multiplicity of properties instantiated. He is rather numerically identical with any property truly attributed to him. Thus, God = Wisdom, God = Goodness, God = Power, God = Justice, and so on. And of course, from this it follows by the principles governing identity that each divine property is identical with every other divine property, which means that in reality there is only one property that God has—a property with which he himself is identical.

Let us refer to this striking formulation of the doctrine as the property view of divine simplicity. Its problems are obvious, and by now widely acknowledged.[3] For one thing, it identifies properties we know to be distinct, properties which are not even co-extensive. In addition, it seems clearly to imply that God, as a property, is an abstract object. On the basis of these and other implications, it would be hard to find many

philosophers who would subscribe to this particular view of
divine simplicity. It is one of Mann's objectives to stress that
this is not the only way a doctrine of divine simplicity can be
formulated. He finds in St. Thomas a subtle distinction which
he thinks can be exploited to make a big difference in the
plausibility of claims about God's simplicity.

St. Thomas, Mann relates, holds not that God is identical
with Wisdom, Power, and Justice, but rather that he is identical with *his* wisdom, *his* power, *his* justice, and so forth. In
this slight variant of expression, Mann sees the key to a defensible formulation of divine simplicity. It is his suggestion that
if we understand this small difference as reflecting an important but elementary metaphysical distinction, the absurdities
which seem to plague the property view of simplicity can be
avoided completely. The distinction he draws is one between
properties and property instances. Roughly, a property is an
abstract object capable of exemplification. A property instance
is a particular exemplification of a property. A great number
of property instances, moreover, are concrete particulars. What
Mann most likely has in mind here is something like a distinction between the rectangularity of this page, as a feature of
the page existing in space and time, and the property of rectangularity, which exists only as an abstract object.

The application of this distinction to the doctrine of divine
simplicity is, then, straightforward. God can be held to be identical with his instantiation of wisdom, his instantiation of
power, and, generally, his instantiation of any property which
holds true of him. From this formulation of the doctrine, it
will not follow that wisdom is one and the same property as
power, and so on, but only that the instance of wisdom we
have in the case of God is one and the same concrete particular
as the instance of power we find in deity. And although this
latter claim may sound a bit mysterious at first, it — unlike the
identification of patently different properties — is in no way
clearly absurd. Furthermore, this formulation of the doctrine
obviously does not make God out to be an abstract object. It
characterizes him rather as an individual property instance, a
special sort of concrete particular.

Let us refer to Mann's formulation as the property instance view of divine simplicity. Like the property view, it is meant to be a comprehensive thesis holding true in the case of every one of God's properties. Unlike the property view, Mann thinks, it is a reasonable position for a theist to hold. Before we examine whether the property instance view can succeed on both counts, we should first note an important difference between it and the property view as yet unmentioned.

Alvin Plantinga has suggested that a major reason theists historically adopted a doctrine of divine simplicity was to accommodate what he calls a 'sovereignty-aseity intuition', a fundamental convinction that God must be such as to depend on nothing distinct from himself for what he is, and such that he has everything distinct from himself within his absolute control.[4] The connection between this intuition and simplicity was forged by the following sort of argument: What God's nature is, and what his character is, consists in his having certain properties rather than others. Now if these properties constitutive of his nature and character were abstract objects distinct from God, he would be dependent on something distinct from himself for what he is. Furthermore, there would then be certain connections between him and these distinct objects which would not be wholly within his control. If there can be absolutely no sense in which God depends on anything distinct from him, and no sense in which anything can be outside his control, then the properties God has cannot have an ontological status distinct from him.

Any such ontological distinction is eliminated by simply identifying God with any property he has. Thus the sovereignty-aseity intuition can motivate a doctrine of divine simplicity. But notice that the view of simplicity required to accomodate such absolute sovereignty and aseity is the property view. The property instance view will not do the job. For it allows that there is at least one property existing distinct from God as an abstract object on which God is, in some sense, dependent for what he is—an instance of that property. So whatever we think about the sovereignty-aseity intuition at work in this argument, we must acknowledge that it will not act as a motivation for adopting a property instance view of simplicity. If this version of the doctrine of divine simplicity is to be a reasonable position for a theist to hold, other reasons must be found for subscribing to it.

Although Mann does not acknowledge this difference between the property view and his own favored property instance view—indeed, he articulates his view after delineating briefly the aseity motivation for a doctrine of simplicity, and without noting the lack of motivational connection with his own formulation—he does in fact suggest some other reason that theists might have for adopting a property instance doctrine of simplicity. In brief, he seems to see the view of simplicity he expounds as the most general account available of the metaphysical nature of deity which will be free of any obviously false implications while at the same time entailing, and allowing for a defense of, some of the other striking and important claims about God which have been propounded as central elements in the tradition of rational theology. Most importantly, Mann contends, his view entails that God is timeless, and, independently, that he is immutable. He suggests further that it has explanatory value with respect to these other doctrines about God's nature.[5] To the extent that these other claims are valued and at the same time thought to be in some need of more general theoretical support, if Mann is right, then there would seem to be at least *prima facie* grounds to recommend his view of simplicity logically distinct from the now irrelevant sovereignty-aseity intuition.

But in order to give any more complete assessment of his view, we must attend to its components a bit more carefully and take a look at the elements of a supporting theory he constructs for it.

II. Rich Properties

It is just absurd to identify God as an abstract object, as the property view seems to do. It is at least not so obviously absurd to characterize God as a property instance if we remember that a property instance is meant to be the sort of thing which can be a concrete particular. But we might well wonder whether in the final analysis this is just as unacceptable a claim. For our clearest examples of what Mann might be intending with his distinction between properties and property instances involve as instances such things as the rectangularity of this page, the linear arrangement of these words, the blackness of this ink. These property instances are all features or aspects of something, and of something apparently more ontologically fundamental than themselves. For the identity of this page could survive the excision of its rectangularity if, for example, its corners were cut off, but the rectangularity of this page conversely could not survive the destruction of the page itself.

Is every property instance merely a feature of something more fundamental than itself? If so, and God is a property instance, the clearly unacceptable consequence will follow that God is a feature of something ontologically more fundamental than himself. This would not be much of an improvement on the view that God is an abstract object. However, Mann introduces a notion which, if acceptable, could be used to block the claim that this characteristic holds true of every sort of property instance. The notion he introduces is that of a rich property.

A rich property is defined by Mann as a conjunctive property having as its conjuncts all and only properties which hold true of a particular individual. These will include, he says, both essential and accidental properties. So in the case of any object, however ontologically fundamental, there will exist a corresponding rich property. It is Mann's suggestion that all objects can be viewed as property instances of their appropriate rich property. On this conception, every individual is numerically identical with a property instance. This will hold true of tables, chairs, pages, Mann himself, and of course, God. Certain property instances thus are not features of anything more fundamental than themselves. These are instances of rich properties. Mann's argument is that on the property instance view of divine simplicity, God is held to be numerically identical with just this sort of property instance, an instance of a rich property. For if God is identical with an instance of each of his properties, it follows that in his case there exists only one property instance, however many properties he has being exemplified. And whenever all of a being's properties are exemplified in one property instance, it will follow that that instance can be nothing other than an instance of what Mann calls a rich property. Thus the view that God is a property instance does not seem to imply after all any sort of unacceptable feature-dependency of God on something more fundamental than himself.

This defense of the property instance view of divine simplicity clearly relies on the conception Mann gives us of a rich property, and that conception itself can appear to be plagued with problems. I am supposed to be an instance of my rich property. And my rich property is supposed to be composed of all my properties. If this is supposed to be inclusive of all the properties I ever will have, a problem arises. For presumably I shall exemplify next year properties I do not now have. There are then components of my rich property which will not have instances in my case until next year. But if a rich property just is a conjunctive property composed, and one assumes, composed essentially, of its conjunct properties, then it stands to reason that the existence of an instance of a rich property essentially depends on the instantiation of each of its conjunct properties. So if some of my rich property's conjuncts are not yet instantiated in my case, no instance of my rich property yet exists. And if I am an instance of my rich property, I do not yet exist. And of course, it follows more generally by the same reasoning that no sort of temporal being ever can exist.

This problem, however, can be held not to impugn the notion of a rich property itself, nor even to be relevant at all to the claim that God is an instance of a rich property, but only to block any claim that an existent temporal being is an instance of such a property. As simple, God would have no temporal parts, and so this problem would not touch his case. But it will block the general claim that every object can be identified as an instance of a rich property, and that in at least this respect, on Mann's view God's ontological status is not altogether without parallel; that is, unless the notion of a rich property should be restricted in some way.

The most obvious restriction that comes to mind would be to limit an individual's rich property to a conjunction of all and only its intuitively essential properties. On this conception, the claim that any individual, temporal or atemporal, is identical with its rich property would avoid altogether the problem just mentioned. Further, it would avoid another problem Mann's more liberal conception can be held to have — a problem of modal uniformity.

I think that Mann could have avoided ever writing on simplicity. The property of having written on simplicity is surely not one of his essential properties. But it is one of the conjunct properties in his rich property, liberally conceived. If we understand a rich property to be individuated by means of, and to be essentially related to, its conjunct properties, and view a property instance as a sort of thing which is essentially tied to the property of which it is an instance, then the commonly accepted and quite reasonable view that all metaphysical identities are necessary precludes one from holding both that Mann is identical with what is as a matter of fact his rich property instance and that he could have avoided ever tangling with simplicity. If an individual's rich property is understood to involve all its properties, then one can identify an individual with the exemplification of its rich property only on pain of holding all its properties to be essential. If we want, as Mann does, to acknowledge individuals as having accidental as well as essential properties, and want to identify those individuals with instances of conjunctive properties, we must include as conjuncts only properties we independently and intuitively recognize as essential to them.

Let us call the sort of conjunctive property with whose instances we can identify the ordinary individuals or substances of our conceptual scheme without modally unacceptable consequences an haecceity. Mann could then hold that every individual is a property instance of an haecceity, and that in this respect the doctrine of a divine simplicity he espouses does not make God any different from anything else. He, like anything else, is a property instance. And he is the sort of property instance which does not exist as a mere feature of something more fundamental then himself. He is an instance of an haecceity.

It is worth noting, however, that on the supporting theory Mann develops, the distinction between an haecceity and a rich property liberally construed collapses in the case of God in an interesting way. How this happens will become clear in the next section. Right now, we need to attend to another implication of his version of divine simplicity. In trying to recommend his property instance view of simplicity, Mann has to render plausible the consequence that the instance of each property God has is identical with the instance of every other divine attribute, as well as defending the central claim that God is a property instance. To this end, he sketches out some elements of a theory of property and property instance. To this end, he sketches out some elements of a theory of property and property instance identity, to which we now turn.

III. Properties, Property Instances, and God

Under what conditions will an instance of a property F be identical with an instance of a property G? In answer to this question, Mann presents the following principle:[6]

> C — Property instances *the F-ness of x* and the *G-ness of y* are identical if and only if (1) the property *being F* is necessarily coextensive with the property *being G* and (2) $x = y$.

On the basis of principle C, the theist who wants to hold that God's omnipotence = God's omniscience need only claim that omnipotence and omniscience are properties which are necessarily coextensive — exemplified by all the same objects in all possible worlds in which either is exemplified. Now, as Mann points out, the theist may have a good deal of difficulty in trying to *demonstrate* the necessary coextensiveness of any conceptually distinct divine attributes, but what is important to note is that this is a position that many theists are inclined to adopt—at least with respect to such properties as omniscience, omnipotence, aseity, necessary goodness, and the like—and many have this inclination who would otherwise tend to shy away from any sort of simplicity doctrine. Indeed, as I have suggested elsewhere, the thesis that at least some divine properties are necessarily coextensive may be an important part of any argument that the God of the philosophers is the God of Abraham, Isaac, and Jacob, that the conception of God as a maximally perfect being is fully consonant with all the deepest concerns of a biblically or revelationally oriented religious faith.[7] It is Mann's contention that this thesis will render more plausible the major consequence of the claim that God is identical with an instance of each of his properties, namely the entailment that each of his property instances is one and the same as each other one—that, for example, his necessary goodness is his aseity, which is his omnipresence, and so on.

But why should we think that C is true? It is one thing to claim that necessary coextensiveness of properties is *necessary* for the identity of property instances, but quite another to go on and claim this to be *sufficient* as well (given, of course, the identity of the property bearer involved). Triangularity and trilaterality are necessarily coextensive properties, as understood in Euclidean geometry. Yet why should we say that an instance of one is one and the same concrete particular as an instance of the other? If many property instances are *features* of objects, isn't three-sidedness a different feature of a given geometrical figure than that of having three angles? In order to allay our suspicions here, Mann introduces an element of a theory about properties which I shall not discuss on its own merits, but whose main thrust and implications we need to note.

Mann suggests as reasonable to hold a principle of property identity according to which necessarily coextensive properties are identical. Acknowledging that there are some apparently counter-intuitive consequences of such a position, he nevertheless argues that it is a fully defensible view to take along the spectrum of possible views on property identity. And if such a principle is adopted, our questions about C vanish. For surely, if F and G are not only necessarily coextensive, but actually one and the same property, there is no question that an instance of F is an instance of G.

Let us look then at some of the implications that C and this supporting claim have for the case of God. God's instantiation of omnipotence will be identical with his instantiation of omniscience only if omniscience and omnipotence are necessarily coextensive. And this can be so only if they actually are one and the same property. The same consequence, of course, likewise holds for any apparent pair of God's properties. So there can be only one divine property instance — one with which God is identical — only if there is not more than one divine property. Thus, as Mann acknowledges, God's rich property is a limiting case of a conjunctive property, one composed of only one conjunct. And on any reasonable essentialist metaphysic, an object such as God must have at least one essential property. So it follows that God is an instance of a property which is essential to him. This is why on Mann's view we have in the case of God a collapse of the distinction between a rich property, liberally construed, and an haecceity.

Now this panoply of distinctions and principles Mann introduces to construct and defend a view of divine simplicity has a number of consequences which require examination. First, for all their differences, the property instance view of simplicity Mann presents and the property view have in common, as has just been pointed out, an entailment we might not initially have anticipated: In the case of God, only one property is involved. On the property view it is one with which God is identical. On Mann's view, it is one whose instance God is.

This consequence is problematic in more than one way. First, there arises from it a problem of modal uniformity, a sort of problem one version of which has already been considered in connection with Mann's original definition of a rich property. Here it arises quite simply. God's properties obviously cannot differ among themselves in modal status if he has in reality only one property. But theists traditionally hold that God is essentially omnipotent, omniscient, and good, yet only contingently or accidentally such that he created this world, called Abram out of Ur, spoke through Moses, and so forth. It follows from Mann's account of divine simplicity, as well as from the property view, that no such modal discriminations can be made with respect to God. And surely this is unacceptable.

Secondly, there may be in addition what we might call a supervenience problem for this conclusion about the divine attributes. The problem is this: Standard conceptions of some divine attributes seem to be conceptions of essentially supervenient properties—properties which can be exemplified only in virtue of other distinct properties being exemplified. Now, the notion of supervenience is quite common in contemporary philosophy and, difficult though it might be to understand completely, is basically a simple notion to grasp. If a property F supervenes a property G, then an instance of F essentially depends on there being some instance of G in association with which it exists, in the sense that no instance of F could exist unless some underlying instance of G existed simultaneously.[8] With this sort of relation in mind, a number of recent philosophers have claimed, for example, that human personality essentially supervenes upon corporeality of a sufficiently intricate sort of structure.

Many theists hold a conception of omniscience according to which God is omniscient in virtue of, at least in part, knowing all true propositions. If the 'in virtue of' locution is taken seriously here, then it would seem that God's omniscience is being held to supervene on his knowing this, his knowing that, and so on. Likewise, many would hold that God is omnipotent in virtue of being able to do any of a suitably delimited set of tasks, or in virtue of having all powers of a certain sort, or in virtue of being able to actualize this sort of state of affairs, and that sort, and so on. In either case, it appears that some divine attribute is viewed as exemplified only in virtue of some other distinct properties being had. So, on this understanding, God cannot be omnipotent or omniscient unless he has more than one property. If he has any such attribute, Mann's view cannot be right. At least one property of God's would supervene upon numerically distinct properties which he would, in addition, have to have.

It might be objected that it is not the case that God is omniscient in virtue of knowing p, q, r, and so forth, but rather that he knows any such true propositions in virtue of being omniscient. But of course no mere reversal of precedence here will solve the supervenience problem. For then God's property of knowing that p will supervene upon God's being omniscient and p's being true. And any case of supervenience among divine properties whatsoever will suffice to block Mann's views.

The only move remaining would be to deny any supervenience relation between God's omniscience and any of his more closely specified properties of knowing. And of course this is what Mann's position dictates. If God is omniscient, then presumably he knows that Mann has written on simplicity (or, possibly, something like 'Mann writes on simplicity from t_i–t_n'). And if he is simple, he is identical with his exemplification of the property of knowing that truth. But then his instance of that property must be identical with his omniscience. On Mann's theory, it certainly seems like this can be so only if the property of knowing that Mann writes at some time on simplicity is necessarily coextensive with, indeed identical with, the property of being ominiscient. Yet I and many others have the former property without, unfortunately, the latter. These properties are not necessarily coextensive, so on principle C, none of their respective instances can be identical, one with the other. It looks as if the only way to avoid the supervenience problem, a move actually dictated by Mann's theory, requires identities which his own principle of property instance identity will not allow.

Even apart from any need to avoid the supervenience problem, the same sort of difficulty arises for Mann's views with respect to other properties. For God is knowledgeable and he is powerful. On the property instance view of divine simplicity, he must be identical with his knowledge and identical with his power, and so these property instances must be identical with each other. But on principle C, this can be so only if knowledge and power are necessarily coextensive, which they are not.

However, in some general remarks he makes when presenting his views, Mann recognizes a distinction which could be used to provide for his extrication from these difficulties. He first makes the, by now, common distinction between great-making properties (properties it is intrinsically better to have than to lack) which admit of degrees, and those which are not degreed. The property of being knowledgeable would be an example of a degreed great-making property, while that of existing a-se could be a fairly clear example of a non-degreed property. Further, among degreed properties we can distinguish those with intrinsic logical maxima from those which admit of unlimited increase in degree. Mann claims that the properties of being knowledgeable and of being powerful are degreed great-making properties with intrinsic maxima. He identifies their maxima as, respectively, omniscience and omnipotence.[9] It is his allegation that while the properties of knowledge and power vary somewhat independently through their less-than maximal degrees, they coalesce into one and the same property in their maxima. Thus, although it is not a general truth that knowledge and power are necessarily coextensive, and certainly not the case that they are identical, it is nonetheless true that omniscience and omnipotence are both necessarily coextensive and, indeed, one and the same property.

With these acknowledged distinctions in mind, it might be thought that Mann could claim that God's knowledge is God's power since God's knowledge is nothing other than his omniscience, his power is none other than his omnipotence, and principle C does countenance his omniscience being identical with his omnipotence. Thus by the symmetry and transitivity of identity it would follow that his knowledge is his power.

But principle C as it stands will not license two of the premises
of this argument — the claim that God's knowledge is his omniscience, and that his power is his omnipotence. For knowledge and omniscience, and power and omnipotence are not
necessarily coextensive properties.

Principle C, however, could be emended to take care of that,
employing the distinctions just drawn among degreed and non-
degreed properties. It then might look something like this:

C1 — Property instances *the F-ness of x* and the *G-ness of
y* are identical if and only if (1) the property *being F* is
necessarily coextensive with the property *being G*, or (2) at
least one of those properties is a degreed property with an
intrinsic maximum, and that maximal degree is necessarily
coextensive with either (a) the other property, or (b) the intrinsic maximum of the other property, and (3) $x = y$.

On this revised version of C, it could be held that the knowledge of God is his omniscience, his power is his omnipotence,
and then that his knowledge is his power.

But what about God's apparently distinct property of knowing that Mann writes on simplicity? C blocks the identification of that property with God's omniscience. And so does C1,
for the property in question is not a degreed property. But,
it could be maintained, it is a sort of determinate of a determinable property — knowledge, or being knowledgeable —
which is degreed. Accordingly, C1 could give way to some C2,
a principle which, employing this distinction, would allow the
identification of God's knowledge about Mann with his omniscience. Here, things begin to get a bit complicated, for then
the principle will look something like this:

C2 — Property instances *the F-ness of x* and *the G-ness of
y* are identical if and only if:
  (1) the property *being F* is necessarily coextensive
  with the property *being G*
or (2) at least one of these properties is a degreed property with an intrinsic maximum, and that maximal
  degree is necessarily coextensive with either (a) the

other property, or (b) the intrinsic maximum of the
other property

or (3) at least one of the properties is a determinate
of a determinable, which itself either (a) is necessarily coextensive with either (i) the other property,
or (ii) an intrinsic maximum of the other property,
or (iii) a determinable of which the other property
is a determinate, or (iv) an intrinsic maximum of
a determinable of which the other property is a determinate, or (b) has an intrinsic maximum which
is necessarily coextensive with either (i), (ii), (iii),
or (iv) above

and (4) $x = y$.

And, as if this were not enough, at least one further complica-
tion would have to be taken into account by any successful
formulation of such a principle for property instance identity.

Consider the property of existing necessarily a-se. No created
being could possible have this property. Now consider the properties of being self-identical, of being such that $2 + 2 = 4$,
and finally, of having some property. These are all properties
had by all created beings. And surely they are necessarily such
as to be had by any being whatsoever. But suppose God has
them. On the property instance view of simplicity, God's instantiation of each of them must be identical with his exemplification of each of his other properties, including that of
existing necessarily a-se. None of these properties is a degreed
property with an intrinsic maximum. Nor is any a determinate
of a determinable. So God's instantiations of them can be identical on C, C1, and C2 only if the properties involved are all
necessarily co-extensive. But since no creature exists necessarily a-se, they are not all necessarily coextensive. If God can have
a property only if his instantiation of it is identical with all
his other property instances, then C, C1, and C2 all force us
to conclude that God is not self-identical, not such that $2 +
2 = 4$, and not such as to have any properties. But this is ab-
surd. So presumably, our principle for property instance identity will have to be complicated further.

And it may seem that a further version, C3, could easily be constructed along the lines of C1 and C2 to allow God to have such trivial properties and to provide for their instantiation in his case to be identical with all his other property instances. However, supposing for a moment that this could be done with any initial plausibility at all, the resulting sort of principle would share with C2 some consequences which should be far from attractive to Mann or any other defender of simplicity. First of all, on any version of the principle from C2 on, it will not follow from the identity of all divine property instances that God has but one property. Yet this seems to be a claim every defender of simplicity has wanted to retain, and it is a claim to which Mann seems strongly committed, in spite of its modally untoward implications. At first, it might be thought that this diversity among divine properties recognized by C2 on would, if embraced, allow a defender of simplicity to avoid any problem of modal uniformity with respect to God's properties. But of course, God's having a multiplicity of properties alone does not allow his properties to differ in modal status. And in fact the rest of the apparatus of Mann's theory precludes their so differing. Furthermore, affirming the additional identities any envisioned emendation of C2 would countenance leads to an even worse problem of modal uniformity. Then we would find ourselves forced to swallow a modal uniformity to the exemplifications of all properties whatsoever.

Consider any exemplification of an apparently accidental or contingent property. God will have the property of knowing this property to be exemplified. And this piece of knowledge will be identical to his omniscience. Thus, it will be essential to him. But if this is so, and God is a necessarily existing being, it will be a necessary truth that the original, apparently contingent property is exemplified, and that it is exemplified by the particular object which otherwise appeared accidentally to have it. It then follows of course that the actual world is the only possible world, that all our properties are essential, and so on. This is the extreme of modal uniformity.

In "Simplicity and Immutability in God," Mann attempts

to avoid a couple of broadly related problems by distinguishing between the content of God's omniscience and the activity by which he knows, and in a similar vein between the results of what he actually wills and the power or activity of his willing.[10] His claim is that anyone who holds a simplicity doctrine is free to maintain that the content of God's knowledge or the results of his willing could have been different from what they are without thereby being committed to the claim that the activity by which God knows and the power by which he wills could have been different. If this is true, it will follow that the extreme modal uniformity problem can be avoided by the defender of simplicity.

First, it should be said in Mann's behalf that these surely are intelligible distinctions to draw. Furthermore, it is eminently reasonable to acknowledge that the contents of God's knowledge and the results of his willing could have been different from what they in fact are. But what we must ask is whether these distinctions can be employed to avoid the extreme problem of modal uniformity by anyone who holds a view of divine simplicty such as Mann's. I, for one, do not see how this is possible. For surely God has the property P of being such that his omniscience has the content that it as a matter of fact has (in the actual world). And on Mann's view of simplicity, as he has formulated it, it follows that God is identical with his instantiation of P and that it is identical with his instance of omniscience. How his omniscience could be what it is, and yet no instance of P exist, a property instance with which his activity of omniscience is supposed to be identical, is hard to understand. Indeed, given the most plausible position on the modal status of such metaphysical identities, the sort of divergence Mann envisions to be possible would in fact be logically impossible.

I have suggested that even if some version of a Mann-style principle of property instance identity could be formulated to allow God to have trivial properties as well as his distinctively divine attributes, and which would render their instances identical to his seemingly many instances of other properties, unacceptable consequences would follow. I now want to make the stronger claim that no such formulation will succeed in even its intial task. To see why, we must examine a problem, as yet unacknowledged, with C1 and C2.

Consider Mann's own power and his own knowledge. Surely, these are distinct property instances, for they can wax and wane somewhat independently of one another. But assuming that omnipotence and omniscience are necessarily coextensive, C1 and C2 as they stand entail that Mann's power is one and the same property instance as his knowledge. Likewise, C2 implies that his knowledge that Washington, D.C. is the capital of the U.S.A. is identical with his power to lift a single copy of the *Times* with ease. And this is clearly absurd. Among Mann's many features, these are obviously distinct.

The problem in both C1 and C2 is that the conditions laid out do not meet up to the full requirements of the bicondi-tionality of their formulation. What are presented as severally necessary and jointly sufficient conditions for property instance identity clearly lack sufficiency. Any claim that *the F-ness of x* is identical with *the G-ness of y* must satisfy the general prin-ciple of the indiscernibility of identicals as well as such specific conditions as appear in Mann's original principle C and its de-scendents if it is to be an acceptable identity claim.[11] Mann's original principle can appear to give us a criterion of property instance identity distinct from the generalized indiscernibil-ity principle often known loosely as 'Leibniz's Law', and for-malizable as:

$$(x) \, (y) \, ((x = y) \equiv (F) \, (Fx \equiv Fy))$$

according to which, roughly, an object *x* is identical with an object *y* if and only if *x* has every property *y* has, and vice versa.

The conditions appearing in C1 and C2 may even enhance the illusion of independence from Leibniz's Law. What must be recognized, however, is that absurd results cannot be avoided unless the conditions laid out in C1 and C2 are seen as no more than partial explications of what is involved in the satisfaction of Leibniz's Law in the case of property instances. *The F-ness of x* cannot be identical with *the G-ness of y* unless every property exemplified by *the F-ness of x* is emplified by the *G-ness of y*, and vice versa. No descendent of C will succeed unless this is stated explicitly in its formulation.

And once we have such a general indiscernibility clause, rendering the right hand side of the principle's biconditional fully sufficient for identity, we shall have a principle which blocks Mann's power being identical with his knowledge, and so forth, but in addition one which blocks God's having any trivial properties. Consider again God's instance of aseity. It has the property of being an instance of a property had only by God. Now, on Mann's theory, God can have the property of being such that $2 + 2 = 4$ only if his instance of that trivial property is identical with, among other things, his aseity. But on Leibniz's Law, this is possible only if the former has the property of being an instance of a property had only by God. And since we all are such that $2 + 2 = 4$, this condition is not met. Therefore, God is not such that $2 + 2 = 4$, and by the same reasoning not self-identical, and not such as to have some property. We have this absurd result again, and this time due to a condition ineliminable from any acceptable formulation of a principle for property instance identity.

More generally, we have by parallel reasoning what we can call the problem of divine uniqueness: Leibniz's Law together with the basic elements of Mann's property instance view of divine simplicity will yield the result that God cannot have both (a) a property which is unique to him, and (b) a property shared by any other individual. For his instance of any property unique to him would itself have the property of being an instance of a property unique to God. And he can have a shared property, one not unique to him, on Mann's view only if his instance of that property would be identical with his instance of every other one of his properties, including in this case the instance of his unique property. But his instance of a shared property would not have the property of being an instance of a property unique to God, and so by Leibniz's Law could not be identical with an instance of a unique divine property. Thus, when the governance of Leibniz's Law becomes a recognized component in the property instance view of divine simplicity, it follows that either (1) All of God's properties are shared, or (2) None of God's properties is shared. If God has an individual essence, or any properties distinctive of deity, (1) cannot be true. And if we can make any justified assertions about God at all, (2) cannot be true. Indeed, (2) is not even coherent except on a non-standard and extremely restricted view of what counts as a property. It is hard for me to see how an acceptance of either (1) or (2) could amount to anything other than a relinquishing of the substance of traditional theism. And neither has the least plausibility. So I conclude that no formulation of a property instance identity principle can function in a view of divine simplicity such as Mann's and be both free of patently absurd implications for individuals other than God (implications such as that Mann's power is identical with his knowledge) and free of such implications for God.

Of course, my argument for this conclusion depends crucially on acknowledging into our scheme of things such properties as those I have used as examples — such properties as knowing that Washington, D.C. is the capital of the U.S.A., having the power to lift the *Times*, existing a-se, being such that 2 + 2 = 4, being self-identical, and being such as to have some property. I suppose my conclusions could be resisted by denying that there are any such properties at all. But this seems to me almost too drastic a course to mention. For it would take quite a bit of argument to dislodge the sort of standard and powerful view of properties which countenances my examples. And neither Mann nor anyone else has succeeded in overturning this sort of view. So I think the foregoing arguments are secure.

It seems to me that the only plausible way to avoid the unacceptable problems I have delineated while still holding to a doctrine of divine simplicity would be to restrict the doctrine to apply only to *some* divine properties, abandoning the comprehensive formulation it usually receives. In light of the problem of modal uniformity, if God is held to have any essential properties at all, he cannot be held to be identical with any property instance which we have strong intuitive grounds to think exists only contingently. That is, no instance of a property which we independently judge to be contingently exemplified by God can be declared identical to him. No utterly comprehensive doctrine of divine simplicity, meant to apply to all God's properties, will avoid having modally unacceptable consequences. Likewise, in light of the problem of divine uniqueness, we cannot with any plausibility declare God to be identical with instances of both properties unique to him and properties he shares with others. Restrictions must be introduced here as well. I think this is a conclusion which is forced on us by what we have seen. The question we must then ask is how the doctrine of simplicity might be restricted to avoid these problems.

IV. Restricted Simplicity and Divine Modalities

The most obvious examples of properties God is traditionally thought to exemplify only contingently are such properties as that of creating this world, calling Abram out of Ur, and speaking to Moses. And these are all examples of what are commonly understood to be relational properties. In particular, they are all such that their exemplification entails the existence of some contingent being distinct from God.[12] The modal status of the nondivine relatum determines the modality of God's exemplification of any such relational property. If a doctrine of divine simplicity were formulated in such a way as to allow such properties to be exemplified contingently, any problem of modal uniformity might be avoided.

Now, of course, not all of God's relational properties are contingent. For presumably he bears relations to numbers, propositions, and the like which are as necessary as the relata involved. So a restriction of divine simplicity intended to avoid contingencies need not exclude all relational properties from its scope. The suggestion rather would be that God can be identified with his instantiation only of properties which are not contingently exemplified relational properties.

And it is arguable that this class of relational properties will not be the only class of properties which needs to be excluded from the doctrine of divine simplicity. For consider the property of intending to create some contingently existent physical reality or other. Most traditional theists would judge this to be a contingent property of God's. Yet it is not relational in the stipulated sense of entailing the existence of some particular contingent reality distinct from God. With such an example in mind, it looks as if someone like Mann should just specify that simplicity hold only with respect to properties we have some good grounds for judging not to be exemplified contingently by God, whether they be relational or non-relational. But of course the doctrine of simplicity cannot comprise all non-contingent properties of deity, as we have seen from the problem of divine uniqueness. The most plausible restriction which can be introduced to block this problem is to limit the doctrine to only those non-contingent properties of deity unique to God, such as, presumably, a-seity, omnipotence, omniscience, and the like. To put it somewhat picturesquely, we would then, with these restrictions, be conceiving of a simple core of deity underlying both God's shareable properties and whatever complex of contingent relations and states might be generated by divine intention and action.

On this restricted view, God would be identical with his mere having of omniscience and with his power of omnipotence, but not with his knowledge of Mann or his calling of Moses. Likewise, his omniscience would be identical with his omnipotence, which would be identical with his omnipresence, which would be the same as his aseity, which would be his necessary perfection. None of these would be held to be identical with his instance of any property he contingently exemplifies. And none would be identical with an instance of any property not unique to deity. And so, on this sort of formulation of a doctrine of divine simplicity, no problem of modal uniformity or of divine uniqueness would arise.

Mann could adopt such a restricted doctrine of simplicity to avoid the problems which seem to plague his comprehensive version. But the question which would have to be asked at this point would be why such a restricted doctrine should be adopted at all. Granted, it avoids problems attending the more comprehensive formulation Mann expounds, but what would be the positive motivation for subscribing to any such simplicity doctrine at all? We have already noted that sovereignty-aseity intuitions fail to motivate any property instance view of simplicity. What is just as important to note at this point is that the other motivation to which Mann appeals falls away as well in the case of the restricted sort of doctrine I have just sketched. For God's being identical only with instances of properties he intuitively is judged to have both uniquely and essentially or non-contingently will not entail his being timeless or his being absolutely immutable. Thus, the restricted version cannot serve the explanatory function with respect to these theistic claims that Mann wants of a simplicity doctrine.

Indeed, it is hard to see what reason we could have at all for adopting the sort of restricted property instance view of simplicity at which we have arrived by following Mann's lead. In many patristic and medieval texts, it appears that simplicity is affirmed so as to secure a sort of constancy among God's core property exemplifications. Metaphysical complexity is equated with a sort of composition admitting of decomposition and dissolution. Theists who viewed complexity in this way found themselves committed to affirming simplicity so as to deny the very possibility that any of the properties constitutive of deity be lost by the individual who is God. However, by getting sufficiently clear on modal matters relating to deity, we can see that this may be held to be precluded apart from any doctrine of divine simplicity.

As Nelson Pike and others have emphasized in recent years, there are numerous propositions about God which can be understood as necessary truths *de dicto*.[13] These are propositions concerning what we might call the defining attributes of deity. In an Anselmian vein, for example, there are numerous great-making properties which are requisites of deity. No individual could "count as" God without exemplifying them. They are in this sense necessary to deity.

Further, a strong classical conception of God will involve numerous necessities *de re*. The great-making properties requisite for deity which are exemplified by the individual who is God will be held to be exemplified by him essentially. He will be such that he cannot cease to have any of the defining attributes of deity and yet continue to exist. Further, one of the properties ascribed to God in this tradition is that of necessary existence. On this conception, the individual who is God cannot cease being God. Moreover, it could not have been the case that he not be God. Some philosophers recoil from attributing the modal status of necessity to God's existence and to at least one of the other defining attributes of deity — the property of being good as an agent. But even these philosophers are free to acknowledge another set of modalities to hold true of the defining attributes of deity — the modalities of *stability*, which I have delineated elsewhere.[14] Briefly, the stability of the defining attributes amounts to its not being possible that any individual who has them have begun to exemplify them, and not possible that he cease having them. If the defining or "core" attributes of deity are stable, then it will not be possible that there be any sort of decomposition among them. What friends of simplicity have sought to secure will be secured.

And finally, it can even be held by a traditional theist that some of the requisites of deity, some of the great-making properties such as omnipotence, omniscience, necessary existence, and the like, are necessarily coextensive. In fact, as I have suggested earlier, this will be held by many theists who have no brief for simplicity. Thus it can be held that the unique, crowning attributes of deity cannot "come apart" in any metaphysical sense at all, without any commitment being generated to a doctrine of simplicity.

With these modal matters in mind, I cannot see any clear motivation for adopting a restricted property instance view of simplicity whatsoever. The modalities of God's attributes provide for all that such a doctrine could reasonably be intended to provide. Now, I would not want to deny that the sort of sovereignty-aseity intuition discussed by Plantinga can act as a powerful motivation to consider seriously a property view of simplicity. For the relation between God and such abstract objects as properties is problematic. There may be ways to circumvent the well known, apparently decisive objections to such a view, although I cannot think of any which are both clear and completely plausible. I do think the attempt made by Mann to circumvent these problems altogether by adverting to a property instance view of simplicity has not achieved what he intended. The only version of Mann's view which can be defended as at all plausible is such that no apparent reason exists to adopt it as a distinctive doctrine about the nature of God at all. Rather than having a significant amount of explanatory virtue as part of an overall theory of God's nature, it appears to be altogether superfluous, offering us no assurances about deity that cannot otherwise, and more straightforwardly, be had.

7

God and the World:
A Look at Process Theology

PROCESS THEOLOGY IS in a number of ways a noteworthy and interesting intellectual phenomenon. For one thing, it is predominantly a movement of very liberal Protestant theologians who derive their basic categories of thought from what may be one of the most elaborate and exotic metaphysical systems ever devised—the philosophical system of Alfred North Whitehead. Of course, what is noteworthy here is not the mere fact that a number of theologians are drawing on the ideas of some philosophical system for use in their theological work. The church fathers derived much of their intellectual framework from Plato and Neo-platonism, St. Thomas and his followers drew on the philosophy of Aristotle, and in more modern times numerous Christian theologians once attempted to appropriate important elements of Hegel's philosophical system for their own purposes. It is extremely difficult, if possible at all, to do much work of a systematic theological nature without employing concepts or making assumptions which are properly philosophical.

What is so remarkable about the application of Whitehead's work in contemporary process theology is that, for the most part, liberal Protestantism and metaphysical speculation over the years have mixed about as well as oil and water. Liberal theologians for more than a century have denounced traditional theology, the theology of the councils, confessions, and catechisms, for what they have considered its unhealthy and distorting dependence on metaphysical, philosophical categories foreign to the language of the Bible. Under the unfortunate influence of the eighteenth-century philosopher Immanuel Kant, most liberal theologians for a great many years have done their best to avoid metaphysics altogether, apparently doubting our ability to arrive at knowledge of the ultimate nature of reality which goes beyond what our physical senses together with the natural sciences tell us. However, in contemporary process theology we find numerous thinkers of a liberal persuasion orienting all of their theological work around the basic concepts of a speculative metaphysical system of enormous complexity whose categories and claims go far beyond the deliverances of sense experience and natural science. This is an interesting development indeed. Yet, for at least two reasons, this new development in theology may not after all really be so surprising.

Not all liberal theologians who have objected to the metaphysical cast of traditional orthodox theology have done so because of general Kantian strictures on the possibility of metaphysical knowledge. A number of them have objected primarily to what they take to be a distinguishing feature of the particular metaphysics which informs orthodox thought. In fact, one of the most common charges raised against traditional Christian thought by modern theological critics has been that the particular philosophical categories it employs to articulate the Christian message are static metaphysical categories incapable of capturing the dynamic tenor of the Bible. The main concepts of classical metaphysics are those involved in the analysis of Being, for example the concepts of substance and attribute. Process thought purports to replace this approach with more dynamic considerations. The concern with Being is replaced with a focus on Becoming, the category of substance yields to that of event, and all of reality is viewed as an ongoing, never ending process. It clearly cannot be said of process metaphysics, as it has been said of its classical counterpart, that it is too static to capture the dynamic nature of Christian thought. It is hard to imagine how there could possibly be a more dynamic conceptuality than process metaphysics. So it is understandable that theologians seeking a dynamic conceptual structure might on this ground alone be attracted to process philosophy.

There is a further consideration, however, which may shed even more light on the attraction process thought has had for many theologians. The relation betwen metaphysics and the natural sciences is somewhat elusive, and in itself poses some complex and interesting philosophical problems. It takes no philosophical acumen at all, though, to realize that classical metaphysics, of a Platonistic or Aristotelian sort, was in its origin and developmental stages a pre-scientific intellectual phenomenon. That is to say, it was developed many centuries before the rise of modern science. It is a tempting illusion to think of ourselves as always standing on the shoulders of those who have preceded us, in such a manner that we see more in every way than they were able to see. A great many modern theologians have been unable to resist this illusion, and consequently often have appeared to prefer nearly anything of recent vintage over the best of ancient and medieval thought. And of course, from this point of view, the more in step with modern science an idea is perceived to be, the better. Philosophically, one of the most interesting features of Whitehead's thought is that it represents the only careful and well developed attempt so far to construct a comprehensive metaphysical system in the light of central discoveries and perspectives of twentieth century physics. Since he was a sophisticated mathematician as well as a philosopher, Whitehead's metaphysical thought itself bears some of the marks of a scientifically responsible system. Thus it is easy to see how theologians dubious about classical metaphysics and enamoured of the modern scientific spirit might be attracted to such a philosophy, even though it is not a system of thought which has been very attractive to other philosophers, or to scientists, interestingly enough.

Process theology is not to my mind a dominant trend in theology. Yet in view of its remarkable popularity in some circles, it merits careful philosophical and theological scrutiny. A critical scrutiny of process theology is especially important due to the great amount of highly persuasive rhetoric in which it often is clothed by its proponents. In many ways, I think, this new theology can be a wolf in sheep's clothing. It is presented for our approval garbed in a fabric of buzz-words which in our time have many highly favorable connotations: process thought is said to recognize and uphold the importance of creativity, novelty, development, evolution, freedom, ecological relatedness, society, and the like. It is difficult to criticize a movement which appears to uphold all the positive and seemingly healthy values of the modern world. But in spite of the positive aspects of process theology, there exist in its tenets serious denials and dismissals of important traditional Christian beliefs. I suggest that our attitude toward process theology needs to be a carefully balanced one: while applauding and learning from its more laudable elements, we must also learn to recognize and reject what, from a Christian point of view, are its more lamentable features.

In this essay, I want to look at a few of the more interesting claims of process theology having to do with the relations that exist between God and the world. The process theologians have done us a favor by insisting that our concept of God be such as to square with the central religions conviction that God can interact with us, his creatures. Some strands of medieval theology stand in tension with the biblical portrait of God as a responsive agent in history. Process theologians have sought to point this out and develop a concept of God more adequate to the biblical picture. By looking at this criticism of one feature of some medieval theology, even briefly, we can come to see something very important about our idea of God.

Unfortunately, not all that process theologians say about God and the world is equally valuable, or even acceptable to traditional Christians. I want to take a look at two points at which numerous process theologians have gone wrong concerning God's relation to the world. First, it is a standard tenet of process thought that God needs the world in order to be who he is. As we shall see, this involves a denial that God freely created the world *ex nihilo*, the denial of a central belief of orthodox Christian thought. I hope to show how the process theologians, starting from a genuine insight, go wrong at this point for no good theological reason. It will be fairly easy to see that we can preserve their insight while avoiding their error on this point.

Second, I want to look at what a number of process theologians have said about God's eternal preservation of his world, and specifically at the idea of immortality they ordinarily endorse. The sort of immortality they promise is very different from the personal after-life in which Christians have believed over the centuries. I hope to show that the one and only argument presented against the traditional view by one of the most prominent process theologians not only is itself unconvincing, but also may be inconsistent with one of the central claims distinctive of process thought.

I aim here neither at completeness nor at any measure of comprehensive scholarship concerning what exactly this or that process theologian has said in one or the other edition of this or that book. Nor shall I concern myself much with the relation between the ideas of process theology I have chosen to discuss and the details of Whitehead's original metaphysical system, to which they are related in one way or another. This self-imposed limitation is possible due to the fact that the specific ideas of process theology I shall examine can be understood well enough for our purposes without the need of any Whitehead exegesis. This limitation is desirable for the sake of clarity so that we can focus our attention more firmly on the substantive theological issues at stake and leave aside the complexities of interpreting Whitehead.

I. God's Perfection and Action in the World

In the twelfth century, St. Anselm, Archbishop of Canterbury, one of the greatest theologians of all time, wrote that he understood God to be "that than which no greater can be conceived"—a greatest conceivable, or maximally perfect being. This was meant by Anselm to be something like a defini-

tional truth: In much the same way that it is true by definition that a triangle has three angles, it is true that God is a
perfect being. Another way of putting this point would be to
say that just as no figure counts as a triangle unless it has three
angles, no individual counts as literally divine unless he is
altogether perfect.

St. Anselm's definition attempts to capture the core of the
Christian concept, or idea, of God. To specify that God is a
greatest possible, or maximally perfect being is not to display
all of the Christian concept of God, it is just a way of sum-
marizing a controlling feature of that concept. Anselm's definition can be thought of as a formula which can be used to help
us arrive at a more complete conception of deity: God is to
be thought of as having a maximally perfect set of great-making
properties, where a great-making property is a property it is
intrinsically better to have than to lack. For example, if it is
intrinsically better to be powerful than not to be powerful,
Anselm's formula will have us ascribe power to God. Likewise,
if it is better to be omnipotent, or unlimited in power, than
not to be omnipotent, we must ascribe omnipotence to God.
The same will hold true for such properties as omniscience and
omnibenevolence. Applying Anselm's formula to intuitions
we have about what properties are great-making properties,
or perfections, we begin to develop philosophically our idea
of God.

Most sophisticated philosophers and theologians over the
centuries seem to have agreed that if there is a God, he must
be a perfect individual. One thing they have not agreed on,
however, is exactly what that perfection must involve. Intuitions can vary about what properties are perfections. A number
of medieval theologians, including such great thinkers as St.
Augustine and St. Thomas Aquinas, had a set of intuitions
about divine perfection not shared by contemporary process
theologians. Some of those intuitions gave rise to the view that
a perfect being must be metaphysically simple or non-composite
in every respect whatsoever. The intuitions operative here seem
to be that anything which is composed of parts or which can

be analyzed into parts depends for what it is on what those parts are. But it is greater not to be dependent on anything else for what one is than to be so dependent. Thus God, the greatest possible being, must lack any sort of part whatsoever, and must be such that his nature cannot be analyzed into parts. This conclusion, which has come to be known as the doctrine of divine simplicity, has had important implications for the conception of God developed by many philosophers and theologians since the early middle ages.

If God has no parts, he has no spatial parts such as arms or legs. He thus cannot be a corporeal being located in physical space. This is an implication of divine simplicity accepted by a great number of orthodox theologians. Likewise, simplicity theologians reason, God can have no temporal parts either— there can be no before and after in the divine life. God is outside time altogether. His eternity is thus not to be understood as unending, everlasting existence through infinitely many moments of time, but rather is to be understood as a-temporality, or timelessness, existence outside the bounds of any temporal framework.

If God is outside time, it follows that he is absolutely immutable, that he cannot undergo any sort of real change, for any real change must occur over time. In any case of real change, an object comes to lack at some time a property it had at a previous time, or it gains a property it lacked at an earlier time. In either sort of case, the object must exist through different times in order to change.

God is described in the Bible as having done different things at different times. At one time he called Abraham out of Ur, at a later time he spoke to Moses, later still he revealed his will to the prophets, and, at the culmination of the biblical account of his dealings with his people, he himself became a man and dwelt among us. This seems to implicate God in change—he changes from doing one thing at one time to doing something different at a later time. In the biblical account, God seems to be ever-changing not only in the actions he initiates but also in his responses to ever changing circumstances and needs on the part of his people. In short, the Biblical portrayal of God does not appear to be the portrayal of an absolutely immutable being. Granted, the biblical God does not change in his character, or, with respect to the basic attributes distinctive of deity, such as omniscience and omnibenevolence, but along with these continuities in who he is, he appears to be characterized by a ceaseless and appropriately changing activity in what he does.

This is a point not ignored by medieval theologians who held to divine simplicity, a-temporality, and immutability. They and their contemporary followers have attempted to explain away the appearance of change on the side of God by drawing some fairly simple distinctions. First, we need to distinguish real change from merely relational change. Suppose that, unknown to me, there is now a man standing exactly two miles to my right, and that suddenly he walks farther away. Due to his move, I come to lack a property I earlier had—the property of having someone exactly two miles to my right. Yet have I undergone any sort of real change; has there been a change *in me*? Most of us would agree that it was not I who underwent a real change here but rather my right hand man, who really changed by moving away. In this story, I lose a property I had, but I can be said to change only in the loosest sort of relational sense: I underwent a merely relational change.

Likewise, suppose some man Smith dreams of vanilla ice cream daily. But then at some point in time he ceases ever to think of vanilla and begins to dream of chocolate. Vanilla seems to lose a property it formerly had—the property of being dreamed of daily by Smith. And chocolate gains that property. Yet have these flavors themselves thereby undergone any sort of real change? Surely not, the real change is in Smith and his imaginings, not in the ice creams of his dreams. They can be said to have changed only in the loosest of senses, having undergone merely relational change.

Defenders of divine immutability attempt to use this distinction to help explain away the appearance of change in God. There are two ways the distinction between real change and merely relational change can be used for this purpose. The simplest is just to apply the category of merely relational change to God and claim that all divine change is merely relational change—God never undergoes real change, change *in himself*, but rather always is characterized only by merely relational change. Suppose that at some point in time God created our physical universe. Defenders of immutability will insist that upon the creation of this world, nothing really changed on the side of God; it merely began to be true at some time that this world existed. Any change here was extrinsic to God, not intrinsic to him. Likewise, they argue, as various biblical characters are spoken to by God throughout the centuries, there is no real change on the side of God, only on the side of those receiving his word. On this view, God changelessly and eternally wills to speak to Abraham at time t, to Moses at $t + n$, and so forth. The claim is that from God's willing to do different things at different times, it does not follow that God's act of willing changes from one of those times to another. Although his will has to do with the changing times, he does not himself really change with those times. His eternal will is changeless in any but a merely relational way.

Notice however that in the two stories used to illustrate the distinction between real and merely relational change, the object or objects said to change in the merely relational sense did undergo the gaining or losing of some property. In each case it was a relational property, a property of standing in a relation to some other object, but a property nonetheless. It is possible for an object to gain or lose a property only if that object is a temporal individual. But God, according to the simplicity/a-temporality/immutability theologians, is not in time. So if gaining or losing a property, and thus existing throughout successive moments of time, is a necessary condition of undergoing merely relational change, God cannot undergo even this loosest sort of change. At this point, the defender of exteme immutability who, remember, needs to explain away the appearances of real change on the side of God, can make either of two moves. He can deny that gaining or losing properties is necessary for undergoing merely relational change, and so characterize that form of change that God can undergo it. Or he can say that in much the same way that we distinguish merely relational change from real change, we must distinguish the mere appearances of merely relational change from the actual occurrence of merely relational change. In this case, he will deny that God ever undergoes even merely relational change.

A realist account of truth typically specifies that a statement about an object is true just in case the object has the property predicated of it in that statement. My statement that the grass outside my office is green is true just in case the object my statement is about — the grass in question — has the property predicated of it — the property of being green. Suppose however that at t a statement made by Aaron that God is speaking to Moses is true. Later at $t + 1$ a second statement of Aaron's that God is speaking to Moses is false, God's having ceased the communication. On the view that God is outside time, this situation cannot accurately be described by saying that God had a property at t which 'he had ceased to have by $t + 1$ — the property of speaking to Moses. For to be so describable truly would implicate God in time as well as change. The classical theologian must deny that Aaron's true statement uttered at t was true in virtue of a property God had at t, because he must deny that God has any properties at any times.

Some theologians have tried to claim that God has all his properties timelessly, but the classical theologian who endorses divine simplicity as well as a-temporality and immutability cannot say even this. For on the standard explication of simplicity, God cannot be said literally to have properties at all, distinct from each other and from him, since that would involve a sort of composition simplicity theologians have found objectionable. Now this aspect of the doctrine of simplicity is itself far from simple and far from easy to understand. And it has been amply criticized elsewhere.[1] So I shall not comment on it here any further. The point to be made here is that the classical theologian who endorses divine simplicity either must interpret the category of merely relational change in such a way that under-going such a change requires no gaining or losing of proper-ties of any sort, or else must deny even this loosest sort of change to God, holding instead that in the case of God we have only the appearance of merely relational change.

Let us suppose the classical theologian takes the latter course and denies that God is capable of change in any sense. His strategy for dismissing the appearance of change on God's part as he interacts with his creatures can turn on the following claim: just as real change in one object can be reflected in merely relational change in another, so real change with respect to God's creatures can be reflected in the mere appearance of merely relational change on the part of God. We are presented then with an analogy. How successfully the theology of simplic-ity, timelessness, and immutability can be squared with the biblical and religious picture of God as an active agent in history will turn at least in part on how well this analogy holds up.

Consider a standard sort of story of merely relational change. A woman's husband is on an ambassadorial trip to a foreign land and dies at the hand of a terrorist, unknown to her for some hours. At the moment of his death, she becomes a widow. But at that time, the change she undergoes is a merely rela-tional change. The circumstances involve no real change in her part. Contrast this with an alternate story in which the murder occurs in her presence, or an even worse story in which she herself pulls the trigger. In neither of these cases is her becom-ing a widow a set of circumstances involving only merely re-lational change on her part. In light of this difference, we can isolate at least three features of any situation in which one ob-ject has undergone nothing more than merely relational change, reflecting some real change in a different object. First, the on-going existence of the really changing object and its having at least most of the non-relational properties it has are matters in some sense causally and metaphysically independent of the object undergoing the merely relational change. Secondly, the real change in question involves no occurrent exercise of power on the part of the object undergoing merely the relational change. And thirdly, the real change is not registered as a piece of knowledge or belief on the part of the individual going through merely relational change.

We find that in each of the three stories I have told to illustrate merely relational change (the man to my right, Smith and the ice cream, and the unknowing widow), all three features are present. And the same will hold true of any story non-controversially portraying a case of merely relational change. But these are features which could never hold true of God and any of his creatures, such that the creature underwent real change and God was properly characterized as exemplifying all the features of merely relational change that the doctrines of timelessness and simplicity will allow. Each of God's creatures depends on God moment to moment for its existence. None can exist causally or metaphysically independent of God. Further, nothing can happen without at least the concurrent operation of God's conserving power. And nothing can come about without God's knowing it. Whenever we have a case of real change reflected in a case of merely relational change, we have an object undergoing the latter which exists in numerous sorts of isolation from the object going through the former. It is impossible for God to exist in such isolation from his creatures that exist. In light of this, it is hard to see how the classical claim could be made plausible that God stands to all creaturely change in much the way in which an object undergoing merely relational change stands to a really changing object. And without plausibility here, the immutability theory cannot be reconciled to the biblical portrayal of God, in which it seems so clear that God changes what he does as his creatures' circumstances require.

Other objections can be raised to the traditional defense of extreme divine immutability. However, I shall mention no more here aside from pointing to the central Christian doctrine it seems most difficult to square this conception of divine immutability with—the doctrine of the Incarnation, the core belief of the Christian faith that God once became a man and entered into our human history as one of us. I have seen no attempt to reconcile extreme divine immutability with the Incarnation which did not fall into some ancient heresy, or invent a new one.[2] I shall not declare categorically that this cannot be done, or that extreme immutability cannot be made consistent with other elements of the biblical picture of God, but the prospects for such a reconciliation seem dim. I think it a sound method of theological reflection for a Christian, when in serious doubt about the coherence of a particular philosophical claim with central biblical claims about God and divine-human interaction, to avoid endorsing that philosophical claim and to explore alternate philosophical ways of articulating the aspect of deity in question.

If God is not immutable in the extreme sense, then he is not an altogether a-temporal individual. Nor is he metaphysically simple. Such are the logical relations among these properties. It is important for us to realize that we can give up extreme immutability, a-temporality, and simplicity without this detracting from the grandeur of our idea of God. For instance, for God to be such that his nature is analyzable into distinct properties and temporal parts is not for God to be dependent in any substantive and objectionable sense on those parts for what he is. On the contrary, those parts can be held to be dependent on him.[3] So deciding that the notion of metaphysical simplicity has no application to God need not involve detracting from the divine perfection. Process theologians have repeatedly called our attention to those features of the classical conception of God, such as simplicity, a-temporality, and extreme immutability, which seem to comport ill with the biblical picture of God and the religious conception of God as in interaction with us his creature, and have rejected vociferously those classical attributions. Their insistence at this point is that our idea of God be controlled by the data of revelation and religious experience seen as normative by the church. Thus, intuitions about what properties are great-making properties — for example, intuitions that it is better to be outside time than to be temporal — are only defeasible indicators of truth: they can sometimes be wrong. The idea of perfection is not itself rich enough to tell us alone what God is like in every way. And we should not expect to develop our idea of God just from the Anselmian formula together with supporting value intuitions. The revelation God has granted us in his Word and in his Incarnation must be attended to as the central source of any detailed conception of what God is like.

By challenging the classical conception of God, process theologians have helped open the eyes of many Christian thinkers to the role of revelation as an important control on purely philosophical theorizing concerning the nature of God. The impact of their challenge is enhanced by their attempt to provide an alternative conception of God which can satisfy the requirements of perfection without creating the problems we find in classical theism.

Consider the claim that God is immutable. This is a claim that nearly all Christians want to endorse in some sense. But there are many ways of understanding it distinct from the classical conception we have been reviewing. Some theologians seem to understand it in the very minimal sense that God is reliable in the conduct of his affairs. They take divine immutability to be no more than God's moral dependability. On the other hand, there is a stronger, more comprehensive construal of divine immutability which stops far short of the extreme classical view. This would be the claim that it is impossible that God change either with respect to his defining attributes, those properties distinctive to and constitutive of deity—such properties as omniscience, perfect goodness, and almightiness—or with respect to his character and basic intentions.[4] For example, God could not ever have begun to be omniscient, nor can he ever cease to exemplify this attribute. This conception of divine immutability excludes certain very important sorts of change from the life of God, but also allows God to undergo the sorts of change involved in his being unceasingly active in his interaction with his creation.

This dual aspect characterization of deity is somewhat like the conception articulated by many process theologians, including prominently Charles Hartshorne, which often is referred to by them as dipolar theism. There is one pole of deity, one aspect of God which is necessarily as it is, and thus is immutable. There is, however, contrary to classical theism, a second aspect of deity characterized by receptivity, responsiveness, and change. On this conception of God, the immutability,required by divine perfection is perfectly compatible with the sort of change required by God's interaction with his created world. In supplementing their critique of the classical conception with such an attractive alternative way of thinking about what God is like, process theologians have provided an important service to modern theology.

II. God's Relation to the World

In many ways, what process theology has said about God and his relation to the world has been of value, and has served as a needed corrective to some elements of traditional thought, as we have seen. Yet there are also process claims about God and the world which I judge to be unacceptable to Christian faith. Let us consider briefly one way in which a genuine insight had by many process thinkers has been translated into a theological commitment which is unacceptable to orthodox Christians. In process thought, every existent object is viewed as essentially related to other existent objects. Essential relatedness is a pervasive characteristic of reality. Prominent process thinkers such as Charles Hartshorne, along with many more traditional theologians influenced by St. Anselm, hold that God necessarily exists. Not only is it as a matter of fact true that God exists, but things could not possibly have been otherwise. God's non-existence is impossible. Now a property is essential to an individual just in case that individual could not fail to have that property without failing to exist. Since God cannot fail to exist, his essential properties are all necessarily exemplified. And so, if every existent individual is essentially related to other existent objects, and God is a necessarily existent individual, there must of necessity exist objects distinct from God to which he is related. And further, since every object distinct from God must be dependent on him as creature to creator, it follows that a created world necessarily exists. God is necessarily a creator. But any property an individual has necessarily, he does not have freely. So it follows that God never was free with respect to whether he would create a world distinct from himself. He may have been free to create this world rather than another one, but he was not free not to create.

On this view, God needs a world to which to relate himself. A number of process thinkers have given a parallel argument for this view, beginning not from the premise that all existent objects are essentially related to others, but from a specifically theistic premise that God essentially exemplifies a certain sort of relation—that of being loving. The sort of love intended here is not self-love, but what we can call 'other-love'. It is thus impossible that God exist without loving another, some individual distinct from himself. But every individual distinct from God is a created being. It is thus impossible for God to exist without a creation. So, again, God has never been free to refrain from creating at all. To be who he is, he needs a world.

The conclusion common to both these lines of reasoning is at odds with a firm commitment of the Christian tradition, the belief that with respect to creation God was utterly free not only concerning what he would create but also concerning whether he would bring into existence any universe at all. I think that process theologians who mount these sorts of arguments are starting from genuine insights about relatedness and divine love: everything that exists is essentially related to other existent individuals, and it is an essential property of deity to be other-loving. But the process theologians' conclusions do not follow from these premises as they seem to think. A traditional Christian, upholding the orthodox belief in God's absolute freedom with respect to creation can capture both these insights by a properly articulated doctrine of the Trinity.

The minimal content of any acceptable formulation of Trinitarianism will specify that within deity there is an internal relatedness. On a traditional understanding of the Trinity, each of the three persons is distinct from the other two. Theologians throughout the centuries have differed over whether to stress the distinctness of these three persons, one from the others, or their unity, which is such that Christians can say there is one God who exists as three persons. There are thus two strands of orthodox thinking on the matter. What is called the social view of the Trinity, or Social Trinitarianism, is an approach which stretches back to at least the Cappadocian fathers, and which has had able development and defense in recent years. The other emphasis, on the unity of deity, which tends to see the three-ness of the Trinity as three modes of the existence of one being, was represented by, for example, St. Augustine, and has actually been the dominant view among theologians. The Augustinian emphasis, I think, has resources for countering the process view we are explaining, but it will be simpler, and possibly more interesting as well, to consider how a social view of the Trinity can capture the process insights at this point while avoiding their conclusion.

In the context of discussing favorably the process argument that the necessity of divine love requires a creation, Barry L. Whitney has written that:

> If one were to reply that love could exist only in God himself among the persons of the Trinity, this would seem to imply an unacceptable "tri-theism" wherein the persons of the Trinity are considered as distinct centers of consciousness.[5]

Is Whitney right in suggesting that a social view of the Trinity implies an unacceptable tri-theism? Or is it possible that three distinct centers of consciousness, three individuals, three persons be acknowledged as God without any unacceptable theological results? These are very difficult questions, which would require a great deal more treatment than can be given them here. But I do want to comment on what many philosophers and theologians appear to have taken to be a decisive argument against any plurality of divine persons, and show how, in seeing what is wrong with it, we may be seeing how a Social Trinitarianism can be a completely orthodox view to hold.

No being is divine unless it has all the defining attributes of deity. Any divine persons must be essentially omniscient, omnibenevolent, and omnipotent, as well as necessarily existent, and so forth. Let us suppose this for the sake of our argument, in line with the Anselmian tradition. With this in mind let us now ask whether there could be two divine individuals or persons.

We can begin with a thought experiment. Imagine two arm wrestlers of exactly equal power, skill, and determination. Their match presumably will end in a stand-off, clasped hands straight up, equidistant from each side of the table. Now imagine two essentially omnipotent and omniscient beings 01 and 02. Suppose 01 wants some contingent object A to exist at some time t. And suppose 02 wants A not to exist at t. At t, what happens? There is here no equivalent to a stand-off. By reflection on this sort of imaginable scenario, numerous philosophers and theologians have been led to conclude that there cannot possibly be more than one essentially omnipotent being. Yet, our thought experiment does not support this strong a conclusion, only the interestingly weaker conclusion that there cannot be multiple, essentially omnipotent and omniscient beings *with opposible wills*. However one philosopher, William Wainwright, has proposed a conceptual claim about persons which, when joined to this weaker conclusion, entails the stronger one that there cannot be more than one essentially omnipotent and omniscient person.[6] The claim is that

> (C) Necessarily, given that two persons are genuinely distinct, it is possible for their wills to conflict.

This is just a claim, in other words, that any two or more persons have opposible wills. If Wainwright is correct about this, Social Trinitarianism of any clearly orthodox sort is ruled out.

But why should we think that Wainwright is correct? It surely does seem to be a necessary truth of a conceptual sort that it is possible for the wills of any distinct persons to *differ*—01 for example willing A, 02 either just having no intention with respect to A, or else willing only that whatever 01 wills concerning A be done. But differing in this way is compatible with their wills being necessarily harmonious, such that it is impossible for them to *conflict*. Unless we have any good reason to endorse Wainwright's stronger claim (C), and I for one do not see any good reason to, we seem to be left with the real possibility that there be multiple, essentially omnipotent persons necessarily harmonious in will. This is a far cry from any sort of pagan polytheism, whose gods were in continual conflict. As long as we recognize the conceptual requirement of necessary harmony in will, a belief in multiple divine persons, in particular three, will be far from any obviously unacceptable sort of tri-theism. And it may well be that the unity of deity among the three persons of the Trinity consists, at least in part, in that very harmony of will.

If we can endorse a social conception of the Trinity, a very simple way of blocking the process arguments for the necessity of creation we are examining will follow. But there is one further argument which can be given against a multiplicity of divine persons which draws on a distinctive claim of process theology. According to leading process thinkers, such as Whitehead and Hartshorne, God develops through time, progressively enriching his experience and thereby surpassing his own previous levels of greatness. According to them, it is a conceptual truth that any divine being is a greatest possible being not in the sense that he is so great *he* could not possibly be greater, but in the sense that he is so great *no other* being could possibly be greater. In short, God's greatness is unsurpassible by any other being. We shall return to the conception of divine perfection in the last section of this paper, but for now I want to look at another argument Wainwright has attempted to construct, this time from the process conception of unsurpassibility to the conclusion that there cannot be more than one divine person. Wainwright very carefully lays out his argument in the following ten numbered propositions:[7]

(1) Necessarily, any perfect being is more perfect at later times then at earlier times. (This follows from the dynamic process conception of perfection.)

(2) Necessarily, if there were two unsurpassable beings A and B, then A at time $t+1$ would be more perfect than A at time t, and B at $t+1$ would be more perfect than B at t. (from 1))

(3) Necessarily, B at $t+1$ is either more perfect than, just as perfect as, or less perfect than, A at t.

(4) Necessarily, if it is more perfect, then B at $t+1$ surpasses A at t, from which it follows that A is surpassable by another being and is therefore not perfect.

(5) Necessarily, if it is less perfect, than A at t surpasses B at $t+1$, from which it follows that B is surpassable by another being and is therefore not perfect.

(6) Necessarily, if it is equally perfect, then since A at $t+1$ is more perfect than A at t, A at $t+1$ is more perfect than B at $t+1$, from which it follows that B is surpassable and is therefore not perfect. Therefore,

(7) Necessarily, if there were two perfect or unsurpassable beings A and B, then either A would not be perfect or B would not be perfect. (from 2 through 6)

(8) Necessarily, if there were two perfect or unsurpassable beings, then there would be two perfect beings at least one of which was not perfect.

(9) It is impossible for there to be two perfect beings at least one of which is not perfect. Therefore,

(10) It is impossible for there to be two perfect or unsurpassable beings. (from 8 and 9)

This is an impressive argument whose only major flaw is that it depends on an artificial conception of unsurpassability which not even process theologians need to hold. The intuition, or claim that God is unsurpassable by any being distinct from himself is captured most naturally by an understanding of unsurpassability according to which a being A is unsurpassable just in case it is impossible that there exist a being B and a time t such that B-at-t is greater than A-at-t. And on this most natural understanding of surpassability the argument given by Wainwright will not work. For the unsurpassability of A will not be judged by how A at t compares to B at $t+n$ (for any positive value of n). To the extent that we have no good reason to accept the construal of unsurpassability on which Wainwright's argument turns, and reason to prefer a more natural construal, we have no reason to judge this to be a good argument against any multiplicity of perfect divine persons. So the possibility of a Social Trinity still stands.

Suppose we endorse a social view of the Trinity, as many orthodox Christians of the past have. Can we account for the essential relatedness of all existent beings and the essentiality of the other-love of God without accepting the process claim about the necessity of creation? Yes, we obviously can, for the three persons of the Trinity exist in eternal and necessary relatedness to one another, a relatedness which includes an intra-Trinitarian relation of love. The necessity for any divine person that there exist an object distinct from himself as an object of relatedness and love does not entail the necessity of a physical universe or the necessity that there exist some contingent being or other distinct from God. So in the light of this understanding of the doctrine of the Trinity, we can capture the insights of process theology at this point without following the process theologians into their quite unorthodox conclusions concerning God's freedom in creation, or, rather, his lack of it.

III. God's Preservation of the World

It is a tenet of process philosophy that the changing aspect of deity reflects and registers eternally every thing, state of affairs, and change in the world. Every contingent being which comes into existence and, then passes away, passes away only from the original physical stage of its existence, retaining a sort of foothold in reality in the mind of God. According to many process thinkers, it is impossible that God ever cease to remember and preserve the objective reality of even the slightest and most ephemeral of entities in this world. God is ever changing with respect to the continually active registration in his omniscient knowledge of every new thing that happens in our world. He is never changing with respect to the strength with which he holds all these things in memory, eternally preserving their objective reality. At one time in the past, it was true that Socrates was drinking hemlock. It is now true that Socrates once drank hemlock, and it always will be true. It can never now become false. According to some process thinkers, this very fact about truth, the fact that truths about the past are forever true, along with the fact that we now can refer to Socrates at all, a being who no longer exists on the earthly stage of reality, reflects the objective preservation of the past in the mind of God.

What happens in this world is thus, to process thought, not merely ephemeral. The ongoing developments of history are not transient, evanescent, and ultimately meaningless. They are eternally preserved, and they make a difference in the actuality of the ultimate being, God. Viewed in this way, process thinkers declare, the events of history are full of eternal significance. God's eternal preservation of the world and all its contents provides for meaning and significance concerning even the smallest details of life.

There is a grandeur about this view which cannot be denied. And it is true that many, if not most, people find a great deal of personal satisfaction and comfort in the thought that, in an ultimate sense, "Here today, gone tomorrow" is not the final truth about things in our world. It is interesting and important to note, though, that in so far as it commands widespread assent and provides widespread comfort, this view about God and the world, at least on the points mentioned here, is not unique to process thought. It is a fully orthodox and traditional religious view. What is unique to, and distinctive of, much process thought on these matters is the way in which the preservation picture is used to provide a conception of human immortality—the final end of man.

Immortality has been a central and driving concern in human thought throughout the centuries. Blaise Pascal, the great seventeenth-century scientist and religious thinker once wrote:

> The immortality of the soul is something of such vital importance to us, affecting us so deeply, that one must have lost all feeling not to care about knowing the facts of the matter. All our actions and thoughts must follow such different paths, according to whether there is hope of eternal blessings or not . . .[8]

And this sentiment has been echoed by many others. Tennyson, for example, once said:

> If there is no immortality, I shall throw myself into the sea,

a pronouncement which many people on first reading find puzzling, since many of us would incline to say rather that if there is no immortality, I shall be as careful as possible, avoiding the sea, great heights, and any other dangers as much as I can. However the point, and profundity, of Tennyson's remark comes to light clearly when we meditate on the words of the nineteenth-century English historian Henry Thomas Buckle:

> If immortality be untrue, it matters little whether anything else be true or not,

and those of Bismarck, who said bluntly:

> Without the hope of an afterlife, this life is not even worth the effort of getting dressed in the morning.

So great has been the importance of the promise of immortality to many of the most eminent thinkers of history. It is a central tenet of the Christian faith that those who love God and appropriate the saving work of Christ on their behalf will exist in communion with him forever. Personal immortality through resurrection into new life with Christ is a fundamental belief of orthodoxy. It is a concern with which any comprehensive theology must deal.

A number of process theologians, including Charles Hartshorne, whose work ordinarily sets a standard for process thought, have re-interpreted the idea of personal immortality and have argued that their version of this idea captures the only real hope we have for eternity. As John Cobb and others have pointed out, Whitehead's metaphysical system itself neither entails nor precludes the continuation of conscious human experience beyond bodily death. Whitehead himself seems also to have been agnostic on this issue. It has been left to other process thinkers to decide what should be said about personal immortality.

The view endorsed by Hartshorne and others is that there is no hope to be had in an eternal and blissful continuation of personal conscious experience beyond bodily death for religious believers, or for anyone. Our lives are rather immortalized, or perserved forever, in the mind, or more specifically, the memory, of God. It is thus in the sense, and only in the sense, that everything else is preserved by God forever, that human beings will have an objective immortality. This is the promise of immortality allowed by Hartshorne.

Of course, this is obviously not the sort of immortality for which most people hope. What difference does it make to me if there are, in effect, divine snapshots of my life preserved forever in the gallery of omniscience? On the Hartshornian picture, my future reality one thousand years from now will be no different in fundamental nature from the present reality of dinosaurs: there will be truths about me, as I was, and I shall be remembered, as I was. What we must ask is why Hartshorne and other process thinkers have abandoned the traditional, full-bodied view of immortality in favor of this thin, mnemonic alternative.

In one of his most recent books, Hartshorne gives, or rather, hints at, only one argument against the traditional belief in a personal after-life. The argument is basically quite simple and is akin to arguments offered by other critics of traditional religious belief who are not process thinkers. It is an argument which arises out of no fundamental tenet of process metaphysics, but rather, as I shall point out, turns on a crucial premise which is actually either inconsistent with some central claim of process thought, or else is such that we have no good reason to think it true. Either way, it cannot be used by a process theologian to get us to abandon orthodoxy on this point and join his ranks.

In *Omnipotence and Other Theological Mistakes*, Hartshorne says:

> Those who want to go on being themselves forever and yet pass on to additional experiences after death are either asking for unbearable monotony, endless reiterations of the same personality traits, or they are asking for a unique perogative of God, ability to achieve self-identity through no matter how great and diverse changes and novelties. Unconsciously they either want to be bored to death, so to speak, or to be God.[9]

The traditional Christian promise to believers is that of a blissful eternity. It could be argued that the notion of a blissful eternity is incoherent: There are at most finitely many sorts of pleasures, or aesthetically positive experiences possible to a person. Throughout an infinite span of time, each type of experience would have to be repeated over and over again. But at a certain point, what was once a positive value would eventually become cloying, or at best unbearably boring. Such an existence would not be blissful. So a life can be blissful or it can be eternal; it cannot be both. The concept of blissful eternity is then something like a concept of square circularity—a conception of an impossibility, a logically incoherent notion.

If this were a good argument, if there could be no blissful eternity, then the traditional Christian promise of everlasting life would have to be rejected, but so would a central tenet of process theology—the claim that God's perfection is eternally progressive, that he eternally surpasses his previous states of value by virtue of the ongoing and ever positive aesthetic experiences he has of the world. For the process God exists in a state which cannot be denied to be one of blissful eternity. If positive value through infinite time is possible in the case of God, the very notion of a blissful eternity is not itself logically incoherent. If it were incoherent, this major claim concerning the progressive perfection of the process God would be ruled out as false, and, moreover, as impossible.

The argument just presented for the incoherence of the notion of a blissful eternity is not a good one. Supposing that there were only finitely many positive sorts of experience to be had, it is only a contingent fact of our psychology that repetition bores and cloys. It is part of the Christian hope that in the resurrected life our psychology, as well as the bodily form of our existence, will be transformed. But this need not alone circumvent the threat of tedium. For what reason do we have to suppose that, for any sense of 'kind' relevant to the ongoing experience of an immortal, transformed soul, there are only finitely many kinds of experience possible? There is no reason that I can see for thinking this, and there is no reason that Hartshorne or anyone else offers. In fairness to Hartshorne, he seems to assume neither that a blissful eternity is impossible, nor that the types of positive experience available in principle are of finite number. He does imply that to enjoy eternal bliss, one would have to be God, But why think this? Why not allow that in order to enjoy such a state of existence one would have to be either God himself, or a being created in and conformed to the image of God? This is what Christians traditionally claim, and Hartshorne has given us no reason to conclude otherwise.

Many theologians have said that part of what it means, in traditional terms, to be in the image of God is to be creative. Creativity, or the capacity for creativity, is a key feature of our nature reflecting what it is to be God. It is one aspect of human nature which images deity. And it is the essence of creativity to be open-ended and inexhaustible. Our union and communion with God in the after-life will not extinguish this feature of ours which reflects his nature. Rather, there is every reason for the Christian to suppose it will be magnified in the hereafter. And it is impossible for an individual to be both eternally creative and at the same time infinitely bored. Human creativity, and what it manifests, is a key to the real possibility of eternal bliss for human beings. One need not wish to be God in order to wish to be in a state of eternal bliss. For an infinite span of life, monotony and deity are not the only two options as Hartshorne claims. His argument contradicts this perspective, implies it is false, but his remarks do absolutely nothing to show it to be false.

In the last analysis, it is hard to see how a process theologian could resist an argument in favor of traditional belief based on the importance of creativity. For the pervasive presence of endless creativity in the world is a central idea of process thought. Some critics even contend that in process theology creativity is more fundamental and ultimate than God. It cannot be denied that it is a most important feature of reality from the process perspective. Once we have a fuller appreciation of what creativity is, we can appreciate a bit more how a creative personal existence can continue on in blissful eternity as traditional Christian theology claims. There is no good reason to abandon the traditional promise in favor of the extraordinarily weak Hartshornian alternative of eternal preservation as a memory in the mind of God.

Process theoglogians most often present all their views to us as a package-deal. And certainly, this is an inveterate human tendency: "Love me, love my dog." But it seems to me very clear that toward process theology we must have an attitude of critical appreciation at best. Process theology has issued some important correctives concerning the medieval conception of God. But process theologians, in a spirit of innovation, often have departed unnecessarily, and dangerously, from the traditional claims of the faith they most often purport to be preserving. I think it is entirely possible to profit from what is laudable in process theology, while eschewing what is lamentable. By exercising critical discernment, we can in the end come from an examination of process thought with an enhanced conception of God and the world.

8

Creation *ex Nihilo*:
Some Considerations

MANY THEISTS BELIEVE that at a certain point in the past, an entire universe sprang into existence, *ex nihilo*. At one moment nothing material or contingent existed; at the next moment the cosmos appeared. Now this position is not usually thought by its proponents to be demonstrably true, but it is held to be a rational position to maintain. St. Thomas, for example, admitted that natural reason could not prove the universe to have had an absolute beginning. But he also insisted that neither could the contrary be proved. And many philosophers would, I think, agree. The doctrine of *creatio ex nihilo* is in fact thought by many people who are not theists to be a position which it can be rational to hold.

Compare this with the famous hypothesis considered by Bertrand Russell that the universe sprang into existence five minutes ago, exactly the way it in fact was at that time. No rational person would consider this a reasonable position to adopt. As the hypothesis was constructed, it would make no empirically detectable difference whether it was true or false. This once led many philosophers enamoured with some form of a verificationist criterion of cognitive significance to reject it as devoid of meaning. But of course in addition to difficulties endemic to that general semantic strategy, there are at least three serious problems with such a quick dismissal of the hypothesis.

First, if the hypothesis itself were meaningless, so would be its denial. But its denial, or at least some proposition which entails its denial, is believed true by all reasonable people. Secondly, even if we accept the profundity of Herbert Feigl's insistence that "a difference must make a difference," are we in any way forced to say that it makes no difference at all whether the universe existed ten minutes ago, merely because it makes no empirically detectable difference? Surely not. To anyone who holds, for example, a retributivist theory of punishment, it makes a tremendous difference whether anything existed before five minutes ago. If there was then nothing, no crimes were actually committed before then, and anyone accused of such a past offense is in fact innocent regardless of what we all seem to remember, and should on that theory of punishment be let go. Further, on the Russellian hypothesis any promises we seem to remember making or having had made to us never in fact were made. Likewise, I never was married, I have no natural parents, and so forth. The total number of moral obligations any of us actually has would on that hypothesis be vastly smaller than we now think. In light of such considerations it is odd that Russell himself and such other insightful philosophers as James Cornman thought the hypothesis to be irrefutable but practically uninteresting. There seem on the contrary to be not only interesting but important ways in which the truth of this hypothesis would significantly "make a difference." Moreover, it can even be argued that although the event alleged to have occurred was not observed by any of us and in fact cannot be confirmed by any subsequent observations, there could have been an observation made relevant to its truth. For it seems that there is a possible world in which all the matter alleged to have sprung into being in the actual world did the same, but in that world did not comprise the totality of the universe, being pre-existed by an observer who could have witnessed at least part of the shocking sight. At one moment none of that matter existed, at the next it did. Finally, it just does seem meaningful to say that at a certain time in the past all physical things suddenly came into being. Indeed, some cosmologists have claimed on completely scientific grounds that there is nothing absurd about, but rather that there is actual evidence in favor of, the hypothesis that some things suddenly spring into existence. And it is at least no obvious fallacy of composition to argue that likewise there is no inherent unintelligibility to the grander claim that it is possible that all things once suddenly appeared.

If the positivist critique of the five minute hypothesis had been correct, any universal *ex nihilo* hypothesis whatsoever would have been ruled out. And thus the position of the creationist would have been seen to be meaningless. It can be argued that any structured object or collection of inter-related objects such as our universe, if it suddenly were to pop into existence, would have the appearance of having been around before. For example, if there were an observer who arrived on the scene along with the scenery, he would sooner or later, supposing him to be endowed with sufficient intelligence, realize that states of objects follow upon, or result from, prior states. Applying his induction to the first state of which he was aware, he would infer quite reasonably that it was preceded by some prior state, and so on. If he were metaphysically inclined and operated with a conceptuality akin to our own, he might find himself reflecting on the conceptual truth that physical objects such as those around him are continuants, the sorts of things that persist through time. Thus he might be led to conclude that those objects of which he had been first aware most likely had been around awhile before he became aware of them. But to that observer it would make no empirically detectable difference whether this was so or not. So on the positivist criterion the claim that there had been any such *ex nihilo* appearance would be meaningless, and no such story could even be seriously entertained.

The positivist critique failed, yet we find that most people think the Russellian hypothesis crazy. And interestingly, most who so regard that speculation consider the theistic creation doctrine to be at least possible for a sane and rational person to accept. From this point of view, what might be wrong with the five minute hypothesis which is not a flaw in the cognate creation claim? Both are claims that an entire universe once sprang into existence *ex nihilo*. What is the relevant difference between the two possibilities? Is there some consideration which might make the claim that everything came into being in, say, 4004 B.C. more reasonable to hold than the Russellian hypothesis? Bishop Ussher would have thought so, and so would Gosse. Both of them thought they had the word of God that the world had appeared *ex nihilo* in the relatively recent past, as Gosse held, fossils and all — to test our faith. This opinion was based on a particular doctrine of revelation, a literalist understanding of the Old Testament, creative chronological calculations from biblical geneologies, and some eminently dubious assumptions about the character and methods of God. Few contemporaries would hold that Ussher and Gosse had hit upon the factor that makes the fundamental difference between the *prima facie* rationality of a creation claim and the absurdity of the five minute hypothesis. In order to account for the difference we must be able to perceive clearly what is wrong with the latter. And what is wrong with it is not that it lacks the backing of revelation.

So what is wrong with Russell's hypothesis? Accepting the truth of that proposition would require rejecting the truth of the vast majority of all the empirical beliefs we hold. Any belief concerning something's having happened or been the case more than five minutes ago would be false. Each of us has innumerably many such beliefs about the past. The only beliefs we now hold about the past which would be compatible with the truth of Russell's hypothesis would be any about something's having happened or been the case during the last five minutes which did not entail anything's having occurred or been the case before that time. And this would be a small set of beliefs indeed. In general, the more of our present beliefs, and especially our present fundamental beliefs, an hypothesis accords with or accounts for, the more reasonable it is for us to accept. The fewer of our beliefs an hypothesis preserves, the less reasonable it is to accept. The five minute hypothesis accords with only a minute fraction of our factual beliefs and offers absolutely no account of why we hold the others. So although the hypothesis cannot strictly be proved false, it is such that it would not be rational for any normal person to accept it.

This epistemic criterion for rejecting the hypothesis has implications which might at first appear counter-intuitive. For example, according to it a rival hypothesis to the effect that the universe was created one hour ago could be more reasonable to accept than Russell's particular formulation, as it could accord with more of our other factual beliefs, beliefs about matters within the past hour. But it does not follow that anyone who actually accepted it would be any less crazy than someone who believed the five minute alternative. The difference in degree of reasonableness is so miniscule as not to be worth practically considering. And of course it follows that the even more bizarre possibility that the universe came into existence two seconds ago — an hypothesis according to which you did not in fact ever read the beginning of this sentence, but only have the apparent memory of having done so — would be even less reasonable to accept than the other hypotheses in question. Difference in degree of reasonableness or unreasonableness is being treated here as a strict function of compatibility or incompatibility either with the entirety of our belief set or else with some fundamental and privileged subset of it. On these grounds, to say that one hypothesis could be more reasonable or less unreasonable than another is not at all to imply that the former would be reasonable to accept. When this is kept in mind, a further implication of the criterion can be seen to be harmless. Suppose you are told at 9:05 A.M. that the universe came to be five minutes ago. By lunch it would be more reasonable to accept that claim than when you first considered it. At that later time it is likely that more of your beliefs would be consistent with the hypothesis that this startling event occurred at 9 than was the case at 9:05. It is not of course the mere passage of time from 9 until 12 that makes the difference, but rather any new beliefs acquired during that time about empirical events occurring or states of affairs obtaining since 9. And as I have pointed out, it makes so miniscule a difference as never to yield a rational justification for adopting such an hypothesis. Regardless of how long we might wait while considering such a claim, and how many new beliefs compatible in this way with it we might acquire, it will always conflict either with more of our beliefs, or at least with more of our important scientific beliefs, than it supports. This will clearly be the case so long as we have well grounded scientific theories about the universe's history to any significant extent resembling present ones.

To push the purported date of the universe's *ex nihilo* appearance farther into the past is thus, all other things being equal, to render the claim more reasonable, or at least less unreasonable, to accept. The claim that it happened a decade ago is better than the claim that it was five minutes ago, but not much. The allegation that it occurred in 4004 B.C. is better than that, but again, not by much. The claim that it happened billions and billions of years ago is completely different. So long as it is in accord with the best extrapolations of current scientific theory, it not only is much better off than these other hypotheses, it is the sort of claim which it could be more reasonable for a well informed, normal person to accept rather than reject or withhold. If the theist were to claim that before "the first three minutes" of our present cosmos the singularity which can be considered our origin itself appeared *ex nihilo*, there would be nothing in the belief set of most well informed people, or in the assured results of any respectable and plausible scientific theory with which it would be incompatible. Thus the epistemic criterion which rules out Russell-type hypotheses would allow this sophisticated theistic claim to be held rationally.

Of course if a person eschews enough of the contemporary scientific world picture, and has what he and his fellows consider good reasons for so doing, he can opt for a much more recent date for creation. The later his date, the more current scientific theory he flouts, and consequently the better his own arguments for the hypothesis have to be. Otherwise, his creationist claim will fail to be a rational position to hold. If a person departs unreasonably from enough of contemporary science, his doctrine of creation will fail in rationality not uniquely on its own, but just in so far as it is connected up with and dependent upon his other unreasonable beliefs.

The doctine of *creatio ex nihilo*, if wisely enough deployed, can satisfy in these respects acceptable standards of rationality. Yet in order to maintain full consistency in his belief set, the theist who holds such a position must beware of what other theoretical positions he adopts, not only in the domain of the physical sciences, but also in such unlikely fields as philosophical semantics and analytic metaphysics. Let me illustrate. It is now, I think, widely agreed that natural kind terms, terms like 'tiger' and 'gold', give rise to what Stephen Schwartz has called 'stable generalizations', universal generalizations over the kind which are known to be true only a posteriori, and yet which have the metaphysical status of broadly logical necessity. These generalizations concern the essence or underlying nature of the kind; that is to say, they display necessary conditions for membership in the kind. According to this position, for example, propositions like 'Gold is atomic element 79' and 'Tigers are animals', if indeed they are true are so of necessity, although they have been discovered to be true a posteriori.

It is most widely agreed that stable generalizations concern the fundamental constitution of members of natural kinds, whether this is spelled out in terms of genetic make-up, molecular constitution, atomic number, or along more macroscopic lines. If all members of a kind K examined are found to have an underlying trait concerning their basic constitution C, then it is held that we have discovered the truth of a proposition of the form

(1) $\square$ (x) (Kx $\rightarrow$ Cx),

which ascribes *de dicto* a necessity of C to members of K. (1) simply amounts to the claim that, necessarily, nothing is a *K* unless it has *C*.

Kripke, among others, has argued that certain propositions concerning the origin of individuals have the same epistemic and metaphysical status as stable generalizations. They are necessary a posteriori truths. For instance, if H. T. and T. F. are my natural parents, I could not possibly have sprung from any other source. No one can know a priori my parentage, but it is an essential property of mine nonetheless. These claims are familiar in the literature. Now some philosophers are tempted, on the basis of the arguments for the necessity of kind constitution and individual origin, to incline favorably toward the claim that having a certain sort of origin is also *de dicto* necessary for kind membership, at least in the case of biological kinds. If all examined members of kind K are found to have an origin of type O (making the range of O, of course, wide enough through disjunction of conditions to accord with evolutionary theory), it can be thought that the truth is discovered of a proposition of the following form:

(2) $\Box(x) (Kx \rightarrow Ox)$

which of course would be the claim that, necessarily, nothing is a K unless it has some origin of type O.

It is easy to see that a theist who believes there to have been a creation *ex nihilo* cannot hold such a position concerning all natural kinds. Allow me to put the argument crudely in order to present it vividly. Suppose we find all examined humans to have had an origin of type G described by scientific accounts of the genetics and micro-biology of natural conception. Can we consider

(3) $\Box(x) (Hx \rightarrow Gx)$

to be a truth we have discovered? Suppose we also hold, for simplicity's sake, that God produced Adam *ex nihilo*, along with an entire universe to boot. Then according to (3), Adam was not a human being, since he did not have the required natural origin. But as his descendants, what does that make us? If Adam was not human, then neither are we. Surely if origin G is a kind-essential property, a human must come from a human, or given evolutionary theory, some other closely related natural organism, which itself must have had the appropriate form of natural origin. But in that case, Cain and

Abel, along with the rest of us following them fail to count as humans.

But if *we* fail to count as humans, then what natural kind is it whose essential origin we have discovered in isolating G? Must we say we have discovered a truth about not humans but *humanoids*, some other natural kind H1? Have we found that

(4) $\square(x) (H1x \rightarrow Gx)$?

But, again, if that is what we discovered, then Adam will fail to count as even a humanoid. And likewise as his descendants, so shall we. And so forth, ad infinitum.

To escape all this absurdity it will suffice to deny that type of origin is a kind-essential property for all natural kinds. Specifically, a Christian may want to hold that there are no such stable generalizations about natural origins for human-kind. And if this is true, then there is no difficulty on this count with the orthodox claim that the man Jesus was fully human even though he had no human paternity. Non-standard origin is compatible with complete humanity.

Suppose that in some laboratory in the distant future scientists were to accomplish the astounding task of concocting *from scratch* (from basic chemicals, etc.) a being with the constitution, organs, appearance, mannerisms, and cognitive abilities of a normal human adult. Suppose he acts like a human, marries a woman, fathers a child, takes a job, and cultivates many close and satisfying friendships. Would this creature *be* human or not? Intuitions may vary on this, but I think it most reasonable to say yes. And if so, then this presents us with some additional backing for the position which the theist, or specifically the Christian affirming a doctrine of creation, may want to hold.

The argument I have produced against holding together the doctrine of *creatio ex nihilo* and the doctrine that for all natural kinds there is an essentiality of origin was presented with an example of the sudden creation of an entire universe containing at least one rational being. But not even fundamentalists hold this sort of account. Whether on good scientific grounds or on a literalistic reading of Genesis or both (a hybrid approach), nearly all creationists will hold that the inorganic and merely organic elements of nature appeared on the scene before humans. But even on the most sophisticated account of cosmological history, the same sort of argument could be constructed. Thus, it seems that a position the creationist must avoid is the theory that for all kinds, there is a type of origin shared by all members and necessary for kind membership. The theist must take care to preserve the consistency of his beliefs in even such unlikely areas as these. But if he does exercise the requisite care, it may indeed be the case that he can be quite reasonable in holding a doctrine of creation *ex nihilo*. So, whether it is derived from appeals to revelation or cosmological arguments, a belief in creation may well be rationally acceptable. At least it cannot be excluded simply on grounds such as the above.

9

Absolute Creation

IN THIS PAPER WE shall examine, in at least a preliminary and programatic way, a point of apparent conflict and potentially fruitful contact between two major metaphysical visions, each rooted in a tradition of thought which has deeply influenced western intellectual history. The two traditions we shall have in view are Platonism and Judeo-Christian theism. The apparent conflict is between what is arguably the central idea of the theistic tradition, the idea of a God as absolute creator of everything which exists distinct from him, and the characteristic, metaphysically powerful claim of present-day Platonism that there are strong theoretical reasons for recognizing in our ontology, or philosophical account of what there is, a realm of necessarily existent abstract objects, objects so firmly rooted in reality that they could not possibly have failed to exist—such things as properties and propositions.[1]

Throughout the centuries, numerous philosophers have tried to construct a thoroughly theistic metaphysic—a general account of reality in which theism, the belief in an omnipotent, omniscient, maximally perfect being, functions not just as one more component in an overall metaphysical scheme, but rather as the central and regulative factor, at least partially determinative of other metaphysical commitments. This has been attempted by, for example, such great philosophers as Aquinas, Berkeley, and Leibniz, and has had in every case many results of quite general philosophical interest. At the heart of any metaphysic, and of any world-view, is its ontology. A thoroughly theistic ontology, one in keeping with the dominant theme of the Judeo-Christian tradition, will be one which places

161

God at the center and views everything else as exemplifying a relation of creaturely dependence on him. Now, the idea of a God as creator of all contingent reality which finds expression in the doctrine of *creatio ex nihilo* is in some ways a quite difficult notion. But its basic thrust is clear enough: All things which need not have existed but do exist are totally dependent for their existence on the creative activity of God. But if the existence of literally all things is claimed to be rooted in divine activity, and if the distinctive claim of Platonism just mentioned is true, then the thorough-going theist must, it seems, claim that the realm of necessity as well as that of contingency is within the province of divine creation, that God is somehow responsible for the existence of all necessarily existent entities such as numbers, as well as for such things as stars, planets, and electrons.

Let us characterize this Platonic realm of necessity as comprising necessary truth as well as necessarily existent objects, and refer to it as "the framework of reality." On the standard view, this framework provides a structure which exists in and delimits every possible world. In particular, it is a structure which would have to be instantiated by any contingent created universe. The focal question we need to address is whether, in addition to holding God responsible for the existence of every contingent reality which is structured by the framework, it can be intelligible and coherent for theists to hold God responsible for the framework itself. The question then is whether any divine creative activity can consistently, and even plausibly, be held by theists to be the source of necessary existence and necessary truth, or to put it another way, whether such existence and truth can in any defensible way be held to be dependent on God.

Although Platonism in general has been viewed historically as congenial to western theism, having been appropriated in various ways by such important theists as St. Augustine, the difficulty of seeing how our question could possibly be answered in the affirmative can appear to indicate a fundamental and central incompatibility between a strongly modalized Platonism and any version of theism holding God to be absolute creator of all. And in fact, when we survey the contemporary literature relevant to this question, we find on the one hand that theists such as James F. Ross who stress the importance and universal scope of divine creation tend to criticize and reject Platonism, whereas on the other hand Platonists such as Nicholas Wolterstorff who are also theists tend to restrict the idea of creation so as not to apply it to the framework.[2] Moreover, in one of the best known recent discussions of theism, abstract objects, and necessity in his book *Does God Have A Nature?*, Alvin Plantinga has considered at great length problems which may be posed by what we are calling the framework of reality for traditional theistic beliefs concerning the sovereignty and aseity of God.[3] In short, in a variety of recent publications, numerous philosophers have expressed worries or raised difficulties concerning the relation between traditional theism and the theoretical recognition of such a framework. Is it then the case that anyone's theism gives him or her a good reason to avoid Platonism, or vice versa, or are these fundamental visions of reality compatible? It will be the suggestion of this essay that a strongly modalized Platonism and a theism stressing absolute creation are indeed consistent, and can be integrated together into what may be the most powerful, comprehensive theistic metaphysic that can be constructed. In particular, I want to propose, and begin both to elucidate and defend, the claim that God is absolute creator of necessary as well as contingent reality, and thus that literally all things do depend on him. In doing so I shall be sketching out a central component of any thoroughly theistic metaphysic which takes contemporary Platonism seriously.

I

It has been suggested by Wolterstorff that any such proposal would be from the start a misbegotten one.[4] The biblical authors do seem to have held a belief that they expressed by saying that everything derives from God.[5] And it is true that no less a theologian than St. Thomas wrote "It must be said that everything, that in any way is, is from God."[6] But in light of the apparent difficulties in claiming God to be creatively responsible for such things as universals, Wolterstorff suggests that it is unlikely that the biblical authors had abstract objects like properties and propositions in mind when they made their claims about God and creation. Likewise, we know that St. Thomas did not mean to be discussing the denizens of contemporary Platonism in his remarks. But surely, it is just as certain that neither the prophets, the apostles, nor the Angelic Doctor had in mind either Alpha Centauri, DNA, protons, or electric fields when they made their creation claims; yet no one hesitates in understanding the doctrine of creation to apply to such items as these. In light of this, it would seem reasonable to attempt to take the traditional doctrine of creation at face value as being absolutely universal in scope, and to face head-on the difficulties that arise when it is applied to the realm of necessity.

In any attempt to display an asymmetrical dependence relation between God and abstract objects, such that they depend on God as their cause but he does not so depend on them, the theist may seem to confront immediately a problem. For presumably, he is wanting to affirm the truth of something like

(1) If there were no God, there would be no abstract objects.

And on a standard account of subjunctive conditionals, having a necessarily false antecedent renders any such proposition true. If, as the traditional theist believes, it is a necessary truth that God exists, then (1) will come out true due to the necessary falsehood of its antecedent. But supposing some abstract objects to exist necessarily—a tenet of current Platonism—truth also gets assigned for the same reason to

(2) If there were no abstract objects, there would be no God.

Now if (1) displays a dependence of abstract objects on God, (2) seems just as well to display a dependence of God on abstract objects. But the theist wants a one-way dependence relation.

There are two possible strategies at this point. The theist can refuse to endorse the standard semantic view which assigns truth to all subjunctive conditionals with impossible antecedents, and on some basis separate the sheep from the goats among such propositions. This would be a semantic maneuver of significant interest, and one which many theists might find attractive for reasons completely independent of our problem. But such a move is not strictly necessary at this point due to a second option. The theist can admit the truth of (2) as well as (1), acknowledge a *logical* dependence running both ways between God and abstract objects (a trivial result of there being necessary existence on both sides) and nevertheless maintain that there is a *causal* or ontological dependence running in only one direction, rendering (1) somehow ultimately more revealing than (2).

There are obstacles to alleging such a causal, or ontological dependence relation. Some accounts of causation just will not work here. For example, no standard sort of counterfactual analysis of such causation can be given. And with necessarily existent entities, it cannot be the case that one brought another into existence at some point in time. It may be largely due to this impossibility that it is generally assumed to be a necessary, or even a conceptual truth that the necessary is the uncaused, and therefore the uncreated and independent — an assumption I intend to challenge. It might be wondered whether there could be any reason at all for the theist to think that there is some causal relation running in one direction and not the other between God and necessary abstract objects. But the answer to this is, at least *prima facie*, straightforward. Independently of our problem, God is thought of as causally active, indeed as the paradigmatic causal agent, whereas such abstract objects are standardly regarded as causally inert. If there can be any causal relation between them, the theist so far does seem to have some justification or rationale for the directionality he sees.

But the crucial question is precisely whether there can be any such causal relation at all. I submit that a traditional theist can rationally hold that there can be, and is. For consider the following characterization of that relation. God traditionally is thought of as personal. A dominant model of deity is that of mind or active, creative intellect. In line with that model, I want to suggest, to begin with, that all properties and relations are God's concepts, the products, or perhaps better, the *contents* of a divine intellective activity, a causally efficacious or productive sort of divine conceiving. Unlike human concepts, then, which are graspings of properties that exist ontologically distinct from and independent of those graspings, divine concepts are those very properties themselves; and unlike what is assumed in standard Platonism, those properties are not ontologically independent, but rather depend on certain divine activities. This view can be extended to the rest of the traditional Platonic domain as well. All necessarily existent propositions, for example, can be thought of as "built up" out of properties. Thus, in the way in which we characterize properties as God's concepts, we can characterize propositions as God's thoughts. So, for example, the proposition that red is a color can be construed as the content of God's thinking: Red exemplifies *being a color*. So the existence of propositions as well derives from an efficacious divine conceiving.[7] And taking numbers to be a variety of property (for example, taking cardinal numbers to be certain properties of properties),[8] we thus have all necessarily existent abstract reality, from necessary mathematical objects to haecceities, to non-mathematical universals, to propositions, deriving existence from God.

But in order to be absolute creator of the entirety of the framework of reality, in order to be responsible for its existence and nature, God must be responsible for the necessary truth of all propositions with this modality as well as for their mere existence as abstract objects. I have characterized propositions as God's thoughts. Some of those thoughts are contingently true, some are contingently false. The latter, of course, are not among his *beliefs*, since God is omniscient. Others of his thoughts have their truth-value with the modal status of necessity. God's responsibility for contingent truth and falsehood consists in his creating *ex nihilo* the contingent entities whose existence, properties, and activities give rise to those truths and falsehoods, as well as consisting in his own engagement in other contingent activities. His responsibility for necessary truths and falsehoods consists in the natures of his concepts. To make this somewhat more precise, consider for example the proposition

(3) $2 + 2 = 4$.

The number 2, the number 4, the relation of addition, and that of equality are all divine concepts, all products of the divine conceiving activity. The existence of the proposition that 2 + 2 = 4 is thus the existence of a divine thought. Its truth is also a function of that divine conceiving activity. For (3) is true in virtue of what the number 2, the number 4, addition, and equality *are*, i.e. in virtue of how God conceives them. Further, God conceives them as being essentially as they are (at least as far as the properties they possess relevant to the truth of (3) are concerned). The number 2, for example, would not be the number it is if it were not such that when added to itself the result is 4. This, we might say, is part of 2's *nature*. Finally, since proposition (3) is itself part of the framework of reality, being built up as it is from necessarily existing abstract objects, it too exists necessarily, that is, God thinks it in every possible world. Thus, given the natures of its constituents, it is not only true in fact but necessarily true. It is in this way then that both the truth-value and the modal status of a necessary truth, or a necessary falsehood, are dependent upon God.[9]

So the suggestion being advanced is that the Platonistic framework of reality arises out of a divine, creatively efficacious intellective activity. It is in this sense that God is creator of the framework. It depends on him. And since God is responsible for the modal status of propositions, it is God who is creatively responsible for the realm of possibility. It has already been suggested in the literature that God's being necessarily good as well as essentially omnipotent renders him a delimiter of possibility—given his existence as necessary, certain worlds which, so to speak, would otherwise have been possible are not among the maximal groupings of propositions to be counted as genuinely possible worlds.[10] Here it is clear that God can be held to be not just a delimiter of possible worlds, but the absolute creator of such worlds, responsible for the abstract existence and intrinsic features of the entire framework of reality. All modalities are in this way seen to be rooted in and dependent upon the intellective activity of God. What we have arrived at is, in effect, a modally updated descendent of the "divine ideas" tradition represented by, for example, St. Augustine.

II

Let us refer to this view, the view that a divine intellectual activity is responsible for the framework of reality, as "theistic activism'. A theistic activist will hold God creatively responsible for the entire modal economy, for what is possible as well as what is necessary and what is impossible. The whole Platonic realm is thus seen as deriving from God. Now it is well known that one famous theist of the past, Descartes, held that God is creatively responsible for mathematical truths as well as for more mundane truths, and exercises sovereign control over them. God is so powerful, Descartes thought, that he could have made the proposition that $2 + 2 = 5$ true. This view, in its full generality, is often referred to as 'universal possibilism'. Its problems are obvious and are almost as well known as the view itself.[11] It may appear at first glance to some as if the view of theistic activism must end up sufficiently akin to Descartes' view as to entail similar problems. But this is false. Activism neither is equivalent to, nor entails, nor shares any clearly untoward consequences with Descartes' possibilism.

Descartes is most often faulted with having been carried away with a desire to exalt God and magnify his omnipotent power to the excesses at which he arrived. On a Cartesian view, God's responsibility for the mathematical and other formal structures of our world is such that he could have endowed it with other such structures, and possibly such that he can change those we have in an exercise of sovereign control. From the perspective of theistic activism, there is a sense in which Descartes failed not by going too far in his assessment of divine activity, but by not going far enough. If it is held that God's activity gives rise to all modalities in addition to *de facto* truth, universal possibilism need not follow at all. Indeed, if we accept the existence of a creaturely framework consisting of necessities, possibilism comes out by simple argument to be either trivially false or conceptually malformed.

Let us represent the Cartesian position in as general a way as possible to be the claim that if an activity of God's is responsible for the framework of reality, it follows that he could have generated a different framework instead, say, one in which $2 + 2 = 5$, or one in which properties of color do not exist, or one in which a property exists which does not serve as a constituent of the framework we in fact have. Now this is a modal claim, a claim alleging a certain sort of divine act to be possible. How shall we assess such a claim? Well, we can survey all the possible worlds there are to see whether in at least one of them this claim would come out true. But then we are asking whether any possible world structured by our framework as it is, complete with its modal character, is such that in it our framework is not generated by God, but rather is replaced by a different one instead. And of course it is immediately evident that the answer to this will be "no". As we have seen already, the framework comes to us with its modal character, so to speak, already "in place." What groupings of propositions constitute genuinely possible worlds is determined at the outset. But, it may be objected, this is a question-begging assessment of the Cartesian claim. To evaluate the suggestion that God could have created a different framework of possible worlds, it may be thought inappropriate to consult just the contents of the framework we have. But in thinking this way, the critic would be attempting to require that we consider the Cartesian claim from a vantage point somehow outside the actual divine activity which generates the range of possible worlds there in fact are. The theistic activist will reply that all modality is a function of the efficacious conceiving activity in which God is in fact engaged. If the claim that God could have created a different framework is supposed to have purchase for its modal element outside the framework which along, according to the activist, grounds all modal claims, then it will be categorized by the activist as a malformed claim, conceptually false at best. There is no Archimedean point outside the actual conceiving activity of God from which we could judge it to be possible that God conceive a framework different from the one which in fact, and of necessity, gives us all possibility and all necessity.

So on the activist view, God necessarily creates the framework of reality. Is this in conflict with the traditional view that God is a free creator? Not at all. The traditional view is that God is a free creator of our physical universe: He was free to create it or to refrain from creating it; he was free to create this universe, a different universe, or no such universe at all. Of course, the range of God's creative freedom must be consonant with his nature as a maximally perfect being. That renders divine freedom interestingly different from human freedom.[12] He could not have done morally otherwise than as he did. He could not have produced a physical universe which was ultimately, on balance, evil. But there are innumerably many ways in which he could have done otherwise than as he did, sufficient for his creation of our worlds being free.

On the view of theistic activism, God's creation of the framework of reality is both eternal and necessary—it never was, never will be, and could not have been, other than it is. But there is a sense, a different sense, in which even it can be considered free. It is an activity which is conscious, intentional, and neither constrained nor compelled by anything existing independent of God and his causally efficacious power. The necessity of his creating the framework is not imposed on him from without, but rather is a feature and result of the nature of his own activity itself, which is a function of what he is.

Ordinarily, when it is said that A causally depends on B, and B is recognized as some rational, free agent, it is implied that B has some control over A, to change A or do away with it altogether. This had led many philosophers to think that when something is not within the control of such a being in these senses, it exists causally independent of that being. I submit that this is not so, that the issues of control and causal dependence are not only distinguishable, but also in some ways separable. The view of theistic activism turns on, and exemplifies, this claim. If this is right, theists can acknowledge the standard Platonist view that God is not in control of abstract objects or necessary truths, in the sense that he cannot annihilate or alter them intrinsically, while at the some time maintaining that these things depend on God for their existence and intrinsic characteristics. The most exalted claims possible are thus secured for the theistic God, while all the implausibilities and problems of Descartes, of universal possibilism, are avoided.

Distinguishing carefully between issues of dependence and control is itself of some significant philosophical interest. For consider as an example the famous Euthyphro problem concerning morality. Is whatever is right right because God wills it, or does God will whatever is right because it is right? It has been thought by many philosophers that if morality is dependent on God, it follows that God could have made it right to torture innocent people for pleasure merely by willing it. This is the extreme position of theistic voluntarism, for which William of Ockham is notorious. On the other hand, if morality rests on objective, necessary truths such as that it is wrong to torture innocent people for pleasure—truths outside God's control—then it is widely that this entails that morality is independent of God.[13] On the view of theistic activism, moral truths can be objective, unalterable, and necessary, and yet still dependent on God. Thus, activism offers us a new perspective on the Euthyphro dilemma for morality.

And this should be no surprise, since theistic activism can be understood, in part, as resulting from an attempt to deal with what can be considered a parallel and more general Euthyphro-style dilemma for modality: Is it merely the case that God affirms the necessity of necesary truths because of the way in which they are true, or are they necessarily true because of the way in which he affirms them? For a theistic activist, a careful distinction between questions of dependence and questions of control allow an answer which can serve as an important component of any thoroughly theistic metaphysic with a Platonist ontology and an S5 modal logic.

III

An important problem may be thought to arise for the claim that God is an absolute creator of everything which exists distinct from him, a problem concerning God's own nature. How, on the view under consideration, are God's own essential properties related to his creatively efficacious conceiving activity? Are they a part of the created framework or not? Of course the whole project of theistic activism is to recognize some divine activity as responsible for the existence of absolutely everything distinct from God. But it would sound at least exceedingly odd to say that God creates the very properties which are logically necessary for, and distinctively exemplified within, his creative activity—properties such as his omniscience and omnipotence—to say that he creates his own nature. In fact, many would find this suggestion incoherent or absurd. To avoid painting himself into such a corner the activist might be tempted to consider placing the essential and distinctive attributes of deity outside the creaturely framework. Then God's creature activity would not appear to be the ultimate act of bootstrapping. But aside from the fact that no such selective exclusion would work in the first place, this move would amount to scrapping the whole project of theistic activism and abandoning the view of absolute creation.

There might appear to be two alternatives available to the activist who wants to avoid the circularity of God's creating his own nature. The first has very little to be said for it. It is a conception of God as "Pure Being," utterly devoid of determinate attributes. As Anthony O'Hear recently put it:

> In this conception, the divine reality is characteristically seen as without positive attributes of its own, for any positive attribute would contaminate the purity of that from which all attributes and all things spring.[14]

But such a view, the dead end of severely apophatic theology, in addition to being based only on a misunderstanding of transcendence as well as a misappropriation of the writings of the great mystics, is blatantly incoherent. Attempting to advert to any such conception at this point would involve the activist's stepping from the conceptual frying pan into the fire.

The second alternative which must be mentioned can have a great deal more said for it. It is a view with a long and respectable history, and with increasingly numerous contemporary defenders. It is the doctrine of divine simplicity, the denial that God has discrete, distinguishable properties which exist as abstract entities disinct from each other and from him. The theistic activist could avoid any problem of circularity or of divine bootstrapping by simply endorsing this doctrine. For if God does not have a nature comprised of distinct properties partially serving to constitute the framework of reality, the problem at issue will not even arise. The doctrine of divine simplicity involves quite an interesting set of metaphysical considerations, and, if acceptable, could provide a powerful rationale for the use of analogy in understanding religious discourse as well as offering a new perspective on the hidden-ness of God, by virtue of placing him firmly outside the framework of creation. Unfortunately, it seems to me that the doctrine has serious difficulties which render it unconvincing.[15] I shall thus not use it, or attempt to modify it for use, at this point. I believe there to be no real problems with the initial, obvious entailment of activism that God has properties, and has some both essentially and distinctively, for whose existence his eternal intellective activity is creatively responsible.

But how can God himself *be* the instantiation of items he creates? Further, if God creates his own haecceity, and the existence of his haecceity is logically sufficient for his existence, as is the case with any necessarily existent being, do we not have the result that on this view God creates himself? And of course, the very idea of self-causation or self-creation is almost universally characterized as absurd, incoherent, or worse.[16]

First, remember that in the claims of activism, there is no implication of any temporal priority of God's conceiving activity to the existence of its framework products. God produces the framework of reality both eternally and necessarily. So one obvious sort of absurdity is avoided by the view. But it might be thought that surely there is another type of priority, a metaphysical priority, which activism does not get right. Surely, it might be suggested, the existence of God must be somehow metaphysically or causally prior to the existence of any products of his creative, causal activity. Otherwise, any explanation of the existence of the framework of reality in terms of the existence and activity of God might seem unacceptably circular.

It can, however, be held that God does create his own nature, and that there is no absurdity or unacceptable circularity about this when properly understood. Consider the following thought experiment as a rough analogy. Suppose there exists a materialization machine, a machine about the size of a normal clock-radio, adorned with various dials. To demonstrate its remarkable ability to create matter *ex nihilo* in ordered arrangements, its inventor holds it waist-high, sets its dial, and materializes a table under it, on which it continues to sit as he releases it from his grip. Suppose that the machine and its products are such that it stands to them in a relation of continual creation; if it were turned off or re-set, the table would vanish. So as it sits on the table, it depends on the table for something—its precise location in space, say, four feet off the flour—but there is a deeper sense in which the table depends on it—for its continued existence. According to the theistic activist, God stands in a relation of logical dependence on his essential properties, but there is a deeper sense in which they depend on him, standing to him in a relation of causal, ontological dependence for their very existence. So far our thought experiment has not produced an analogy close enough to this. For God depends on what he produces in his very activity of production. The machine does not depend on the table for its ability to materialize or its occurrent activity of materialization. So consider an extention of the story.

The knobs of the materialization machine begin to wear out as their inventor experiments with producing all sorts of ordinary, and extraordinary, objects. Just as they are about to become unuseable, they are set to produce, in a matter of seconds, new knobs qualitatively indistinguishable from the original knobs when they were first mounted on the machine. The old ones are pulled off, and presto, the new ones appear, as the machine continues to operate. Realizing that he will never have to buy spare parts for the machine, our inventor now proceeds systematically to replace each of its parts seriatum with parts materialized by the operation of the machine. The end state of this process is the materialization machine, sitting on a table, continually producing all of its own parts, batteries included. With this, we come as close as we can to an analogy for what the activist claims about God. The machine, like God, is creating that on which it depends for its ability to create and for its occurrent activity of creation. If the end-state of the replacement story is conceivable, if it is conceivable that the materialization machine be in this state at any time, it seems also conceivable that such an activity take place at every time, or eternally. And that is like what we have in the case of God.

Now this story, of course, does not give us a perfect analogy. The machine is not creating its own properties, just some of its property instantiations, or all its own parts. The case of God is interestingly different, but not to such an extent, I think, as to deprive the analogy of all value. It presents us with a conceivable situation modeling in central ways what the activist alleges about God.

But, strictly speaking, there is no need of any such analogy to defend the implication of activism now in view. The value of the analogy is mainly heuristic, or pedagogical. It just seems to me that there is nothing logically or metaphysically objectionable about God's creating his own nature in precisely the way indicated. But what of the apparent implication that if God creates his nature, and the existence of his nature is logically sufficient for his existence, then he creates himself?

First of all it should be said that, in so far as there is absolutely no implication of temporal priority in any sense, the idea of self-causation or self-creation may not be so absurd a notion after all. However, this does not matter, since the claims of activism do not entail that God creates himself. God stands in a relation of logical dependence to his nature (a trivial result of the strict necessity of both relata). His nature stands in a relation of causal dependence to him. It simply does not follow that God stands in a relation of causal dependence to himself. Relations of logical dependence are always transitive. Relations of continuous causal dependence are always transitive. But we have no good reason to think that transitivity always holds across these two relations. If God creates some bachelor, the existence of this bachelor is logically sufficient for the existence of some unmarried man. It follows that God creates some unmarried man. But the transitivity we thus see across the causal and logical dependence relations holds only in case the unmarried man is one and the same individual as the bachelor. Unless the doctrine of divine simplicity is true, God is not identical with his nature. Since I have rejected the doctrine of divine simplicity, I can reject as well the inference that from God's nature causally depending on God, and God's logically depending on his nature, it follows that God causally depends on himself. Thus the view that God is absolute creator of everything distinct from himself does not entail that God is self-caused, or self-created.

IV

Not everyone will immediately appreciate the importance of a view like this. Even devout theists have been known to belittle such matters. Blaise Pascal, for example, once expressed this sort of attitude by saying "Even if someone were convinced that the proportions between numbers are immaterial, eternal truths, depending on a first truth in which they subsist, called God, I should not consider that he had made much progress towards his salvation."[17] But, soteriological considerations aside, I think that the view of God as an absolute creator, with its modal component of theistic activism, has many implications of great importance for a thoroughgoing theism, and implications as well which will be of significant general philosophical interest. For example, it yields a subtly new understanding of self-existence. If activism is true, a self-existent being is an uncaused being. A self-existent being is not to be characterized only as a being whose existence follows from its own nature, in the sense that in every possible world in which its nature exists, it exists. For this is true of all necessarily existent abstract objects, which on the view of absolute creation are not self-existent entities. A self-existent being, rather, is a necessarily existent individual caused to exist by no other being. On the view under consideration, appropriately, only God fits the bill.

Consider in addition one further theological perspective the view yields. It is well known that the Protestant theologian Paul Tillich was loathe to speak of the existence of God as the existence of one determinate entity among others. Numerous other theologians and philosophers have likewise hesitated to characterize God as an individual, giving as one reason for their hesitation the worry that if God is thought of as a determinate, existent individual, then one who believes in God seems merely to have just one more item in his inventory of reality than the non-believer; whereas, these religious thinkers insist, the reality of God should make much more difference in one's world-view than this. On the view of absolute creation, God is indeed a determinate, existent individual, but one whose status is clearly not just that of one more item in the inventory of reality. He is rather the source of absolutely everything there is; to use Tillich's own characterization, he is in the deepest sense possible the ground of all being.

Of course, in addition to yielding new insights for theology, the rapprochement developed between Platonism and theism generates many interesting philosophical implications. In particular, we have here a view which both retains the commitments of realism concerning the objective existence and status of abstract entities and modal truths, while at the same time capturing the conviction of anti-realists and conventionalists that such items must be in some sense mind-dependent. And this in itself is quite significant.[18] Furthermore, the position adumbrated has many components which clearly merit further philosophical investigation, such as the metaphysical status and proper analysis of the causation claimed to be operative in God's generation of the framework, as well as such general topics as the nature of any dependence relations between necessarily existent entities. With the picture presented here, I hope to have provided one focus for such further work.

The picture of God as creator of all conveyed to us by traditional Judeo-Christian theism is in many ways an interesting and powerful one. Just how interesting and powerful can be indicated when it is developed in light of the commitments of contemporary Platonism. I have not been concerned to argue for the truth of either theism or Platonism here. The present task has been merely to suggest the extraordinary compatibility of core elements of these two profound metaphysical visions.

10

Necessary Beings

IN A RECENT PAPER, R. Kane has challenged the modal onto-logical argument for the existence of God in a new and interesting way.[1] I think that an examination of this challenge will yield some important insights concerning the metaphysics of modality and the epistemic status of modal claims, as well as illuminating the Anselmian conception of God.

I

The structure of standard modal ontological arguments is basically quite simple. First, the concept of God is explicated in the Anselmian way as that of a greatest possible, or maximally perfect, being. Then it is laid down, or argued by appeal to value intuitions, that a maximally perfect being must have as an essential property that of existing in every possible world, or of being a necessarily existent entity. Next, it is shown that if it is possible that there exist such a being, one does in fact exist. For if it exists in any possible world, it exists in all, including the actual world. And finally, it is suggested that it is at least possible that such a being exist. So, the conclusion is drawn, in the actual world there is a maximally perfect being.

One principle frequently employed in the construction of such an argument is the theorem distinctive of S5 modality, the principle that a proposition which is possibly necessary is necessary. The proposition that God exists is, on the Anselmian view, necessarily true if true at all. Since it is possibly true, the Anselmian reasons, it is possibly necessary. But then, according to the axiom of S5, it follows that it is a necessary truth that God exists. Kane points out that, of course, the actual existence of God can be inferred in such an argument with the use of a weaker modal principle, what is widely known as the B-principle, the proposition that $\Diamond\Box p \rightarrow p$. But no modal argument for the existence of God will work with anything weaker than the B-principle. So, Kane reminds us, the Anselmian wanting to defend a modal ontological argument for the existence of God must hold at least that the B-principle is true, as well as holding that his conception of God as a maximally perfect being with an essential property of necessary existence is such that the proposition that God exists is possibly true.

Now how is the Anselmian to defend these two claims he needs for his argument to work? The B-principle can be defended in various ways, and does seem to capture very common modal intuitions, as Kane acknowledges. In fact, it is by appeal to these common intuitions that the Anselmian is most likely to defend this principle. But what of the other claim needed, the claim that maximal perfection is possibly exemplified? Kane seems to think that the defense of this claim will involve not appeals to intuitions of any type, but rather only the application of a certain sort of test, that of self-consistency (p. 338). Taking the Anselmian standardly to assume that "the possible corresponds to what is not self-contradictory and the necessary to that whose negation is self-contradictory" (p. 344), Kane appears to hold that the Anselmian's only strategy for defending his possibility claim will be to display his conception of God—a perfect being who necessarily exists—as free from formal inconsistency.[2] If it is the case that the Anselmian conception's being apparently free of self-contradiction, or internal inconsistency, on careful inspection is a good guide, or the only guide, that it is in fact free of inconsistency, and the lack of inconsistency is the same as or entails being possible in the broadly logical sense, then by displaying apparent consistency, the Anselmian would be demonstrating, or at least defending, his claim that it is possible that God exists.

But it is Kane's contention that a use of this strategy involves commitments which will lead the Anselmian into a logically incoherent ontology. To get as clear a view of this as possible we need to redescribe the consistency defense of the claim that maximal perfection is possibly exemplified. First, consider all the properties essential to being a maximally perfect being conceptually distinct from those of existence and necessary existence. Call their full conjunction 'the existentially neutral conception of a maximally perfect being'. This conception will involve properties like omnipotence, omniscience, goodness, and so forth. In order to defend his claim that it is possible that a perfect being exist, the Anselmian must, according to Kane show that (1) there is no formal self-contradiction internal to the existentially neutral conception of maximal perfection, and (2) there is no inconsistency produced by adding to this conception the property of necessary existence. Numerous philosophers, such as R. G. Swinburne, have attempted to argue for (1) in recent years, and have done so with an impressive measure of success.[3] Moreover, as I have suggested elsewhere, the Anselmian conception of God is such that it would be a very difficult task for the critic to establish that it did contain inconsistency within its existentially neutral component.[4] Despite continual attempts to show otherwise, the existentially neutral Anselmian conception of God seems totally free of self-contradiction. And further, there is indeed no evident self-contradiction produced by adding to the existentially neutral conception of maximal perfection the property of being necessarily existent. So, in line with the strategy Kane attributes to the Anselmian, it seems that on these grounds we have an adequate defense of the claim that God's existence is possible.

But at this point Kane would have us consider the very general conception of a less-than-perfect necessary being (as he abbreviates it, LPN). An LPN will be any being which lacks at least one (possibly many) of the perfections God has, but which does have the property of being necessarily existent. An LPN could be a philosopher with necessary existence, an evil demon with this same foothold in reality, or a ballpoint pen which could not possibly fail to exist. Surely the existentially neutral conceptions of innumerably many such things are such as to contain no formal inconsistencies. And adding the property of necessary existence to any such conception seems in no way to generate a formal self-contradiction. So by the same strategy attributed to the Anselmian, it seems that we have made a case for the possible existence of LPNs.

If the B-principle is true and the foregoing consistency defense of the possibility of God's existence is a good one, then the Anselmian can conclude that a maximally perfect being exists. But, Kane suggests, the Anselmian must also agree, by the same sort of possibility argument, and the force of the B-principle, that uncountably many LPNs exist as well. And this creates, he contends, a severe problem for the theist. It is not just a Gaunilo-style problem of ontological profligacy for the Anselmian, but worse, Kane alleges. It is a problem of logical inconsistency with the tenets of traditional theism.

The inconsistency is said by Kane to arise as follows. It is a firm tenet of traditional theism, and of Anselmian theism in particular, that God alone is self-existent, existing *a-se*, and that all things distinct from God are dependent on God for their existence. But, in Kane's words

> This would not be true of LPNs. Their existence is also *a se*. It does not come from God, but is from their own natures; and it cannot be taken away by God, unless (contrary to the common view) God can do what is logically impossible.[5]

Thus, if there are LPNs, it cannot be the case that all things distinct from God are dependent on God for their existence. Thus, Kane thinks that because of their theological commitments and because of what they require in order to construct and defend a modal ontological argument for the existence of God, Anselmians are confronted with an inconsistent tetrad of propositions:[6]

(i) God is the first cause of all things (in the sense that the existence of all other things depends upon God's will or action).

(ii) The B-principle is true (at least for notions of necessity applicable in traditional theological contexts).

(iii) A perfect being is logically possible.

(iv) LPNs are logically possible.

But since (i)–(iv) entail that a perfect God exists who is a cause of the existence of all things distinct from him, and that less-than perfect beings distinct from him exist who can have no cause of their existence, (i)–(iv) generate an ontology whose description is logically inconsistent.

It is Kane's basic contention that the modal ontological argument can be shown to be sound only if (iv) can be shown to be false. Thus, he suggests, in addition to having to argue that all maximally perfect beings are necessary, the Anselmian who defends such an argument must establish also the converse of this, the proposition that all necessary beings are maximally perfect. Is Kane right? I want to suggest that what he says is wrong in a number of interesting ways. The Anselmian is not committed to the conception of possibility Kane seems to attribute to him, nor to the particular strategy for defending possibility claims Kane alleges. Further, it can be held that propositions (i)–(iv) do not form an inconsistent tetrad. If the Anselmian's judgments of possibility were as lenient as Kane says, no incoherent ontology would clearly result, only a bloated one. But, finally, Anselmian modal judgments are not so lenient as to produce even this.

II

Broadly logical possibility is not to be defined as consistency in first order logic. On one standard theory of natural kind terms, the proposition that water is not H_2O is not possibly true, although it does not contain or formally yield a contradiction. It is impossible that Socrates never be a person, even though such a claim about him does not contain any narrowly logical inconsistency. And the example of mathematical propositions such as Goldbach's Conjecture, the Continuum Hypothesis, the Axiom of Choice, and Fermat's Last Theorem, which are such that either they, or their negations are impossible, without either being formally inconsistent, are well known. Less well known is the fact that the Anselmian, of all people, has special reason to reject this definition. For the Anselmian holds that in addition to existing in all possible worlds, God exemplifies necessarily the properties of omnipotence, omniscience, and goodness. Because of this, God has the unique ontological role of being a delimiter of possibility. To put it simply, some maximal groupings of propositions which, if *per impossible*, God did not exist would constitute possible worlds, do not count as genuinely possible worlds due to the constraints placed on possibility by the nature of the creator. Certain worlds can be described with full consistency in first order logic but are such that, for example, their moral qualities preclude their even possibly being actualized or allowed by an Anselmian God.[7]

Consistent describability is at best a defeasible indicator of broadly logical possibility. Common defeaters of such indications are, as the examples above would suggest, most often if not always modal intuitions concerning *de re* essences which are or can be integrated into some ramified and plausible theory — of natural kinds, of object identity, of mathematical propositions, of God and the structure of creation. In fact, however, consistent describability may be no more than an ideally necessary condition of broadly logical possibility, the discovery of which yields on its own no independnt warrant to a possibility claim. I suspect that positive epistemic warrant accrues to possibility claims only if there is some such modal intuition in favor of the truth of the claim or of claims of its type. A discovery that what is claimed to be possible can be described without apparent contradiction would then do no more than enhance, or, better, secure the *prima facie* warrant provided for the claim by intuition. No such discovery would grant positive epistemic status on its own, apart from considerations of intuition.

With this in mind, let us look again at the Anselmian's defense of a modal ontological argument. As Plantinga made clear in *The Nature of Necessity*, the modal ontological argument is not a successful piece of natural theology, an argument deriving the conclusion that God exists from only premises and inference forms acceptable to all rational people.[8] Its premises and inference forms will be acceptable only to people who have the right sorts of supporting intuitions. But this does not render the argument useless in (ideally) helping people to attain, and trace out a justification for, explicitly theistic belief. For one does not have to be a consciously convinced theist already to discover in oneself the intuititions on which the argument turns. The B-principle, for example, is supported by the intuitions of many non-theists as well as many theists. What about the claim that maximal perfection is possibly exemplified, or to put it differently, that it is possible that there exist a maximally perfect being with the essential property of necessary existence? Can the Anselmian establish, or provide positive warrant for this claim merely by producing the simple consistency argument Kane attributes to him? I think the answer is: clearly not. A defeasible defense of the claim could consist in such an argument, a defense against someone who asserts the negation of the claim. But positive warrant is provided only by an appeal to intuition. Many people intuitively judge the existentially neutral conception of maximal perfection to be possibly exemplified, and this intuition is enhanced or secured by the failure of anyone to demonstrate this conception to contain inconsistency. Further, it is intuitively judged by many not only that such perfection is compossibly exemplified with necessary existence, but that the former entails the latter. It is not our failure to find any formal inconsistency between these components of the Anselmian conception of God which warrants the belief that it is possibly exemplified, but rather these intuitions. Its apparent freedom from inconsistency only allows those intuitions to retain their *prima facie* epistemic status.

Is then the belief that a perfect being is possible on a par with the belief that LPNs are possible? Is anyone committed to the former necessarily committed to the latter? In order to answer these questions as clearly as possible, we must distinguish two categories of LPNs. First, there are less-than-perfect (in the sense of lacking some divine perfection) abstract objects with necessary existence, such as numbers, properties, and propositions. Then there is the category of less-than-perfect non-abstract, or concrete entities with necessary existence. All of Kane's illustrations of LPNs are drawn from this latter category, which would encompass necessarily existent human beings, stones, trees, electrons, and ballpoint pens. Now if I am right, judging such imagined entities to have descriptions free of formal contradiction is not sufficient for warrantedly judging them to be possible in the broadly logical sense. Their logical possibility must have some intuitive support. The claim that some non-abstract LPNs possibly exist has absolutely no support from the intuitions of most Anselmians. In fact quite the contrary is true. Traditionally, it has struck many theists as obvious that any physical object, for example, is possibly destroyed. Be that as it may, it remains true that for most Anselmians the source of epistemic warrant for the claim that God is possible is not shared by the claim that non-abstract LPNs are possible. So a commitment to and defense of the former does not commit the Anselmian to the latter.

However, the case is a bit different with abstract LPNs. A significant number of Anselmians have mathematical and ontological intuitions supporting the claim that many of them are possible. And accordingly, many Anselmians are Platonists, or, better, realists concerning such items as properties and propositions, holding that they have both objective and necessary existence. One thing that Kane fails to recognize is that such an ontological commitment may be fully consistent with the traditional view of God as causally responsible for the existence of everything distinct from him. But of course, in this Kane is not alone. For example, in his recent book *Theism,* Clement Dore states that "logically necessary beings are not causally dependent," echoing a view held by probably most contemporary philosophers, a view often enunciated with a great deal of confidence if not with much by way of supporting argument.[9] Since a necessarily existent entity cannot come into existence at any time, it is assumed that there can be no sense in which it causally depends on anything else for its existence. This common assumption, however, is I think false.

A quite traditional Augustinian picture of the Platonic realm sees such items as concepts or thoughts in the mind of God, dependent for their existence on an eternal, creatively efficacious divine intellective activity. This picture is fully compatible with the modal status of such items being one of broadly logical necessity, as long as the causally productive divine activity responsible for their existence is assigned that status as well.[10] And since a self-existent being is one which causally depends on no individual distinct from itself for its existence, such abstract LPNs would not exist *a-se*, being dependent for their existence on God.

What has blinded most philosophers to this possibility is a confusion or conflation of the distinct issues of dependence and control. It is true that God would lack control of abstract LPNs, in the sense that he could not annihilate them, or bring new ones into existence, but it does not follow that any which do exist do not depend on God for their existence. And a lack of such control is not such as to impugn divine omnipotence, ranging as it does only over the logically possible.

With the strongly modalized Augustinian picture in mind, we can see that the four propositions alleged by Kane to form an inconsistent tetrad need pose no problem for the Anselmian defender of an ontological argument at all. First, what warrants the Anselmian in endorsing (iii) — a perfect being is logically possible — has no direct connection with or implication for his attitude toward (iv) — LPNs are logically possible. It can be perfectly rational to affirm (iii) and deny (iv). But if (iv) is read as asserting only that *some* LPNs are possible, many Anselmians will accept its truth, because of their intuitions about some abstract LPNs. Yet, in light of the Augustinian picture, this view need not lead to a problem of consistency for the Anselmian, given his other theological commitments. And further, should there exist some rare Anselmian who intuits the possibility of a non-abstract LPN, perhaps even he could draw on the distinction between issues of causal dependence and issues of control to maintain the consistency of (i)–(iv). In any case, we can see that to defend his position and avoid inconsistency, it is not necessary for the Anselmian to establish that all necessary beings are perfect as Kane contends. On the contrary, it seems that many Anselmians as a matter of fact are fully consistent and justified in accepting the necessary existence of abstract entities which lack divine perfections. And those who refuse to credit non-abstract LPNs with the modal status of possibility are fully consistent and justified in holding that position as well.

So to sum up a bit of what has just been said: On the only reading of (iv) which would be endorsed as true by many theists, the modalized Augustinian picture clearly allows it to be held that propositions (i)–(iv) do not form an inconsistent set. On the reading of (iv) which more plausibly threatens inconsistency — the one concerning non-abstract LPNs, imagined entities which do not as clearly conform to the Augustinian picture — theists can be fully justified in refusing to endorse it as true.

III

A bit more needs to be said about the epistemic status of the modal judgments made by the Anselmian, and any contrary judgments made by a non-Anselmian or anyone to whom the modal ontological argument does not appeal. What exactly is the status of a modal intuition, or for that matter of a metaphysical intuition of any kind? What reason, if any, does anyone have to trust such intuitions? Of course, by 'intuition' I do not mean to refer to anything inherently mysterious, to a cognitive faculty whose very existence is dubious at best. Someone intuitively judges a proposition to be true just in case on merely considering the proposition, it appears true to him, and that appearance does not derive entirely from perceptual belief-forming mechanisms. An intuitively formed belief seems to be a sort of naturally formed belief, a belief whose acceptance does not derive from evidence, testimony, memory, inference, or sense experience (in the sense in which a perceptual belief derives from sense experience). And it seems that there are degrees of intuitive support a proposition can have — some intuitions are stronger than others.

The epistemic status of intuition is a surprisingly neglected topic in contemporary philosophy, especially in light of the frequency with which disputing philosophers find themselves ending an argument with a confession of conflicting intuitions, a confession which often signals the end of further discussion as well. I'll not attempt here a general treatment of intuition, but I do think it important to say something about the Anselmian's reliance on intuition.

To ask why anyone should rely on intuition can seem like asking why anyone should believe what seems to him to be true. But, at least for relatively esoteric intuitions, such as that maximal perfection is possibly exemplified, the question arises as to why any such propositions should seem to anyone to be true. Whence come these convictions? Do we have any reason to think they are due to a reliable belief-forming mechanism?

Our practice as language users provides a context in which it makes sense that we have linguistic and (narrowly) logical intuitions. Likewise, it can be argued, our social relations provide a context in which some moral intuitions are explicable. But for relatively abstruse metaphysical and modal intuitions, it is hard to see how any naturalistic account would be plausible. Do intuitions about haecceities or about the modalities of natural kind membership have evolutionary survival value? It is hard to see how. The Anselmian, however, does have available the elements of an account of some such intuitions. For the Anselmian's intuitions about God, or more generally, all those intuitions which together yield the Anselmian conception of God, generate without intentional contrivance an overall belief set in which it makes sense that there should be some such intuitions and that they should be, at least a core of them, reliable. For if an Anselmian God exists and creates rational beings whose end is to know him, it makes good sense that they should be able to come to know something of his existence and attributes. It makes sense that he create them capable of recognizing important truths about him as well as about themselves. Such a being could, in his creation of us, render us at least capable under the right conditions of having reliable intuitions such as those which yield the Anselmian conception of God and provide for a modal argument to his existence. So once he comes to believe in the existence of such a being, the Anselmian can retrospectively provide some reason for thinking that those intuitions which brought him to belief, or which strengthen his cognitive hold on that belief by way of a modal ontological argument are formed by a reliable belief-producing mechanism.

Of course there are two distinguishable questions I have just allowed to become interwoven. First, there is the question of providing some reason for thinking any modal intuitions are true. Secondly, there is the question of explaining why we have such intuitions. The non-theist can make some plausible progress on the first question in so far as he can integrate together his modal intuitions, with each other, and into ramified, coherent, and plausible theories about the nature of the world. Significant strides can be made in this direction by a completely non-theistic, essentialist metaphysic, for example. When modal intuitions both survive simple logical tests of consistency and also contribute to overall theories in this way, there is some indication that they are trustworthy intuitions. But anyone who has a plausible account of the origin of such intuitions, such that they are traceable to a reliable belief-forming mechanism, has so much the more warrant for taking them to be reliable, all other things, as we like to say, being equal. In so far as the Anselmian has a more natural explanatory account of this kind of his intuitions than the non-theist with contrary intuitions has of his, the Anselmian's natural preference of his own intuitions is epistemically enhanced and had a higher epistemic status than the contrary preferences of his opponent.[11]

So I think that anyone who finds himself with the modal intuitions needed for an ontological argument can find himself justified in relying on those intuitions. And of course anyone who lacks a supporting intuition for a specific modal claim is justified in refraining from accepting that claim, so long as it has for him no other indirect support which should be overriding.

So it can be reasonable to judge that a maximally perfect being is logically possible, in the broadly logical sense, while not judging of some or all LPNs that it is possible that they exist. And a mixed judgment on LPNs may even be the most reasonable of all for many Anselmians, and certainly is coherent: an acceptance of the possibility, and thus the existence of some abstract LPNs, along with a refusal to accept the possible existence of any non-abstract LPNs. One interesting question which remains is whether, and if so how, the theist can be justified in *denying* that any concrete LPNs exist. For this seems to be something many theists would deny — that there could be any necessarily existent demons, humans, or material objects of any kind.

Some theists seem to have direct intuitions that such things are impossible. And indirect arguments to this conclusion can be constructed from other intuitions. Consider for example the following argument, which I present without necessarily endorsing, just to give an example of the sort of argument a theist could deploy at this point.

Remember that a theist stressing the universal scope of divine creation and causal activity can accept the possibility of some LPNs, and their actuality, only if he endorses something like a modally up-dated Augustinian picture of them as dependent on God for their eternal and necessary creation. Thus, he can give as a reason for thinking concrete LPNs not possible any reason he has for thinking God would not engage in such a creative activity to produce such beings as necessary humans, necessary trees, and so forth.

Some theists find it intuitively plausible to think it is a necessary truth that

(D) Any non-divine created person has a *prima facie* duty to be thankful to God for his existence.

and consider it a conceptual truth that

(T) Thankfulness to a person is possible only for what could have been otherwise.

Given that not even a *prima facie* obligation can exist to do the impossible, such a theist can conclude that God cannot create a non-divine person with necessary existence. Granted that if, *per impossible*, such a person were created and were ignorant of his astounding ontological status, he could adopt all the psychological, phenomenological elements of thankfulness to God. But according to (T) the relation he would objectively bear to God would not be one of thankfulness. Further, if he learned the truth about himself, and accepted (T), he could no longer even take himself to be thankful to God. And many theists are committed to holding that it cannot be the case that learning the full truth about himself would render it impossible for any created non-divine person to be thankful to God for his existence.

But what about concrete LPNs which are not persons but rather material objects? As was mentioned earlier, some theists intuit that no material object is possibly necessary. For some who lack that intuition a companion argument to the one just developed can be constructed. For any material object can be held to be possibly such that it is a part of the natural causal environment of some created non-divine person. And some theists think that it is a necessary truth that

(D') It is possible for a created non-divine person to be thankful to God for any part of his natural causal environment.

But if any material object were necessarily existent, then given the truth of (T), (D') would be false. So anyone who holds the requisite modal propositions on intuitive grounds could argue that in the category of concrete LPNs, neither persons nor material objects are such that God could make it possible that they exist with this modal status. And granting that this is an exhaustive partitioning of non-abstract LPNs, the argument could justify holding that no such imagined beings are possible.[12]

But of course in order to avoid all the charges raised by Kane, the Anselmian need not endorse any such argument at all. All that is required is that he stick to his modal intuitions and avoid any modal commitment which does not in any way have for him intuitive support.

11

Pascalian Wagering

"Either God is or he is not." But to which view shall we be in-clined? Reason cannot decide this question. Infinite chaos separates us. At the far end of this infinite distance, a coin is be-ing spun which will come down heads or tails. How will you wager? Reason cannot make you choose either, reason cannot prove either wrong.

IN THIS VIVID AND memorable passage, Blaise Pascal began to develop the famous argument which has come to be known as 'Pascal's Wager'.[1] The Wager is widely regarded as an argu-ment for the rationality of belief in God which completely cir-cumvents all considerations of proof or evidence that there is a God. Viewed as such, it has both excited and aggravated philosophers for years. Some have applauded it as a simple, down-to-earth, practical, and decisive line of reasoning which avoids altogether the esoteric, mind-boggling intricacies and apparently inevitable indecisiveness of the traditional theistic arguments that year after year continue to be revised and re-evaluated. They seem to share the view of Pascal himself who once wrote that

> The metaphysical proofs for the existence of God are so remote from human reasoning and so involved that they make little im-pact, and, even if they did help some people, it would only be for the moment during which they watched the demonstration, because an hour later they would be afraid they had made a mistake.[2]

Others have been exceedingly offended by the very idea of wagering on God in hopes of obtaining infinite gain, and shocked by the suggestion that rational belief can be established by wholly non-evidential, or non-epistemic means. Such philosophers have succeeded in raising an impressive number of objections to Pascal's case, objections which in the eyes of many render the argument of the Wager a failure. In this essay, I propose to examine this common view of the Wager as intended to secure the rationality of religious belief without any regard to purely epistemic matters. I want to suggest that such a view involves a misunderstanding of the Wager based on a neglect to take seriously an important feature of its original context, manifested by those initial remarks which Pascal used to launch his argument, and from which this paper began. A proper understanding of the epistemic context within which the Wager was intended to be used can provide us with a way of answering a number of the most standard and imposing objections to this interesting argument.

I

In attempting to show on prudential grounds that everyone ought to be a theist, Wager enthusiasts often seek to maximize the rhetorical force of their argument by conceding almost everything to the epistemically reasonable atheist and then producing from his own premises their desired conclusion. The rhetoric of their presentation often develops like this. First, it is pointed out that rational gamblers seeking to maximize their gains over the long run bet in accordance with the highest mathematical expectation, where expectation is established with the formula

(E):   (Probability × Payoff) − Cost = Expectation

and is ranked for all possible bets in the contest or game situation. Then the confident Pascalian announces that in this life we are all in a forced betting situation in which the possible wagers are that there is a God and that there is no God. The situation is said to be forced in the sense that not acting as if there is a God—not praying, not seeking God's will for one's life, not being thankful to God—is considered to be equivalent to acting as if there is no God, practically speaking.[3] So one either acts as if there is a God, thereby betting on God, or one does not so act, thereby betting there is no God. Which bet should a rational person make? To answer this question, we must make assignments to the expectation formula and compare outcomes for the bets of theism and atheism. And this is where the rhetorical flourishes come into play whose assumptions result in disaster for the argument.

Let atheism be assigned an extremely high probability, and theism accordingly a very low one, the modern-day Pascalian suggests. It will not matter, so long as neither value is 0 or 1. And so long as theism is even a possibility, it is claimed, its probability is greater than 0, however small, and atheism's is less than 1. Now consider the question of cost. What does it cost to be an atheist? The Pascalian is typically ready to concede that it costs nothing. For, remember, in betting situations the cost is figured under the presumption that the outcome is unknown. So atheism cannot be said here to cost the loss of eternal bliss. And further, any values of the religious life whose descriptions do not entail the existence of God, such as the aesthetic pleasures of liturgy, and the social fulfillment of religious community, are in principle available to atheists as well as theists, if they are sufficiently shrewd. Even the comfort of believing in an after-life need not be the exclusive possession of theists. So even in this life atheism can be conceded to bear no cost. But religious belief, on the contrary, can be acknowledged to exact quite a cost from the believer. An adherent to typical theistic religions finds himself under all sorts of prohibitions and rules not recognized by the nonbeliever. So, the Pascalian is often quick to agree, the cost of betting on God is great.

Unlike standard betting situations, we have not to this point had determinate, precise assignments of probability and cost, but rather have contented ourselves with very general, comparative indications. According to the view of the Wager under consideration, this does not matter, however, since the values we must assign to the payoff variable will work in the formula for expectation in such a way as to render any precision with respect to the other variables irrelevant. Theism promises infinite, eternal reward. Atheism at best carries with it a promise of finite rewards—whatever pleasure in this life would have been prohibited to the theist. So the Pascalian claims.

Respective expectations of atheism and theism are then figured and ranked as follows. In the case of atheism, multiplying a very high probability by a great finite payoff, and subtracting no cost at all will yield at best a very large finite value. For theism, on the other hand, the product of an infinite payoff and any positive finite probability, however small, will yield an infinite expectation, regardless of how great a finite cost is subtracted. So theism has an infinitely higher expectation than atheism. Thus, the rational person seeking to maximize his gains in this betting situation ought to bet on God.

II

Many objections have been raised against Pascal's Wager. I want to focus for a moment on those which I think to be particularly problematic for the sort of presentation of the Wager just elucidated. Let us refer to that development of the argument as the epistemically unconcerned version of the Wager, a version in which it does not matter what the precise epistemic status of theism or of atheism is, as long as neither is certainly true. Such a version is vulnerable to a number of objections.

First of all, many people who accept (E) as a formula appropriate for use in normal betting situations may hesitate or refuse to use it in this situation. For the conditions under which it is appropriately used may not obtain with respect to this quite unusual bet. In normal situations, for which the formula was constructed, possible payoffs are always finite in value. The insertion of an infinite value here so over-rides considerations

of probability and cost as to render them nearly irrelevant. Can
(E) be expected to serve its ordinary function with such an extraordinary assignment to one of its variables?

Likewise, in normal betting situations there is usually a controlled range of divergence between probability values when
the cost of some bet is high. And, again, it is in such situations that (E) has its appropriate application. Often, this feature
of a betting situation is not perceived as being so important.
And it need not be, so long as there is, as there usually is,
a direct correlation and otherwise proper sort of relation between magnitude of cost and magnitude of probability. But
in this version of the Wager, there is an inverse correlation
between these factors. Under such conditions, degree of divergence between probabilities becomes a concern. The epistemically unconcerned version of the Wager purports to work regardless of the disparity between the probabilities of theism
and atheism, even if, for example, there is only a one in a
trillion chance, or less, of theism's being true. It can be rational to distrust the formula's application under such conditions. Further, there is some serious question about the use
of probability assignments at all by this version of the Wager.
It seems clear that the only interpretation of probability relevant and useable here is the subjective one; yet, how are even
subjective probability assignments supposed to arise out of the
mere insistence that theism is not demonstrably impossible?
Its mere possibility need not be taken to endow it with any
positive probability at all.

Thirdly, (E) clearly functions to aid a rational gambler in
maximizing his gains over the long-run. And this it does, since
long-run success is compatible with the losing of many individual bets along the way. Now, despite the fact that one
often hears Pascalians insist on the formula's appropriateness
in this case since "there is no longer run than eternity," it is
clear that in the bet concerning God we do not have a situation of repetitive wagering, in which ultimate maximization
of gain is compatible with numerous losses along the way. And
so again it could be argued that conditions do not obtain in

which the rational bettor is best guided by (E). But of course, if (E) is not used, this form of the Wager does not work.

A fourth objection to the Wager we must consider, one raised and developed by numerous critics in recent years, is the Many Claimants Objection, one which is often characterized as resulting from a partitioning problem. The Wager, it is said, partitions the variously possible bets on the issue of God inadequately, presenting us with only two options, theism and atheism, when in reality there are many, perhaps innumerably many. And this is much more than an easily correctable oversight. First of all, there are numerous different versions of theism extant, all vying for our credence. For any which promises eternal bliss, and many do, (E) will yield an infinite expectation, as long as there is the slightest positive probability that it is true. And if mere possibility yields some positive probability, as the epistemically unconcerned version of the Wager alleges, matters are even worse. For if it is even logically possible that there exists a being who promises infinite eternal reward to all and only those who deny the existence of all other claimants to worship, including the Christian God, (E) yields a dilemma equivalent to a practical contradiction: a rational person both ought and ought not bet on, say, the Christian God. Further, as if this were not enough, not even will it be the case that some theism or other will be preferable to all forms of atheism. For consider the apparent logical possibility that there is no God and that by some weird law of nature there will be an infinite, eternally blissful after-life for all and only those who in this life live as convinced atheists. On the basic assumptions of the epistemically unconcerned version of the Wager, the expectation associated with this form of atheism will also be infinite. Clearly, we have here a serious problem.[4]

Most recent commentators have seen one or more of these objections as decisive against the Wager, sufficient to show it to have no rational force. And this is, I think, a correct judgment with respect to the epistemically unconcerned version of the Wager. But it is neither the only version of a Wager-style argument nor, I believe, the sort of version we should attribute to Pascal. When the formula (E) is allowed to work on very low probability values, even those so low as to be approaching 0, and the positive probability of a bet is thought to be provided by the mere logical possibility of its outcome, a context is created in which the production of absurd results is unavoidable. But this is not the context of the original Wager.

It is almost anyone's guess as to what Pascal's planned defense of the Christian faith would have looked like in detail had he lived to complete it. One thing that is clear though is that it was not an epistemically unconcerned project. In fact, even a fairly casual reading of the *Pensées* will show that Pascal felt it important to try to defeat *prima facie* evidential considerations which could be held to count seriously against the truth of Christian beliefs, considerations such as, for example, the hidden-ness of God, and the rejection by most of his Jewish contemporaries of the Christian claim that Jesus was the long awaited Messiah sent from God. Furthermore, although he engages in no natural theology at all, Pascal does marshal together quite a few considerations in favor of the reliability of the Bible and the trustworthiness of Christian claims. We have no reason to think that he intended his Wager argument to operate in complete isolation from any purely epistemic considerations. In fact quite the contrary is indicated even by the remarks with which he launched the argument. Recall the claim in the quote from which we began this essay that "Reason cannot decide this question." If epistemic conditions were such that Christian theism could properly receive a very low assignment of subjective probability by any well-informed rational person, and its denial a correspondingly high value, it would not be the case that "reason cannot decide this question." I think we have here sufficient textual indication that the Wager argument was intended to work only for people who judge the theism Pascal had in mind and its denial to be in rough epistemic parity.

If reason cannot decide whether the Christian God exists or not, there cannot be a clear preponderance of purely epistemic considerations either way. Thus there cannot be a great disparity between the assigned probability values of theism and atheism. If it can be rational for a person to judge these positions to be in rough epistemic parity, it can be rational to dismiss altogether one objection to the Wager we considered, the one in which hesitation is expressed concerning the application of (E) to situations with greatly disparate probability values. The objection in this context becomes irrelevant.

Likewise, the hesitation to employ (E) with an infinite value for one of its variables is groundless unless there is reason to believe that allowing such a value assignment will have obviously absurd or unacceptable consequences. A moment's consideration will show that the only problematic and absurd consequences of applying (E) with an infinite payoff value are displayed in the famous Many Claimants problem, a problem which as we have seen results only from the additional assumptions as well that (1) apparent logical possibility should be translated into some positive non-zero probability value, and (2) the Wager formula can and should be employed regardless of the probability disparity between possible bets. But if both these assumptions are rejected, the Many Claimants problem does not arise, and the importation of an infinite value into (E) has no clearly problematic results.

So holding the Wager to be appropriate only under conditions of rough epistemic parity between Christian theism and its denial avoids altogether three otherwise interesting and worrisome objections. What about the fourth we considered? We do not have here a repetitive wagering situation in which short term loss is compatible with long term gain. There is only one bet; it is either won or lost. But if (E) is thought not to be relevant, how is a decision between theism and atheism to be made? If theism and atheism are in rough epistemic parity, no decision between them can be made on purely epistemic grounds. Some form of agnosticism would be the appropriate doxastic stance if no considerations other than purely epistemic ones could or should enter into such decisions. But, according to Pascal, this is betting against God. One's doxastic stance is a form of, and a function of, behavior which amounts, in the context, to the placing of a bet. And surely there are values other than purely epistemic values which are relevant in the placing of a bet. What sorts of values? Just the ones which function in (E). So even though the wager concerning God is not only one episode in a repetitive wagering situation, there seems to be no good alternative to (E) to employ here when choosing one's bet. So given our restriction of the Wager argument to conditions of rough epistemic parity, this objection is neutralized as well.

This view of the wager is an improvement over the epistemically unconcerned version then in two respects. It seems to be more in line with Pascal's original intentions, and it is immune to certain difficult objections which plague the more contemporary version. But this version of the wager can have use for a rational person only if it can be reasonable to judge Christian theism and its denial to be in rough epistemic parity. Pascal seems to have thought this was possible. But others have offered reasons to think otherwise. So this is an issue which will merit some consideration.

III

There are two possible ways in which theism and atheism can be in rough epistemic parity for a person. It seems possible for a person rationally to think that there is no positive evidence or any other epistemic ground for thinking that there is a God, nor any good evidence or other epistemic ground for thinking that there is not. Such a person might be aware of traditional arguments for both positions but find all of them flawed to such an extent that he reasonably judges none of them to endow either conclusion with any positive epistemic status. And he might lack any other purely epistemic consideration either way. For example, he could also lack any natural inclination to believe either way, and so find himself with neither a properly basic theistic belief nor a properly basic atheistic belief. Let us say that with respect to the issue of theism versus atheism, such a person would find himself in epistemically null conditions. The other way in which theism and atheism can be in rough epistemic parity for a person obtains when each is judged to have some positive epistemic status, but neither is more evident than, or clearly outweighs, the other. Let us say that a person who reasonably makes such a judgment is in epistemically ambiguous conditions regarding theism and atheism. Initially, it would seem that if either epistemically null, or epistemically ambiguous conditions can reasonably be thought sometimes to obtain, we have reason to believe that a version of the Wager requiring rough epistemic parity can be formulated as a potentially useful decision making device.

Both N. R. Hanson and Michael Scriven, however, have argued that it is impossible to be in epistemically null conditions with respect to any positive existence claim. In the posthumously published 'What I Don't Believe,' Hanson wrote:

> When there is no good reason for thinking a claim to be true, *that* in itself is good reason for thinking the claim to be false.[5]

and, accordingly

> a 'proof' of x's non-existence usually derives from the fact that there is no good reason for supposing that x *does* exist.[6]

In the line with this, Scriven wrote in *Primary Philosophy* that:

> The proper alternative, when there is no evidence, is not mere suspension of belief; it is disbelief.[7]

Applying this to the question of theism, Scriven went on to say that

> Atheism is obligatory in the absence of any evidence for God's existence.[8]

If epistemically null conditions could obtain for any proposition p and its denial -p, then according to Hanson and Scriven, it seems, we would be forced to disbelieve p, thereby believing -p, and to disbelieve -p, thereby believing p. But this is absurd, so epistemically null conditions cannot obtain both for a proposition and its denial. The absence of a positive epistemic consideration in favor of p will just be a positive epistemic consideration in favor of $-p$, and vice versa.

On close inspection of their arguments, however, it becomes clear that Hanson and Scriven are not concerned to make a completely general claim about the epistemic dynamics of just any sort of proposition whatsoever, but rather that they want to lay down a rule for the evaluation only of positive existence claims, propositions which assert that some sort of object exists. One feature of such propositions Hanson points out is this: It is possible in principle to gather conclusive evidence concerning a positive existential generalization; whereas, it is not possible in principle to gather such evidence for the denial of an unrestricted, positive existential, a proposition of the form of an unrestricted universal generalization. Hanson sees this asymmetry as setting the logical backdrop for what we can call the Hanson-Scriven Thesis:

HST   For any rational subject S and any positive existence claim P, if S is in possession of no good evidence or any other positive epistemic ground for thinking that P is true, then S ought to adopt the cognitive relation to P of denial.

Now of course, the evidential asymmetry between unrestricted positive and negative existentials does not entail or in any other way dictate the HST. But the intuitive force the HST has had for many philosophers need not be impugned in the least by this fact. For it just seems that in many ordinary situations we do govern our assent by something like it.

Suppose I am seated in my office, which is neither excessively large nor unusually cluttered. The proposition suddenly occurs to me that there is a large Boa Constrictor in the room. I make a quick but cautious thorough inspection of the place. Suppose I find absolutely no trace of such an animal anywhere in the office. What is the most rational stance for me to take concerning the suddenly entertained proposition? Affirmation?

Certainly not. Agnosticism? Surely this would be just as inappropriate. The only rational stance to take in absence of any evidence or any other positive epistemic consideration at all will be one of denial. And that judgment seems to accord perfectly with the HST. Any number of such examples from everyday life could be produced as well which seem to show that Hanson and Scriven have indeed captured in their thesis one of our ordinary principles for rational judgment. And if we are committed to such a principle, we are committed to refusing to allow the claim that epistemically null conditions concerning both theism and atheism can obtain for any rational subject. The absence of any evidence or any other positive epistemic consideration for theism will just count as providing a good, decisive consideration for atheism.

An ingenious rejoinder to Hanson and Scriven has been devised by Alvin Plantinga.[9] Plantinga asks us to consider the proposition

> (1) There is at least one human being that was not created by God.

Since it is, he suggests, a necessary truth about God (at least about the God of orthodox Christian theology) that

> (2) If God exists, then God has created all the human beings there are,

any set of epistemic considerations in favor of the truth of (1)—evidence, arguments, etc.—will have to contain an argument that there is no God. But suppose that

> (A) There is no good argument against God's existence.

Then we shall have in consequence no good argument for (1) and so, according to Hanson and Scriven, we must believe its denial:

> (1′) All human beings are created by God.

Now suppose also, Plantinga suggests, that

> (B) There is no good argument for God's existence,

a supposition which surely would be dear to the hearts of both Hanson and Scriven. Then when considering

(3) There is a God

we find that we are obliged to believe its denial

(3') There is no God.

But then, Platinga continues, assuming that

(C) There are no good arguments for or against the existence of God,

the Hanson-Scriven view forces us to believe

(4) There is no God and all human beings are created by him

which is awkward and embarrassing enough for anyone, but which also, along with the obvious truths that

(5) Some human beings exist

and that

(6) No human being was created by God unless God exists

entails a contradiction. And certainly, no principle which produces this sort of absurdity is worthy of rational acceptance.

But, of course, we can well imagine that Hanson and Scriven would reply that this attempted refutation of their principle just begs the question against them. For on their principle, assumption (C) could never be true. The absence of any good argument *for* the existence of God would just itself provide us with a good argument *against* the existence of God. The epistemically null situation portrayed by (C) could not obtain. So this argument against the principle espoused by Hanson and Scriven cannot after all show it to be unacceptable.

Is there anything wrong with their principle? It has stood for years in the literature, unrefuted, and apparently endorsed by many philosophers. Further, it has the apparent backing of common intuitions about the proper governance of our assent, as illustrated by the story of the Boa Constrictor. However, it is easy to show that such backing is apparent only for the specific HST formulation we are considering and which is necessary for blocking the possibility of epistemically null conditions obtaining for both theism and atheism.

Circumstances in which the lack of any positive epistemic considerations (evidence, etc.) for some positive existence claim P rationally oblige a subject S to deny P rather than to withhold on it are those in which S reasonably believes he is in *good epistemic position* with respect to P, where being in good epistemic position relative to a proposition is understood in such a way that any subject S is in good epistemic position relative to P if and only if (1) P is such that if it were true, there would exist positive epistemic considerations indicating or manifesting its truth, and (2) S is such that if there existed such considerations, he would, or most likely would, possess them. When I have completed my search for the Boa, I am in good epistemic position to assess the claim that such a thing exists in my office. *In that position*, and only in that position, lack of any positive epistemic consideration for the claim amounts to as decisive a consideration against the claim as one could want. It is only when a person reasonably believes himself to be in good epistemic position for assessing an existence claim that an absence of any evidence or other positive epistemic consideration for it can warrant and require his denial of the claim.

So the HST should be revised to read something like

(HST′) For any rational subject S and any positive existence claim P, if S rationally believes himself to be in good epistemic position relative to P, and S is in possession of no good evidence or any other positive epistemic ground for thinking that P is true, then S ought to adopt the cognitive relation to P of denial.

Suppose that someone believes there to be no positive epistemic support for theism. Can he also believe there to be no such support for atheism? Can he rationally judge himself to be in epistemically null conditions regarding both claims? According to the HST', he can so long as he is rationally unsure whether he is good epistemic position relative to theism, or rationally believes himself not to be in such position.

A rational person lacking any positive epistemic considerations can certainly be agnostic about his epistemic position on theism. For suppose he thinks there to be no good evidence or any other positive epistemic consideration either way. Either the Christian God exists or he does not. If the Christian God exists, any failure to have positive considerations of this (any lack of evidence, or of a natural inclination to believe, etc.) may be due to the noetic effects of sin. And on the other hand, if there is no such being, a failure to see that there is not may be due to low-grade effects of a deep psychological need not to know. In either case, one who lacks evidence or other positive considerations would not be in good epistemic position, having his cognitive abilities clouded in one way or another. Realizing these possibilities can rationally warrant agnosticism with respect to one's epistemic position on this issue.[10] And that condition is sufficient for one's rationally judging the situation to be epistemically null, and on purely epistemic grounds withholding on both theism and atheism. HST' does not require otherwise.

Any perceived condition of epistemic parity between a proposition and its denial can be expressed in a subjective probability assignment of ½ to each option. And for anyone in a condition of epistemic nullity with respect to Christian theism and its denial who is willing to register this with a probability estimation (a function of expectations) of "50/50", Pascal's wager can be formulated to suggest prudential reasons for venturing in behavior beyond the agnosticism which only epistemic considerations alone would require.

But of course, as I have indicated earlier, Pascal did not believe that any well informed inquirer would find himself in epistemically null conditions concerning Christian theism and its denial. So on this count it might seem unimportant to have argued the possibility of such conditions obtaining with respect to these alternatives. Furthermore, anyone willing to

assign a subjective probability assignment to these two alternatives of ½ each, despite being bereft of any positive epistemic consideration for either, seems clearly to be adopting
the procedure of assigning positive probability values on the
ground of logical possibility alone, a policy which I have suggested is unwise, and has been partly responsible for actually
weakening the reasoning of the Wager. So on its own, it is
not so important to have established, against the contentions
of Hanson and Scriven, the possibility of epistemically null
conditions obtaining here.

What is important is seeing how an HST-style principle requiring denial under conditions of no positive grounds for an
existence claim must be qualified. For such a principle could
be reformulated quite naturally and easily for circumstances
in which the epistemic considerations relevant to such a proposition (distinct from any arising from the application of such
a principle itself) were ambiguous, or counterbalanced in such
a way that there existed no sufficient consideration for the
purely epistemic endorsement of the proposition. Such an ex-
tension of the original HST might be thought to be in full
accord with the basic intent of its proponents. And such a principle could be taken to rule out the possibility that any rational, well informed inquirer be in epistemically ambiguous
conditions with respect to any positive existence claim and its
denial. But this is precisely what Pascal envisioned to be possible
in the case of Christian theism and its denial. Once we have
seen how the original HST must be qualified in such a way
that it allows epistemically null conditions to obtain here, it
surely will require no separate argument to see how a properly qualified version will allow the possibility of conditions
of epistemic ambiguity. And surely, many people confess to
finding themselves in just such conditions on the issue of
Pascal's concern, seeing some reason to think Christian theism
to be true, some reason to think it false. This perspective is
very naturally reflected by such subjective probability assess-
ments as "roughly 50/50". In any situation of rough epistemic
parity the famous and much maligned Principle of Indifference

can even be produced to yield a probability assignment of exactly ½ for each of the two competitors.[11] If it is rational for anyone to make such an assignment as a reflection of his subjective doxastic state, it is reasonable, so far, to think that Pascal's Wager has a context of rational application.

IV

It seems to have been Pascal's conviction that a person's epistemic condition with respect to theism and atheism is a function of his attitudes, desires, and other commitments, and that in turn these are a function of the sorts of patterns of behavior he liked to call 'habit'. It is a dangerous illusion to think of our epistemic capacities as existing and operating independently of the other features of our lives. The person who loves God, according to Pascal, is able to see that everything is created by him (781). The person with contrary passions is bereft of this perspicacity. It was Pascal's view that there exists evidence for the truth of Christian theism which exceeds, or at least equals, evidence to the contrary (835). But he was convinced that it is a person's passional state which will determine how he sees the evidence, and what he does on the basis of it.

The enjoinder to wager on God is the recommendation, on prudential grounds, to adopt a Christian form of life to the extent that one is able. Pascal thought that an entry into that sort of life pattern would have a long-term and cumulative effect on a person's attitudes, desires, and epistemic state. As contrary passions were bridled and finally put aside, he was convinced that anyone who formerly was incapable of seeing or knowing God would attain this capacity, and only with the onset of such a capacity could true faith come.

It is not an assumption of the Wager that God will reward a person for a deliberate, calculated charade of belief undertaken and maintained on grounds of the grossest self-interest. So the famous objection of William James, who was offended by such an assumption, misses the point. There is no doubt that the argument as constructed by Pascal appeals to self-interest. But its intent and goal is to induce a wager whose outcome will yield true faith, an attitudinal state in which self-interest takes its rightful and surbordinate place as a behavior motivation. Furthermore, the Wager need not be formulated as an appeal to self-interest at all. It can be presented as an appeal to altruism. One then bets on God so that one will be in a proper position non-hypocritically to urge others to do so, thereby potentially providing them with the greatest amount of good one possibly could.

Likewise, other moral objections to the Wager are easily defeated. James found it morally offensive that God would reward those who want reward. Terence Penelhum apparently has found it repugnant that God would punish anyone who did not otherwise believe for failing to follow such a course of attempted aggrandizement.[12] Both James and Penelhum impose a conception of the eternal economy on the argument which it in no way requires and then object to their own creations. In particular, they have what we may call an inappropriately externalist conception of after-life. One reads Pascal's original wager passage in vain for the language of rewards and punishment. He does not there portray God at all as either granting or withholding benefits in accordance with how people bet. It seems on the contrary that a more internalist conception of eternal beatitude can both accord with Pascal's own Wager presentation and serve to neutralize the James and Penelhum type of objection. One's state after bodily death is then viewed as being in proper moral and spiritual continuity with one's earthly existence. Those who have hungered and thirsted after righteousness are satisfied. Those who have not, are not. Now, it might appear odd to characterize all those who align themselves with the Christian God as those who hunger and thirst after righteousness. In particular this may seem an inappropriate description of those who are, on Pascalian grounds, wagering on God. However, as indicated already, this is the sort of mind-set meant to eventuate from the particular wagering behavior recommended. Further, the infinite "payoff" as characterized in the Christian tradition, if delineated carefully enough, just may not appeal to a person with no taste for moral and spiritual good. For the heaven of Pascal is not the heaven of, say, popular Islam. It is not an infinite expansion of sensual delights. In fact it is the sort of infinite bliss which will be attractive only to those with at least a latent capacity to exemplify the attitude characterized biblically as a hunger and thirst for righteousness. And only such as these are, in the theology of Christian theism, able to commune with God at all.

It is not my intent here to defend Pascal's Wager against all extant criticism, although I think it eminently more defensible than most recent commentators have allowed. My primary aim has been merely to suggest that when we attend carefully to some important clues in Pascal's text, we can see that the sort of argument he intended is immune to numerous potent objections which have been raised against contemporary versions of the argument differing in important respects from his own. When these objections have been cleared away, it becomes possible to consider more seriously other philosophical and religious questions raised by the whole idea of Pascalian Wagering.

12

Rationality and the
Christian Revelation

> Now there was a man of the Pharisees, named Nicodemus, a ruler
> of the Jews. This man came to Jesus by night and said to him
> "Rabbi, we know that you are a teacher come from God; for no
> man can do these signs that you do unless God is with him. (John
> 3:1–2)

Since at least the time of Nicodemus, people have reasoned
about the identity of Jesus. It has been the most widespread
view of Christians throughout the centuries that it is eminently
reasonable to believe Jesus to be, not just a teacher come from
God, but God himself, incarnate in human nature. In the letter
to the Hebrews, it is said that:

> In many and various ways, God spoke to our fathers by the proph-
> ets; but in these last days he has spoken to us by a Son, whom
> he appointed heir of all things, through whom also he created
> the world. He reflects the glory of God and bears the very stamp
> of his nature, upholding the universe by his word of power (Heb.
> 1:1–3a)

Christians have always believed that the supreme self-disclosure
of God has occurred in the life and death of Jesus. He who
has seen him has seen the Father. It is the insistence of traditional orthodox Christians that this is true precisely because
Jesus was himself literally divine. More precisely, it is the claim
of traditional Christology, and the central commitment of distinctively Christian belief, that Jesus was, and eternally is, God
the Son, the Second Person of the divine Trinity in human

nature. To reveal himself to us, God became one of us. To save humanity, he took on humanity.

In recent years, however, the fundamental Christian claim about Jesus has undergone a barrage of criticism. Numerous critics, including many prominent theologians who continue to align themselves with the Christian church, have alleged that it is no longer possible that it be rational for well informed intelligent people to accept the doctrine of the Incarnation. This allegation has been made in a number of ways and stands nowadays as a foregone conclusion in many centers of higher education, including numerous seminaries and schools of divinity. I believe it is a view which richly deserves to be challenged.

In this essay, I want to examine some important facets of this question as to whether it is possible that it be reasonable or rational to believe Jesus to be God Incarnate. In particular, I want to take a look at some considerations which have been thought by many recent critics to constitute obstacles for a positive answer to this question and see how a perspective on the Incarnation can be developed which will allow these potential obstacles to be overcome. Thus, we shall be dealing here with some basic epistemic matters concerning the doctrine of the Incarnation. My aim here, however, is not to marshal evidence or other sorts of epistemic support in favour of the doctrine. I shall not try to prove, argue, or in any other way show that Jesus was God Incarnate. Not even the more modest task will be attempted of showing that all Christians ought to adopt this traditional understanding of Jesus over any of the alternative conceptions of him developed by a number of contemporary theologians, although I believe this is the case. On this occasion, I shall focus on what are, in principle, only some of the epistemic dynamics of the incarnational claim — some of its logical relations to the sorts of epistemic considerations in the light of which its rational affirmation would be possible or impossible. What I do hope to indicate, in a positive vein, is that contrary to what many critics have argued in the recent past, it is possible that it be rational to believe Jesus to be God Incarnate. To put it a bit more strongly, I hope to go some way toward showing that none of the major criticisms of a philosophical nature directed against the doctrine of the Incarnation in the last few years provides any good reason at all to think that it cannot be rational to believe that the pinnacle of divine revelation has consisted in God's coming among us as one of us. The belief that Jesus was God Incarnate can be an eminently rational belief to hold.

The present essay will be an exercise in Christian philosophical theology, an intellectual enterprise which I take to be a necessary component in any comprehensive, broadly orthodox theology. Of course, Christian theology is not just apologetics. It is not even primarily apologetics. Yet, especially in our time, it must prominently involve apologetics. And this is something we need not regret. For in attempting to answer our critics, we very often come to see features of our beliefs we otherwise might have overlooked. It is my hope that in taking even a brief look at each of the challenges I want to address, we shall begin to attain a richer perspective on one of the most central and important Christian beliefs about the self-disclosure of God.

I. God in Christ: The Possibility of Rational Belief

In the past, many people, including some friends of the Christian message as well as numerous foes, have believed the doctrine of the Incarnation to be ultimately beyond the scope of reason. Some have believed this because they have taken the doctrine to be inexpungibly obscure to the point of being without clear sense or determinate, cognitive meaning. If it were beyond the scope of reason on this ground, or on any other ground, it would not be such that belief in it could be rational, or in accord with reason.

What are we to make of this sort of view? I think it will be interesting here to quote at length a line of reasoning presented some time ago by John Wisdom:

It has been said that once at least a higher gift than grace did
flesh and blood refine, God's essence and his very self—in the
body of Jesus. Whether this statement in true or false is not now
the point, but whether it's so obscure as to be senseless. Obscure
undoubtedly it is but senseless it is not. For to say that in Nero
God was incarnate is not to utter a senseless string of words nor
merely to express a surprising sentiment; it is to make a statement which is absurd because it is against all reason. If I say of
a cat, 'This cat is abracadabra' I utter a senseless string of words,
I don't make a statement at all and therefore don't make an absurd statement. But if I say of a cat which is plainly dead 'In this
cat there is life' I make a statement which is absurd because it
is against all reason. The cat is not hunting, eating, sleeping,
breathing; it is stiff and cold. In the same way the words, 'In Nero
God was incarnate' are not without any meaning; one who utters
them makes a statement, he makes a statement which is absurd
and *against* all reason and therefore *not* beyond the scope of reason. Now if a statement is not beyond the scope of reason then
any logically parallel statement is also not beyond the scope of
reason. . . . The statement 'In Jesus God was incarnate' is logically
parallel to 'In Nero God was incarnate.' The latter we noticed is
not beyond the scope of reason. Therefore the statement 'In Jesus
God was incarnate' is not beyond the scope of reason.[1]

It is not merely the case that we have no reason to believe that
Nero was God Incarnate; that would be compatible with our
also having no reason to believe he was not God Incarnate.
And in that case, the claim, and claims of its type, could be
beyond the scope of reason. Wisdom's point is that we have
very good reason, as decisive a grounding as we could want,
for believing that the wicked man Nero was *not* God Incarnate. And surely to this, everyone in possession of the Judeo-
Christian conception of God would agree. Any claim that Nero
was God Incarnate we would label as nonsense or absurd. Now
it happens to be the case that many critics of orthodox Christian doctrine within the contemporary academic theological
community have called the traditional claim that Jesus was
literally God Incarnate nonsense or absurd. But even these

critics, or at least the vast majority of them, surely would recognize something clearly wrong with the Nero claim which is not wrong with the parallel claim about Jesus. The Nero claim is nonsensical or absurd on properly epistemic grounds, and thus in an epistemic sense — It stands in flagrant contradiction to all we know about the character of the man Nero, in light of the concept we have of God. It is something about Nero himself, his particular personality and character, which would make a claim to his deity particularly absurd, and markedly inferior in an epistemic sense to the parallel claim about Jesus. It is this that Wisdom would have us attend to.

The Christian claim has been said by some critics to be nonsensical or absurd in a logical, or semantic, or conceptual sense. That this is not the case can be held to be evinced by the comparative difference in *prima facie* epistemic status we sense between the claim about Nero and the claim about Jesus, given what we know about the two of them on the human level. Thus, as Wisdom indicates, neither of these statements is unintelligible. And neither is beyond the scope of reason. The difference we feel between them witnesses to that.

If Wisdom has indeed successfully indicated to us that the doctrine of Incarnation is not beyond the scope of reason, has he shown that the possibility is open that it may be rational or reasonable to endorse this doctrine? The answer to this question is clearly "No," for the claim that Jesus was God Incarnate could fall within the scope of reason in much the same way as would a claim that, for example, Jesus was a married bachelor, for all that Wisdom shows. Wisdom does draw our attention helpfully to a difference between the Nero claim and the Jesus claim. But the claim of deity for Nero could be absurd in a way in which the claim of deity for Jesus is not absurd without its following from this that the claim about Jesus is not absurd in any sense at all, and such that it is even possible that it be rational to endorse it.

As a matter of fact, various contemporary theologians have thought the incarnational claim about Jesus to be patently incoherent and thus absurd in a logical or conceptual sense. From this point of view, it would be possible to believe Jesus to be God Incarnate and to be rational in so believing only if one rationally could fail to see the patent incoherence of the claim. A certain significant degree of ignorance or obtuseness would be required, if this were to be possible at all. A number of philosophers have offered persuasive arguments in recent years to the effect that it is possible rationally to believe the impossible, or necessarily false. However, if 'incoherent' means more than merely 'necessarily false', if 'patently incoherent' means something more like 'analytically false' or '*a priori* impossible', then it is less likely, to say the least, that anyone would be able rationally to believe a patently incoherent doctrine, for it is highly unlikely that belief in the truth of an analytically false, or *a priori* impossible, proposition can reasonably be ascribed to a person at all. If a patently incoherent proposition is such that one cannot understand it without seeing it to be false, and it is impossible to believe a proposition to be true without understanding it, and, moreover, it is impossible to believe a proposition to be true while seeing it to be false, then should the doctrine of the Incarnation be patently incoherent, it would not be possible rationally to believe it, because it would not be possible to believe it at all. Furthermore, understood in this way, it is clear that nothing could count as a positive epistemic consideration in favour of the truth of a patently incoherent claim. If the incarnational claim endorsed by traditional Christians had this status, there could be no positive epistemic ground for believing it true. As, for example, Grace Jantzen has said:

> If the claim that Jesus is God incarnate is on an epistemological level with 'Jesus was a married bachelor' then no matter how much evidence we could discover for his having said so, his disciples and others having believed it, and the early church having affirmed it, the claim must still be rejected: such 'evidence' would be strictly irrelevant.[2]

And this is certainly correct. Nothing can count as evidence or any other form of epistemic grounding for belief in a proposition the very understanding of which suffices for seeing its falsehood.

The charge of patent incoherence has been repeated in various forms quite often in recent years by critics of the doctrine of the Incarnation. Basically, the sort of argument most of them seem to have in mind is roughly something like the following: On a standard and traditional conception of deity, God is omnipotent, omniscient, incorporeal, impeccable, and necessarily existent, among other things. Moreover, by our definition of 'God', such properties as these are, so to speak, constitutive of deity—it is impossible that any individual be divine, or exemplify divinity, without having these properties. To claim some individual to be divine without being omnipotent, say, or necessarily existent, would be on this view just as incoherent as supposing some individual to be both a bachelor and a married man at one and the same time. By contrast, we human beings seem clearly to exemplify the logical complement (or "opposite") of each of these constitutive divine attributes. We are limited in power, restricted in knowledge, embodied in flesh, liable to sin, and are contingent creations. Jesus is claimed in the doctrine of the Incarnation to have been both fully human and fully divine. But it is logically impossible for any being to exemplify at one and the same time both a property and its logical complement. Thus, recent critics have concluded, it is logically impossible for any one person to be both human and divine, to have all the attributes proper to deity and all those ingredient in human nature as well. The doctrine of the Incarnation on this view is an incoherent theological development of the early church which must be discarded by us in favor of some other way of conceptualizing the importance of Jesus for Christian faith. He could not possibly have been God Incarnate, a literally divine person in human nature.

As I have addressed this challenge to the doctrine of the Incarnation in great detail elsewhere, I shall give only a relatively brief indication here of how it can be answered.[3] A lengthy response is not required in order for us to be able to see how this currently popular sort of objection can be turned back. A couple of very simple metaphysical distinctions will provide us with the basic apparatus for defending orthodoxy against this charge, which otherwise can seem to be a very formidable challenge indeed.

As it is usually presented, the sort of argument I have just outlined treats humanity and divinity, or human nature and divine nature, as each constituted by a set of properties individually necessary and jointly sufficient for exemplifying that nature, for being human, or for being divine. Such an argument depends implicitly on a sort of essentialist metaphysic which has been around for quite a while, and which recently has experienced a resurgence of popularity among philosophers. On such a view, objects have two sorts of properties, essential and accidental. A property can be essential to an object in either of two ways. It is part of an individual's essence if the individual which has it could not have existed without having it. It is a kind-essential property if its exemplification is necessary for an individual's belonging to a particular kind, for example, human-kind. Human nature, then, consists in a set of properties severally necessary and jointly sufficient for being human. And the same is true of divine nature. The critic of the Incarnation begins with the simple truth that there are properties humans have which God could not possibly have, assumes that these properties, or at least some of them, are essential properties of being human, properties without which one could not be fully human, and then concludes that God could not possibly become a human being. The conclusion would be well drawn if the assumption were correct. But it is this assumption that we must question.

Once a distinction betweeen essential and accidental properties is accepted, a distinction employed in this sort of argument against incarnation, another simple distinction follows in its wake. Among properties characterizing human beings, some are essential elements of human nature, but many just happen to be common human properties without also being essential. Consider for example the property of having ten fingers. It is a common human property, one had by a great number of people, but it clearly is not a property essential to being human. People lose fingers without thereby ceasing to be human. Further, consider a common property which safely can be said to be a universal human property, one had by every human being who ever has lived — the property of standing under fifteen feet tall. Obviously this is not an essential human property either. At some time in the future, an individual might grow beyond this height, certainly not thereby forfeiting his humanity. So it is not a safe inference to reason simply from a property's being common or even universal among human beings that it is an essential human property, strictly necessary for exemplifying human nature.

The relevance of this distinction to the doctrine of the Incarnation should be obvious. It is common for human beings to be less than omnipotent, less than omniscient, contingently existent, and so on. And any orthodox Christian will quickly agree that apart from Jesus, these are even universal human properties. Further, in the case of any of us who do exemplify these less than divine attributes, it is most reasonable to hold that they are in our case essential attributes. I, for example, could not possibly become omnipotent. I am essentially limited in power. But why think this is true on account of human nature? Why think that any attributes incompatible with deity are elements of human nature, properties without which one could not be truly human?

An individual is *fully human* just in case that individual has all essential human properties, all the properties composing basic human nature. An individual is *merely human* if he has all those properties *plus* some additional limitation properties as well, properties such as being less than omnipotent, less than omniscient, and so on. Some examples of this *merely x/fully x* distinction may help. Consider a diamond. It has all the properties essential to being a physical object (mass, spatio-temporal location, etc.). So it is fully physical. Consider now a turtle. It has all the properties essential to being a physical object. It is fully physical. But it is not merely physical. It has properties of animation as well. It is an organic being. In contrast, the gem is merely physical as well as being fully physical. Now take the case of a man. An embodied human being, any one you choose, has mass, spatio-temporal location, and so forth. He is thus fully physical. But he is not merely a physical object, having organic and animate properties as well. So let us say he is fully animate. But unlike the turtle he is not merely animate, having rational, moral, aesthetic, and spiritual qualities which mere organic entities lack. Let us say that he belongs to a higher ontological level by virtue of being fully human. And if, like you and I, he belongs to no higher ontological level than that of humanity, he is merely human as well as being fully human.

According to orthodox Christology, Jesus was fully human without being merely human. He had all properties constitutive of human nature, but had higher properties as well, properties constitutive of deity, properties which from an Anselmian perspective form the upper bound of our scale. What is crucial to realize here is that an orthodox perspective on human nature will categorize all human properties logically incompatible with a divine incarnation as, at most, essential to being *merely human*. No orthodox theologian has ever held that Jesus was merely human, only that he was fully human. It is held that the person who was God Incarnate had the full array of attributes essential to humanity, and all those essential to divinity.

I am suggesting that armed with a few simple distinctions the Christian can clarify his conception of human nature in such a way as to provide for the coherence and metaphysical possibility of the traditional doctrine of the Incarnation. But I am sure it will be objected by many that to use these distinctions to explicate what Chalcedon and the rest of the church has had in mind about Jesus is to land oneself in some well known absurdities. On the Chalcedonian picture, Jesus was omniscient, omnipotent, necessarily existent, and all the rest, as well as being an itinerant Jewish preacher. But this has appeared outlandish to most contemporary theologians. Did the bouncing baby boy of Mary and Joseph direct the workings of the cosmos from his crib? Was this admittedly remarkable man, as he sat by a well or under a fig tree actually omnipresent in all of creation? Did this carpenter's son exist *necessarily*? These implications of orthodoxy can sound just too bizarre for even a moment's consideration.

A couple of ancient claims are sufficient to rid orthodoxy from any such appearance of absurdity. First of all, a person is not identical with his body. Even a modern materialist who holds that all personality necessarily is embodied need not deny this. So the necessary existence of God the Son, with its implications that he cannot have begun to exist and cannot cease to exist, does not entail that the earthly body in which he incarnated himself had these properties. Secondly, a person is not identical with any particular range of conscious experience he might have. With this in mind, we can appreciate the early view that in the case of God Incarnate, we must recognize something like two distinct ranges of consciousness.[4] There is first what we can call the eternal mind of God the Son with its distinctively divine consciousness, whatever that might be like, with its full scope of omniscience. And there is a distinctly earthly consciousness which grew and developed as the boy Jesus grew and developed. It drew its visual imagery from what the eyes of Jesus saw, and its concepts from the languages he spoke. The earthly range of consciousness, and self-consciousness, was thoroughly human, Jewish, and first century Palestinian in scope.

To be as brief as possible here, we can view the two ranges of consciousness as follows: The divine consciousness of God the Son contained, but was not contained by, the earthly range of consciousness. Further, there was what can be called an a-symmetric accessing relation between the two (think of two computer programs or informational systems, one containing but not contained by the other). The divine mind had full access to the earthly experience being had through the incarnation, but the earthly consciousness did not have such access to the content of the over-arching omniscience of the Logos. This allows for the intellectual and spiritual growth of Jesus to be a real development. It also can help account for the cry of dereliction. We have in the person of Jesus no God merely dressed up as a man. No docetic absurdities are implied by this position. Nor is it Nestorian. Nor Appolinarian. There is one person with two natures, and two ranges of consciousness. He is not the theological equivalent of a centaur, half God and half man. He is fully human, but not merely human. He is also fully divine. There is, in this doctrine, no apparent incoherence whatsoever. Thus, there seem to be no good logical or conceptual grounds for thinking that there can be no rational belief that Jesus was God Incarnate.

But before concluding too hastily that it is at least possible for belief in the Incarnation to be rationally grounded, we would do well to consider briefly a problem which has been raised by Francis Young. Young has said:

> . . . it is now accepted by the majority of Christian theologians that Jesus must have been an entirely normal human being, that any qualification of this implies some element of docetic thinking, and that docetism, however slight, undermines the reality of the incarnation.
>
> I therefore pose the following conundrum:
> If Jesus was an entirely normal human being, no evidence can be produced for the incarnation.
> If no evidence can be produced, there can be no basis on which to claim that an incarnation took place.[5]

If it is assumed, as I would suspect it is by Young, that the belief that Jesus was God Incarnate cannot be a reasonable or rational belief to hold unless there can be evidence on which to base it, this argument, or conundrum, immediately becomes an argument to the effect that, on a certain assumption concerning what the doctrine of the Incarnation itself requires with respect to the humanity of Jesus, we find that it cannot be reasonable or rational to believe that Jesus was God Incarnate.

It is true that in order to avoid the docetic tendency which some critics have claimed plagues traditional theology, we must maintain the full, complete humanity of Jesus. But Young has a genuine problem here for incarnational belief only if in order to avoid docetism we also would have to hold that Jesus was *merely* human, and thus different from ordinary human beings such as you or me in no metaphysical way which could possibly be empirically manifested. But as we have seen, there is an important distinction to be drawn between being fully human and being merely human. Jesus can be fully human without being merely human. At least, that is the orthodox claim as I have articulated it. His complete humanity is thus compatible with his belonging to the higher ontological level of deity as well, and being such that his deity as well as his humanity is manifest in his life. We need not hold that Jesus was merely human in order to avoid docetism and uphold the doctrine of the Incarnation. If we did hold this, it is clear that we would be fleeing docetism only to fall into the grasp of psilanthropism, and thereby relinquish the doctrine just as certainly, only in a more currently fashionable way. On a careful understanding of the logic and metaphysics of the Incarnation, we can thus see that Young's 'conundrum' cannot even arise. So, once again, we find that what has been taken to be a problem for the traditional position that it is possible for belief in the Incarnation to be rational is in actuality no problem at all. None of the considerations we have examined so far has had the slightest tendency to block in principle the possibility of rationally discerning God in Christ.

But there is one more major sort of objection many recent critics have lodged against the doctrine of the Incarnation, along with the beliefs about divine-human relations it presupposes. The doctrine of the Incarnation is one component in a much larger doctrinal scheme encompassing the themes of creation, fall, and redemption. Contemporary critics of the traditional renderings of these themes often have pointed out that they originally where enunciated and developed in pre-scientific conditions and thus within the context of a very different sort of world-view from the one which modern scientifically minded people have today. They have then usually gone on to suggest that religious claims which may have made a great deal of sense in their original context have lost much, if not all, of their plausibility in the modern age. It is interesting to note that this is a general point made repeatedly in recent years by many prominent professors of Christian theology as well as by critics avowedly outside the communion of the church.

Now, I think we must recognize that many professedly Christian theologians during the past century or so have appeared a bit overly ready to beat a hasty retreat in the face of almost any specious argument or other consideration against the traditional affirmations of the faith they are supposed to be representing. Often they seem inclined to relinquish or "reinterpret" important doctrines on no better grounds than that those beliefs can appear to some secular critics to be somehow out of step with the march of science. There have been those such as Rudolf Bultmann, for example, who claim to be unable to believe in the literally miraculous while at the same time availing themselves of the comforts of modern technology. But of course such cases as these may be of more interest to psychologists than to anyone seeking to determine the objective status, truth value, or rationality of orthodox Christian beliefs. Occasionally, however, an interesting and even challenging philosophical or theological problem can be extracted from the often vague misgivings of such critics of orthodoxy. Let us consider various ways in which such a challenge might be thought to arise here against the doctrine of the Incarnation.

It has been suggested many times during the past two hundred years that this doctrine, which made a great deal of sense to many people living within the geocentric world-picture of Ptolemaic cosmology, is rendered in some sense absurd by modern accounts of the immensity and nature of our universe. The problem seems to be something like this: During the times when the Chalcedonian understanding of Christ was developed and reigned supreme, it was believed by great numbers of people, including the best educated, that we human beings live in a relatively circumscribed universe, the entirety of which has been created for the benefit of human life, which represents the special crowning act of divine creation, situated, appropriately at the hub of the cosmos, around which all else literally as well as figuratively revolves. Within such an overall perspective, it would have seemed in no way incongruous, but rather could have appeared supremely fitting, that the Creator of all take such interest in his human creatures as to step into his world himself and take a part in the human drama, being enacted, as it was, on the center stage of the universe. An anthropocentric world-view provided the cosmological backdrop and framework for a literally anthropomorphic theology — God become a man. The importance of the earth and the importance of humanity rendered this incarnation of deity intelligible and appropriate.

However, during the past few centuries this world-view, and the framework it provided, has been destroyed, chipped away bit by bit by the onslaught of scientific discovery until nothing of it remains. Actually, it is quite a variety of scientific discoveries, assumptions, hypotheses, speculations, and methodological implications which have seemed to many people to have had the net result of demoting human-kind from its traditionally exalted place in the universe to what can appear to be a relatively unexceptional and terribly insignificant role in the cosmic process. I shall not attempt to delineate here the variety of negative effects modern science has been perceived to have on religious doctrine. Numerous books exist which thoroughly document the so-called "history of the warfare between science and theology." But it will be of some interest to at least indicate a couple of points at which scientific developments have been thought to have this de-valuing impact on our view of humanity, and thus on the system of Christian doctrines, including centrally that of the Incarnation, in which the value of human beings seems clearly to be assumed to be great.

Some critics appear to think that the sheer size of the universe renders humanity unimportant in the cosmos, and Christian doctrine thus implausible. Of course, it is no modern novelty to juxtapose the immensity of the universe to the religious emphasis on man. The psalmist, for example, wrote long ago:

> When I consider Thy heavens, the work of Thy fingers, the moon
> and the stars, which Thou hast ordained: What is man that Thou
> dost take thought of him? And the son of man that Thou dost
> care for him? (Psalm 8:3,4)

This is an expression of an attitude of wonderment, and perhaps astonishment, that amidst the grandeur of the heavens, human beings should be especially valued by God. The attitude of modern critics, however, is that of simple disbelief. Of course, the psalmist was not aware as some of us are today *how* immense the heavens might be. But it is a bit difficult to see exactly what it is about distinctively modern knowledge of the scale of the universe which is thought to show the absurdity of any religious beliefs based on the assumption that the earth and human beings are important to the Creator of all.

Now, it is clear that in many contexts size and value are in direct correlation, the latter depending on the former. For example, all other things being equal, a large army is of greater value than a small one, if one seeks protection of one's country from an enemy. But this dependence of value on size is only relative to some contexts having to do with instrumental value, and clearly does not hold true in either all or even most such contexts. And when it comes to considerations of intrinsic value, the sort of value ascribed to human beings by Christian theology, questions of size or physical magnitude are simply irrelevant. It is just absurd to argue: Small therefore unimportant. Critics often accuse Christian theologians of being anthropomorphic in their thought. But here it seems to be the critics who are anthropomorphizing, or better, anthropopathizing, with the assumption that if there were a God, he would not deign to notice or value anything as small and insignificant on the cosmic scale as the earth and its inhabitants. On the Christian picture, God is sufficiently unlike a man that his attention and care can extend fully to every part of a universe, however large, to the point of being infinite in space and time.

So I think we are safe in concluding that if any discovery of modern science undercuts the Christian belief that God so valued us that he became a man, it will not be any discovery concerning the sheer size of the universe. But as with the link between relative size and value, there have been traditionally believed to be a number of other signs, or even requisites, of human importance which have been undercut by the advance of the sciences. For example, in many primal religions an equation is held between spatial centrality and importance. Anthropologists have found many tribes who hold as a sacred belief the claim that their village, or a fire in the center of the village, is located at the center of the world, or at the center of the entire cosmos. Their importance to the gods is held to be tied to their central location. Such a view also can be seen in the Ptolemaic cosmology and in the many theological and philosophical speculations arising out of that cosmology. In light of this apparently natural equation of importance and spatial centrality, reflected also in non-spatial uses of the notion of centrality, it is easy to understand the resistance many Christian theologians and clerics once felt toward any transition away from a geocentric cosmology. But again, outside a very few contexts of instrumental value considerations, it is simply wrong to think there to be a necessary link between spatial centrality and value. Modern critics who cite the transition from a Ptolemaic to a Copernican to a contemporary cosmology as counting against or as undercutting traditional Christian claims that the earth and humanity are sufficiently important as to render appropriate a divine incarnation on earth are making the same mistake with respect to value theory as the ancients whose views they deride.

There are other lines of reasoning which have been used to support the conclusion that the doctrine of the Incarnation is a cosmologically incongruous claim, but all of them suffer from the same, or similar, sorts of glaring debilities as those two arguments we have just examined. It is a bit surprising to find that a challenge to Christian belief which seems to have such widespread emotional appeal for critics has so little substance when examined closely.

II. Experience and Affirmation

If it is possible that it be rational to believe Jesus to be God Incarnate, how is it possible? On what grounds, or in what circumstances, could a person be rational in believing Jesus to be literally God in human nature? What is required for rationality here? What will suffice? Can it be that any Christians who hold to an incarnational Christology, or more simply ascribe deity to Jesus, are rationally justified in so doing? And if so, how so?

If we survey a good deal of relatively conservative theological literature relevant to the topic, we often find writers of an orthodox bent producing arguments of one kind or another for the deity of Jesus, arguments which they apparently attempt to use to ground the propriety or reasonableness of affirming the doctrine of the Incarnation. A number of these arguments can be put quite concisely as producing their common desired conclusion from a simple two premise structure. Among the arguments frequently to be found are, for example, the following:

(1) *The Soteriological Argument*
   (a) Jesus can forgive us our sins and offer us salvation.
   (b) Only God can forgive us our sins and offer us salvation; thus
   (c) Jesus is God.
(2) *The Liturgical Argument*
   (a) Jesus is properly worshipped.
   (b) Only God is properly worshipped; thus
   (c) Jesus is God.
(3) *The Revelatory Argument*
   (a) Jesus reveals God perfectly.
   (b) Only God can reveal God perfectly; thus
   (c) Jesus is God.

Such arguments, of course, hardly ever appear in such pared-down form. Usually, the (a)-premise is defended as part of the distinctively Christian proclamation throughout the centuries and as either given in Christian experience or assumed in Christian practice. The (b)-premise is seen as a product of conceptual truths concerning the concepts involved: in each case the concept of God and, respectively, the concepts of sin, forgiveness, and salvation in the first argument, that of worship in the second, and revelation in the third.

These are clearly instances of deductively valid argument forms. And if the (b)-premise in each case is a conceptual truth, it follows that it will be reasonable to accept the conclusion of each argument if it is reasonable to accept its (a)-premise. But of course, it is also true that it is reasonable to accept the (a)-premise in each case only if it is reasonable to accept the claim of deity for Jesus. And that is precisely the question at issue. Such arguments as these clearly can serve a function within the context of an incarnational Christian faith — the function of explicitly displaying important logical relations between and among various central commitments of such a faith. A function they cannot perform is that of endowing incarnational belief with a rationality or reasonableness it otherwise would lack apart from their construction.

Can there be a deductively valid argument for the truth of the doctrine of the Incarnation which can function in such a way as to provide a person with a rational belief in it which, without the argument, he would not have, all other things being equal? In order to enhance our perspective on this question, let us look at one more relevant form of deductive argument.

In one of his contributions to the Incarnation debate, Brian Hebblethwaite sketched a number of arguments for the preferability of the Chalcedonian characterization of Jesus over the reduced claims for his status propounded in more recent times.[6] In a response to Hebblethwaite, Keith Ward wrote:

Hebblethwaite introduces the remarkable argument that 'if God might have become a man, but did not, then the reduced claims for what God has done in Christ fail to satisfy'. It is difficult to formalize the argument; but it seems to go like this: 'if x is logically possible; and if we think it better that x, then x.' It is the sort of argument sometimes produced for the doctrine of the Assumption of Mary: 'God could have done it; he should have; so he did.'[7]

Consider for a moment Ward's attempt to formalize the argument he finds in Hebblethwaite. He first offers us the schema

(A) 1. x is logically possible
    2. We think it better that x; thus,
    3. x

and then apparently means to paraphrase it, or at least apply it in such a way that a parallel schema, each of whose premise-forms he apparently takes to be entailed by the corresponding premise-forms of (A), will result which relates directly to theological argument:

(B) 1. God could have done x.
    2. God should have done x; thus,
    3. God did x.

It is Ward's contention that using arguments of the form of (A) in theological matters will yield arguments of the form of (B), and will have, to say the least, untrustworthy results. Ward seems to view the sort of theological argument represented in (B) as having all the benefit of theft over honest toil — that of providing an easy route to results we have no right to.

Of course, the first thing that should be pointed out about what Ward says and seems to assume here is that (A) clearly neither is equivalent to (B) and thus properly paraphrased by it, nor does it even entail (B). The many qualifications we must introduce into a careful definition of omnipotence have taught us that (A)–1 does not entail (B)–1. And certainly (A)–2 does not entail (B)–2. We can be wrong about what states of affairs would be or would have been, better than others; moreover, even when we are right in such judgments, we are not always discovering divine obligations to bring about such states of affairs.

Since (A) does not entail (B), (A) can be a fallacious form of argument without its following that (B) is as well. And this, as a matter of fact, is the case. Arguments of the form of (A)

are obviously fallacious. The world does not necessarily conform itself to our preferences. But, interestingly, arguments
of the form of (B) are not fallacious. The (B) schema is a deductively valid one, given the concept of God as a necessarily good
being. If we could know, concerning some possible action, both
that God could have done it and that he should have done
it, then we also could know that he did it. Applying this to
the doctrine of the Incarnation, if we knew or had reason to
believe the two premises in the following argument, our knowledge or reasonable belief would be transmitted to its conclusion:

(C) 1. God could have become incarnate in human nature
       as Jesus of Nazareth.
    2. God should have become incarnate in human nature
       as Jesus of Nazareth; thus,
    3. God did become incarnate in human nature as Jesus
       of Nazareth.

As I have indicated already, a couple of simple metaphysical
distinctions will suffice to defend the truth of (C)–1. But, in
light of the epistemic realities for religious belief with which
we live, it is difficult to see how anyone might be in better
epistemic position with respect to (C)–2 than with respect to
(C)–3. It is thus hard to see how the reasonableness of a belief
that (C)–3 could be thought to be based on or grounded in
an argument such as (C) operating on an independently reasonable belief that (C)–2 and (C)–1, given the epistemic conditions we are all in with respect to God's actions, and the principles of his actions.

It seems to me that vast numbers of Christians are reasonable
in believing Jesus to be God Incarnate, and it is my guess that
many of them have never reflected on or in any other way entertained proposition (C)–2, the claim that God should have
become incarnate, and have no reasonable belief that it is true.
Moreover, many who have considered it would, I suspect, maintain a properly pious agnosticism about it, while whole-
heartedly and reasonably endorsing the doctrine of the Incarnation. And further, I would expect that any Christians who

would affirm (C)–2 would do so on the basis of, among other things, their prior belief that Jesus was God Incarnate. So even in their case, the reasonableness of the latter belief would in no way depend on the reasonableness of the former—quite the opposite.

I have introduced this excursus into Ward's remarks along the way to making a very simple point. If it is reasonable to believe Jesus to be God Incarnate, that reasonableness is not likely produced by means of, or grounded in, any such deductive argument. It seems to be the case that deductive arguments for the Incarnation will always have at least one premise whose positive epistemic status is no greater or more obvious than that of the doctrine itself. In the Soteriological, Liturgical, and Revelatory arguments, it will be reasonable to believe the premise in question, at best, *if and only if* it is reasonable to believe Jesus to be God Incarnate. In the argument (C), gleaned from Ward's remarks on Hebblethwaite, it will be reasonable to believe the more controversial premise at best *only if* it is reasonable to believe in the Incarnation. In none of these cases do we find a prior, independent reasonableness transmitted to and conferred upon the incarnational belief from more evident beliefs. So if it can be, or is, reasonable to believe Jesus to be God Incarnate, then most likely that reasonableness will neither consist in nor be provided by the having of such a simple deductive argument.

It is natural to ask next whether some form of inductive, or nondeductive, argument could render belief in Jesus' deity reasonable. Consider for a moment that form of reasoning in which Nicodemus engaged concerning Jesus, and from which this chapter began. We can represent the structure of his argument as

(N) 1. Jesus performed a certain class of acts *M* (acts such as traditionally have been classed as miracles)
　　 2. No one can perform acts of class *M* unless he is a teacher come from God; thus,
　　 3. Jesus was a teacher come from God.

And again, this is a deductively valid argument concerning the status of Jesus. As Nicodemus appears to have reasoned to the conclusion that Jesus was a teacher come from God, many Christians of conservative theological orientation talk as if they themselves have reasoned, or as if they are convinced that a rational non-believer could reason, from empirically ascertainable facts about the circumstances, character, and deeds of Jesus to the much stronger conclusion that he was and is God Incarnate. They could have in mind an argument such as (N), where M now presumably would include, say, postresurrection activities of the risen Christ, and which would employ a substituted second premise such as

2'. No one can perform acts of class M unless he is God,

from which it would follow validly that Jesus was God. Or they could have in mind a probabilistic transform of the revised (N), in which case the simple, categorical claim of deity for Jesus would not validly follow, but the weaker claim that it is probable that Jesus was divine would. Or it could be the case that many Christians who reason about Jesus in the tradition of Nicodemus have something in mind which cannot be captured by any such simple, two-step deductive argument. Perhaps there is a complex non-deductive form of argument to the best explanation which they have in mind, and which cannot be so simply represented. Thus, they would argue that the best explanation for a certain range of facts about Jesus is that he was God Incarnate.

On the one hand, it is clear that most mature Christians who affirm the divinity of Jesus see their belief as anchored in the empirical realm. They see their incarnational belief as in accord with their own personal experience, with the experience of other Christians throughout the centuries, and with the apparent though sometimes elusive manifestations of deity in the empirical realm which the New Testament documents appear to record surrounding the person of Jesus. But on the other hand, it seems not to be the case that there is any single, isolable form of non-deductive argument typically relied upon by such Christians to get from distinct facts about the portrayal of Jesus in the New Testament, from facts about the experience of Jesus on the part of fellow believers through the ages, or from features of their own experience to a conclusion that Jesus is God the Son, the Second Person of the Divine Trinity. Nor is it obvious that any account of their reasonableness in so believing must involve the production of such an argument.

It does not seem that the reasonableness of incarnational belief is provided by deductive arguments from premises it is independently reasonable to believe, nor does it seem to be provided by any single sort of non-deductive argument consciously entertained or used by believers. Could it then be a simple function of direct experience? Could it be the case that traditional Christians have just *seen* Jesus to be God Incarnate, and that their belief in his deity, thus generated, is reasonable precisely in light of that experience?

Grace Jantzen once wrote:

> Clearly, any doctrine which wishes to affirm that Jesus of Nazareth is God the Son, the Second Person of the Holy Trinity, is going well beyond the boundary of empirical observability. Indeed, what would it be *like* to make that sort of observation? Even the question seems misphrased. No list of empirical data, whether these are taken strictly as sense data or more broadly as observation of speech and behaviour patterns could ever entail the conclusion reached by the centurion in the Gospel: "Truly this man was the Son of God."[8]

Sense data reports underdetermine statements about physical objects. Reports about the disposition and behavior of physical objects (such as arms, legs, mouths, and even brains) arguably underdetermine claims about the distinctively mental properties of persons. And claims about the divine can seem to be even more remote from any reports about what is experienced in the empirical realm. For example, a few years ago an article appeared in which it was argued that not even God could know from observation, or even from observation enhanced by inductive reasoning, that he is God, i.e. that he exemplifies the distinctively divine attributes.[9] Consider omnipotence alone. No matter how many extraordinary tasks a being has attempted to perform and has carried out successfully with no difficulty or strain whatsoever, it will not follow from his record of accomplishments, however astounding, that he is literally omnipotent. Thus, no matter what we observe a being do in the empirical arena, a full report of our observations will not entail the proposition that the being in question is omnipotent. If seeing that an individual is God requires seeing that he is omnipotent, necessarily good, omnipresent, omniscient, ontologically independent, and the like, then the prospects for just directly seeing that Jesus is God look pretty dim, to say the least.

But does experiencing Jesus as divine require this sort of 'seeing-that' relation? Clearly, in undergoing the processes which sense data theorists have characterized as the having of percepts or sense data, we most often reasonably take ourselves to be experiencing physical objects. Likewise, in experiencing the dispositions and behaviors of certain sorts of physical objects in certain sorts of circumstances, we reasonably take ourselves to be experiencing or observing the mental qualities of other persons, e.g. their anger, happiness, irritation, tranquility. It is true that if the observational experience of a table were to be reported in purely sense data language (supposing that to be possible), the report would not entail any appropriately related proposition about a physical object. But this does not prevent our sense experience being experience of physical objects. Likewise, the lack of entailments between reports about Jesus cast in this-worldly terms and the appropriate propositions concerning his deity need not preclude the possibility of an experience of Jesus as the infinite God Incarnate through the sort of finite range of experience of him available to an ordinary human believer.

Suppose that, as many theologians have suggested through the centuries, there is an innate human capacity which, when properly functioning, allows us to see God, or, to put it another way, to recognize God when we see him, in the starry heavens above or in the moral law within. If there is such a capacity to recognize God both in his products, and where he is distinctively present and active, and if he is personally present and active in the life of Jesus of Nazareth as the ultimate subject of that life, then we would expect him to be recognized in his incarnate form by those whose relevant capacity for seeing is sufficiently unimpeded.

Many children believe that Jesus is divine upon being told so by their elders. They believe it on testimony. They do not believe it on the basis of any argument or inference from the general reliability of testimony, from the particular reliability of the elders in question, or from any fact or belief about testimony at all. They just believe it on the occasion of being told it, like so much else they believe. And surely they are not irrational in so believing. But perhaps small children are not yet at any age of epistemic accountability. Perhaps. As children mature, we expect them to start hooking up their beliefs into coherent pictures of the world. What was once a properly basic belief for the young child, a belief not based on any epistemically more secure beliefs by standard basing relations, and not requiring such basing, may later come to stand in such relations in the young person's noetic structure that it is no longer among his basic beliefs, but that it is nonetheless still among his beliefs that it is reasonable for him to have.

Likewise, many people who become Christians, or who come to see Jesus as divine, come to believe in his divinity upon seeing the portrait of him in the Gospels, or upon experiencing what they take to be his presence in prayer or his power transforming their lives. They do not base their belief on any argument or inference from the details of the scriptural account or from the features of their own personal experience. They merely find themselves believing on having some such appropriate originating experience or experiences, experiences which they take to be experiences of God Incarnate. But as the Christian who holds such a belief matures in his faith, he comes to know much better the testimony of scripture and of other believers to the reality of what he has taken himself to have experienced. I want to suggest that the Christian who originally attains a belief that Jesus is God Incarnate either from testimony or from his own experiences, of the sorts indicated, can reasonably take up such a belief, and as he matures, reasonably take much of what he subsequently learns of the Christian story, and from his own experience, to be corroboration of that belief. Instances in the life of Jesus, for example, as recounted in the Gospels, can reasonably be thought by a responsible reader to attest to his divinity. As we have seen in discussing the conundrum for incarnational belief which Francis Young attempted to formulate, the metaphysics of the Incarnation allow Jesus' divinity to be manifested through displays of knowledge and power often categorized as miraculous, as well as in other ways. And, despite what some critics seem to imply, one need not be exceedingly naive concerning the vicissitudes of New Testament criticism in order to be reasonable in so reading the Gospels as to find corroboration in them for a belief in the Incarnation.

The dynamics of reasonable belief are extremely complex and are far beyond the scope of the present essay to lay out in any general way, even for the restricted, though highly controversial, class of religious beliefs such as the one which is our proper focus. One feature of reasonable belief maintenance, however, which should be mentioned here is the following: Whenever one holds a belief which is challenged by apparently powerful considerations which one understands, one's maintaining of the belief will continue to be reasonable to the same degree only if one is able to locate a sufficient response to the newly introduced challenge. For many sophisticated Christians of an orthodox persuasion in recent years, the challenges to the doctrine of the Incarnation which we have been reviewing in this study have constituted potentially the most difficult obstacles to the continued reasonableness of their belief that Jesus was God Incarnate. The availability of such perspectives as I have been attempting to sketch out constitutes, I think, a response to those challenges sufficient to block any negative net impact on the reasonableness of endorsing the incarnational claim. A traditional believer who has grown in the maturation of his faith and who has faced and met such challenges as those we have considered can be held to have attained the sort of corroboration and defense of his incarnational belief which can secure the reasonableness of his maintaining that conception of the status of Jesus which most often arises from the simple founts of testimony and experience.

If there is an innate human capacity which, when properly functioning, allows us to recognize God when we see him, then if Jesus is God Incarnate, it is clear that there are widespread and deeply rooted impediments to this capacity's functioning. It seems likely, in light of what has just been adumbrated, that a reasonable belief that Jesus is God Incarnate will arise and flourish only with the removal of some of these impediments from the life of a person. And this is just the insight we can derive from the original Nicodemus story when we see that Jesus' response to Nicodemus' simple *modus tollens* argument, whose conclusion fell well short of the mark, is not the glaring *non sequitur* it can initially appear, but rather is a profound indication of the truth, or rather of the only way to come to the truth about who he is. The story, in John 3:1-3, from which we began this essay, will bear repeating:

> Now there was a man of the Pharisees, named Nicodemus, a ruler of the Jews. This man came to Jesus by night and said to him, "Rabbi, we know that you are a teacher come from God; for no one can do these signs that you do, unless God is with him."

And then the key:

> Jesus answered him, "Truly, truly I say to you, unless one is born anew he cannot see the kingdom of God."

In Matthew 17:15-17 we find this exchange between Jesus and his disciples:

> He said to them: "But who do you say that I am?" Simon Peter replied, "You are the living Christ, the Son of the living God." And Jesus answered him, "Blessed are you, Simon Bar-Jona! For flesh and blood has not revealed this to you, but my Father who is in heaven.

And in the Apostle Paul's first letter to the church at Corinth (I Corinthians 12:3), we find the succinct claim that

> . . . no one can say "Jesus is Lord" except by the Holy Spirit.

A full account of the epistemic status of Christian doctrine would be quite complex and would require, at its core, what we might call a Spirit Epistemology. The remarks of the present essay have been laid out in broad strokes and have hinted at no more than a very few elements of such an account in even the case of the one tenet of orthodox Christian belief which is our present concern. Yet, despite the severe limitations of what I have undertaken to say here, it seems to me that on the basis of the few considerations we have been able to reflect on, however briefly, we can conclude that from these quarters, there seems to be no obstacle in principle to the acceptability of the widespread Christian assumption that it is possible that it be rational to believe Jesus to be God Incarnate.

Notes

INTRODUCTION

1. J. L. Tomkinson, "Divine Sempiternity and A-temporality," *Religious Studies* 18 (June 1982), 177.
2. Ibid., pp. 186–187.

1. THE GOD OF ABRAHAM, ISAAC, AND ANSELM

1. W. R. Matthews, *God in Christian Thought and Experience* (London: Nisbet, 1930), 104.
2. This parallel was first suggested to me by Chris Menzel.
3. For a full account of the conditions under which this can plausibly be held, see essay 10, "Necessary Beings."
4. For a defense of the claim that there are such maxima, see William Mann, "The Divine Attributes." *American Philosophical Quarterly* 12 (April 1975), 151–159.
5. The attempt is made in R. G. Swinburne's, *The Coherence of Theism* (Oxford: Clarendon Press, 1977), chapter 8 and p. 202, and in *The Existence of God* (Oxford, Oxford University Press, 1979), 97–102.
6. Morris Lazerowitz, "On a Property of a Perfect Being," *Mind* 92 (April 1983), 257–263.
7. For the arguments referred to, see Norman Kretzmann, "Omniscience and Immutability," *The Journal of Philosophy* 64 (1966), 409–421, and David Blumenfeld, "On the Compossibility of the Divine Attributes," *Philosophical Studies* 34 (July 1978), 91–103.
8. I have tried to show this with respect to some difficult problem cases in a number of recent papers, including "Impeccability," *Analysis* 43 (March 1983), 106–112; "Duty and Divine Goodness," essay 2 of this volume; and "Properties, Modalities, and God," essay 5. For a well known, extensive argument to this effect, see Swinburne's book *The Coherence of Theism*.

2. DUTY AND DIVINE GOODNESS

1. The principle stated here circumvents well known counter-examples to the stronger Principle of Alternate Possibilities. See for example Harry Frankfurt's "Alternate Possibilities and Moral Responsibility," *The Journal of Philosophy* 66 (1969), 829–839.

2. Jonathan Edwards, *Freedom of the Will*, ed. Paul Ramsey (New Haven, 1957), 283.

3. The argument here treats God as a temporal agent lacking power to change the past, but this is strictly unnecessary for the generation of our problem. Note also that the inference bears a superficial resemblance to, but on reflection can be seen not to commit, a famous modal fallacy.

4. Bruce Reichenbach, *Evil and a Good God* (New York: Fordham University Press, 1982), chapter 7.

5. Nelson Pike, "Omnipotence and God's Ability to Sin," *American Philosophical Quarterly* 6 (July 1969), 208–216.

6. I argue this in "Impeccability," *Analysis* 43 (March 1983), 106–112.

7. I have argued this in a manner relevant to the present discussion in essay 5, "Properties, Modalities, and God."

8. The arguments appear in "Properties, Modalities, and God," section IV.

9. R. L. Franklin, *Free Will and Determinism* (New York: Humanities Press, 1968), 41.

10. See Brand Blanshard, "The Case For Determinism," in *Determinism and Freedom in the Age of Modern Science*, ed. Sidney Hook (New York: New York University Press, 1958).

3. THE NECESSITY OF GOD'S GOODNESS

1. See, for example, Bruce Reichenbach's *Evil and a Good God* (New York, Fordham University Press, 1982), chapter seven.

2. Lawrence Resnick, "God and the Best Possible World," *American Philosophical Quarterly* 10 (October 1973), 313–317.

3. See, for example, Bruce Reichenbach, "Must God Create the Best Possible World?" *International Philosophical Quarterly* 19 (June 1979), 203–212; and George Schlesinger's "The Problem of Evil and the Problem of Suffering," *American Philosophical Quarterly* 1 (July 1964), 244–247.

4. See Robert Adams, "Must God Create the Best?" *Philosophical Review* 81 (1972), 317–332.

5. Here and elsewhere, the theist will depart from a standard view

of subjunctive conditionals with necessarily false antecedents and separate the sheep from the goats, affirming some, such as the one just given in the text, on good grounds, while denying others.

6. Nelson Pike, "Omnipotence and God's Ability to Sin," *American Philosophical Quarterly* 6 (July 1969), 208–216.

7. Peter Geach, *Providence and Evil* (Cambridge, Cambridge University Press, 1977), chapters one and two.

8. For examples of the Anselmian response, see Joshua Hoffman, "Can God Do Evil?" *Southern Journal of Philosophy* 17 (1979), 213–220; and Jerome Gellman, "Omnipotence and Immutability," *The New Scholasticism* 51 (1977), 21–37.

9. The most complete elucidation of omnipotence to date appears in Alfred J. Freddoso and Thomas P. Flint, "Maximal Power," in *The Existence and Nature of God*, ed. Alfred J. Freddoso (Notre Dame, The University of Notre Dame Press, 1983), 81–113. This is an account fully consistent with what I have said.

10. Theodore Guleserian, "God and Possible Worlds: The Modal Problem of Evil," *Nous* 17 (May 1983), 221–238.

11. Ibid., 234.

12. Reichenbach, *Evil and a Good God*, chapter seven, and Stephen Davis, *Logic and the Nature of God* (London, MacMillan Press, 1983), chapter six. See also Theodore Guleserian, "Can Moral Perfection be an Essential Attribute?" *Philosophy and Phenomenological Research* 45 (1985), 219–241.

13. The discussion can be found in essay 2, "Duty and Divine Goodness."

14. I have produced the arguments for this most fully in essay 5, "Properties, Modalities, and God."

15. "Duty and Divine Goodness," section IV.

16. R. G. Swinburne, *The Coherence of Theism* (Oxford, Oxford University Press, 1977), 146 and 202. The argument is repeated in *The Existence of God* (Oxford, Oxford University Press, 1979), 97–102. See also Keith Ward, *Rational Theology and the Creativity of God* (Oxford, Basil Blackwell, 1982), chapters 6 and 8.

17. W. R. Carter, "Omnipotence and Sin," *Analysis* 42 (March 1982), 102–105.

18. "Impeccability," *Analysis* 43 (March 1983), 106–112.

19. In fact, the same reasoning shows that regardless of whether omnipotence and omniscience are exemplified necessarily or contingently, if they are strongly enduring properties of God—such that he cannot cease to have them if he exemplifies them at all—it also follows that if he is good at any time, he can never thereafter cease to be good.

20. Pike, "Omnipotence and God's Ability to Sin," 210–211.

21. R. H. Kane, "Nature, Plenitude, and Sufficient Reason," *American Philosophical Quarterly* 13 (January 1976), 23–31.

22. See J. N. Findlay's "Can God's Existence be Disproved," *Mind* 57 (1948), 176–183.

23. Saul Kripke, "Naming and Necessity," in *Semantics of Natural Language*, ed. Donald Davidson and Gilbert Harman, 2nd ed. (Dordrecht, D. Reidel, 1972), 266 (Lecture One).

24. Guleserian's meta-modal intuition which conflicts with those of the theist is backed up by no such grounding framework.

25. See essay 1, "The God of Abraham, Isaac, and Anselm."

4. PERFECTION AND POWER

1. W. R. Carter, "Impeccability Revisited," *Analysis* 45:1 (1985), 54.

2. See Desmond Paul Henry, *The Logic of St. Anselm* (Oxford, Clarendon Press, 1967), 156–157.

5. PROPERTIES, MODALITIES AND GOD

1. It should be clear, or at least should become clear, that I am presenting the modalities of stability as being only distinct from, not logically independent of, the standard modalities of necessity and possibility. The former are just a result of combining the latter in certain ways with the metaphysical notions of beginning-to-be and ceasing-to-be.

2. I owe the disjunctive formulation of this category to an example presented by Chris Menzel.

3. For anyone who hesitates treating existence as a property of individuals and modally characterizing its exemplification, all that I have said here can be translated simply into talk about the necessary and stable exemplification of an object's essential properties. An individual has strongly stable existence, for instance, just in case it instantiates its essential properties in a strongly stable manner.

4. Richard Swinburne, *The Coherence of Theism* (Oxford: Oxford University Press, 1977), 214.

5. See for example the book Jonah, chapter three, and Genesis 18:23–32.

6. Temporalists, theists who hold that God is a temporal individual, often claim that their position accords with the biblical depiction of God better than does the traditional philosophical view that God is atemporal or timeless. I think temporalists are justified

in distinguishing the pervasive biblical belief *that* God is an agent in time from particular biblical assertions *about* his temporal agency. In keeping with this distinction, I am concerned here to articulate a conception of divine immutability compatible with the former, not necessarily all of the latter. Thus, neither I nor any temporalist is bound to square his philosophical views with a literalist reading of the problematic passages.

7. I have advanced the second argument, and an earlier version of the first in "Impeccability," *Analysis* 43 (March 1983), 106–112. That paper is a response to an article whose entire argument turns on a failure to distinguish the modalities of stability from the standard notions of necessity and contingency.

8. The qualification is introduced since a sinless being is conceivable who is in a state of moral innocence and lacks even the concept of sin. Such a being could not intend never to act in a way which for him was inconceivable. And he need not intend never to sin in order to be sinless. But clearly God is not such a being.

6. ON GOD AND MANN: A VIEW OF DIVINE SIMPLICITY

1. William E. Mann, "Divine Simplicity," *Religious Studies* 18 (1982), 451–471; and "Simplicity and Immutability in God," *International Philosophical Quarterly* 23 (1983), 267–276 (a version of this paper originally was read at the American Philosophical Association Eastern Division meeting in 1981).

2. The contemporary literature on simplicity consists in only a handful of articles and some short discussions in a few books devoted primarily to other topics. The articles include Daniel Bennett, "The Divine Simplicity," *The Journal of Philosophy* 66 (October 1966), 629–637; Richard R. LaCroix, "Augustine on the Simplicity of God," *The New Scholasticism* 51 (Autumn 1977), 453–469; William J. Wainwright, "Augustine on God's Simplicity: A Reply," *The New Scholasticism* 53 (Winter 1979), 118–123; and a response by La Croix entitled "Wainright, Augustine, and God's Simplicity: A Final Word," *The New Scholasticism* 53 (Winter 1979), 124–127. Especially noteworthy is a recently published essay by Norman Kretzmann and Eleonore Stump entitled "Absolute Simplicity," *Faith and Philosophy* 2 (October 1985), 353–382. The literature however, may soon grow significantly, as a number of papers are now being prepared by philosophers who seek to analyze and evaluate the doctrine in one form or another.

3. For the best known contemporary discussion of these problems,

see Alvin Plantinga, *Does God Have a Nature?*, (Milwaukee: Marquette University Press, 1980), 26–61.

4. Ibid.

5. This becomes especially clear in Mann's later article "Simplicity and Immutability in God."

6. Mann, "Divine Simplicity," 465.

7. This is discussed in essay 1, "The God of Abraham, Isaac, and Anselm."

8. An instance of *F* need not depend for its identity on the continuing existence of a particular instance of *G*; rather, it requires only some instance or other of *G*.

9. Interesting discussions of these distinctions and claims are to be found in Mann's earlier piece, "The Divine Attributes," *The American Philosophical Quarterly* 12 (1975), 151–159.

10. See Mann's "Simplicity and Immutability in God," 272–276.

11. The way in which the principle of the indiscernibility of identicals governs the acceptability of identity claims is sketched out in chapter six of my *Understanding Identity Statements*, (Scots Philosophical Monographs, Aberdeen: Aberdeen University Press, 1984).

12. Problems with this distinction were alleged by La Croix but can easily be circumvented.

13. See for example Pike's "Omnipotence and God's Ability to Sin," *American Philosophical Quarterly* 6 (July 1969), 208–216.

14. I have discussed the modalities of stability in essay 5, "Properties, Modalities, and God."

7. GOD AND THE WORLD: A LOOK AT PROCESS THEOLOGY

1. For recent criticisms, see Alvin Plantinga *Does God Have a Nature?* (Milwaukee: Marquette University Press, 1980), 26–61, and essay 6, of this volume, "On God and Mann: A View of Divine Simplicity."

2. For some of the best attempts to develop and defend the classical conception in recent years see Norman Kretzmann and Eleonore Stump, "Eternity," *The Journal of Philosophy* 68 (1981), 429–458, and William E. Mann "Simplicity and Immutability in God," *International Philosophical Quarterly* 23 (1983), 267–276.

3. For an adumbration of this view see essay 10, "Necessary Beings." A further articulation of the view is attempted in essay 9, "Absolute Creation."

4. Barry L. Whitney "Divine Immutability in Process Philosophy and Contemporary Thomism," *Horizons* 7 (Spring 1980), 67.

5. Ibid.

6. Wainwright discusses this in a paper entitled "Monotheism," presented at the Research Conference in the Philosophy of Religion held at the University of Nebraska-Lincoln in April 1984, sponsored by the National Endowment for the Humanities.

7. In Wainwright: draft of "Monotheism" read at Nebraska.

8. Blaise Pascal, *Pensées* trans. A. J. Krailsheimer (New York: Penguin Books, 1966), 156.

9. Charles Hartshorne, *Omnipotence and Other Theological Mistakes* (Albany, New York: State University of New York Press, 1984), 35.

9. ABSOLUTE CREATION

1. Henceforth, the term 'Platonism' shall be used only to refer to the view that abstract objects such as properties and propositions have objective ontological status. Many Platonists understand their position to entail that these objects are metaphysically and causally independent entities. I hope to show that such independence need not be thought to follow from even the strong form of abstract object realism which holds these entities to have the modal status of necessity. Thus, by 'Platonism' I do not mean to refer to a position which espouses such independence.

2. See James F. Ross, "Creation II," in *The Existence and Nature of God*, ed. Alfred J. Freddoso (Notre Dame: University of Notre Dame Press, 1983), 115–141, and Nicholas Wolterstorff, *On Universals* (Chicago: University of Chicago Press, 1970).

3. Alvin Plantinga, *Does God Have A Nature?* (Milwaukee: Marquette University Press, 1980).

4. Wolterstorff, *On Universals*, chapter 12.

5. See for example *Romans* 11:36.

6. *Summa Theologiae*, I, Question 44, First Article.

7. The view being articulated is compatible with a limited existentialism according to which not all propositions are necessarily existent, in particular, singular propositions like *Reagan is a farmer*. This proposition, for example, might be thought of as the content of God's thinking (though of course not *believing*): Reagan exemplifies *being a farmer*, and hence might plausibly be taken to exist in a world only if Reagan does, since there can be good reasons to hold that not even God can think *of* a particular object that never exists. This point is due to Christopher Menzel.

8. See, for example, George Bealer, *Quality and Concept* (Oxford: Clarendon Press, 1982), chapter six.

9. Possible truth can be handled similarly. A proposition like

Reagan is a farmer is possible in virtue of how God conceives Reagan's nature, i.e. in virtue of the fact that the divine idea which Reagan essentially and uniquely exemplifies is such that it is possibly co-exemplified with the property of being a farmer. One thus might understand the truth value of propositions like *Possibly, Reagan is a farmer* or *Possibly, Reagan does not exist* in terms of Reagan's haecceity.

10. This is argued in essay 3, "The Necessity of God's Goodness." Problems which arise from this view are further discussed in essay 2, "Duty and Divine Goodness."

11. For recent discussions of possibilism's problems, see Plantinga's *Does God Have A Nature?*, 95–146, and Eleonore Stump's review of that book in *The Thomist* 47 (1983), 616–622.

12. On this see essay 2, "Duty and Divine Goodness," and Thomas P. Flint's "The Problem of Divine Freedom," *American Philosophical Quarterly* 20 (July 1983), 255–264.

13. See Norman Kretzmann, "Abraham, Isaac, and Euthyphro: God and the Basis of Morality," in *Hamartia: The Concept of Error in the Western Tradition*, ed. Donald Stump et. al., (New York: Edwin Mellen Press, 1983).

14. Anthony O'Hear, *Experience, Explanation, and Faith: An Introduction to the Philosophy of Religion* (London: Routledge and Kegan Paul, 1984), 51.

15. These are delineated in essay 6, "On God and Mann: A View of Divine Simplicity."

16. For example, Clement Dore in *Theism* (Dordrecht: D. Reidel, 1984) states that "nothing can be the cause of its own existence" (p. 51); in *Experience, Explanation, and Faith*, O'Hear remarks that "Self-causation is a nonsense, strictly speaking" (p. 122); and, speaking of the existentially self-sufficient being whose existence is aimed at by the Cosmological Argument, Keith Ward has said with great assurance that "it certainly cannot depend upon itself for its existence . . .", *Rational Theology and the Creativity of God* (Oxford: Basil Blackwell, 1982), 10.

17. Blaise Pascal, *Pensées*, trans. A. J. Krailsheimer (New York: Penguin Books, 1966), 169.

18. The suggestion that there could possibly be a reconciliation of insights from these two apparently exclusive and fundamental stances toward the abstract and modal realms has been made recently by Plantinga in his Presidential Address to the Western Division of the American Philosophical Association, "How to be an Anti-Realist," and by R. M. Adams in "Divine Necessity," *The Journal of Philosophy* 80 (November 1983), 751, although neither has yet attempted

to develop that suggestion. Some implications of the reconciliation as developed here for the Anselmian conception of God and the ontological argument are traced out in essay 10, "Necessary Beings."

10. NECESSARY BEINGS

1. R. Kane, "The Modal Ontological Argument," *Mind* 93 (1984), 336–350.

2. That Kane ascribes to the traditional Anselmian a consistency conception of logical possibility can be inferred fairly directly from remarks on pages 338 and, especially, 342–343. He says ". . . it seems clear that traditional thinkers like Anselm . . . would have agreed that they were talking about logical necessity and possibility in this broadly logical sense" (pp. 342–343), a few sentences after using the phrase 'logical possibility in the broadest, unconditional sense' to express the conception of modality "where the logically possible is that which is not self contradictory, and the logically necessary is that whose negation is self contradictory" (p. 342). His talk of possibility "in the broadly logical sense" here can be a bit confusing on this point, in that "broadly logical" possibility is usually contrasted in recent literature with possibility in the "narrowly logical" (i.e. first order consistency) sense; whereas Kane appears to use the phrase only to mark a contrast with what is often called 'relative possibility' (a conception of modality on which universal symmetry of accessibility relations does not hold). It is not clear that Kane himself endorses the consistency conception of possibility. Some of the argument of his paper can be taken as an attempt to show that the Anselmian will get into trouble by accepting this conception, a conception which can appear to be involved in one way of defending the proposition that maximal perfection is possibly exemplified.

3. See for example Swinburne's book *The Coherence of Theism* (Oxford: Clarendon Press, 1977).

4. I have argued this in essay 1, "The God of Abraham, Isaac, and Anselm."

5. Kane, "The Modal Ontological Argument," p. 347.

6. Ibid., p. 348.

7. This line is developed in essay 3, "The Necessity of God's Goodness."

8. Alvin Plantinga, *The Nature of Necessity* (Oxford: Clarendon Press, 1974), 219–221.

9. Clement Dore, *Theism* (Dordrecht: D. Reidel, 1984), 15.

10. This picture is developed and defended in essay 9, "Absolute Creation."

11. For a brief general argument that the theist can better account for our knowledge of necessary truths see R. M. Adams, "Divine Necessity," *The Journal of Philosophy* 80 (November 1983), 749–752.

12. Of course, if he is justified in judging a certain reading of (iv) to be inconsistent with (i)–(iii), a theist can be justified in denying the truth of this reading of (iv), rather than merely refusing to accept it, for the very reason that it is judged logically incompatible with other of his commitments, namely (i)–(iii).

11. PASCALIAN WAGERING

1. Blaise Pascal, *Pensées*, trans. A. J. Krailsheimer (New York: Penguin Books, 1966), 150.

2. Pascal, pensée 190, page 86. Hereafter citations from the *Pensées* will all be from the edition cited above, and will be given by the pensée numbering therein adopted.

3. Such a claim has been made or implied by many theists in different contexts. Recently, for example, Peter Geach has written: "Now for those who believe in an Almighty God, a man's every act is an act either of obeying or of ignoring or of defying that God . . . ", "The Moral Law and the Law of God," in Paul Helm, ed. *Divine Commands and Morality* (Oxford: Oxford University Press, 1980), 173. It is easy to see how ignoring and defying God could be categorized together as acting as if there is no God.

4. One of the best recent explications of this sort of problem is Michael Martin's essay "Pascal's Wager as an Argument for Not Believing in God," *Religious Studies* 19 (1983), 57–64.

5. From N.R. Hanson, *What I Do Not Believe and Other Essays*, ed. Stephen Toulmin and Harry Woolf (Dordrecht: D. Reidel, 1972), 323. I have explored the views of Hanson and Scriven in "Agnosticism," *Analysis* 45 (1985), 219–224, from which the present section derives some of its points.

6. Hanson, 310.

7. Michael Scriven, *Primary Philosophy* (New York: McGraw Hill, 1966), 103.

8. Ibid.

9. The argument is presented in Plantinga's major paper "Reason and Belief in God," in *Faith and Rationality*, ed. A. Plantinga and N. Wolterstorff, (Notre Dame: The University of Notre Dame Press, 1983), 27–29.

10. I lay out a different ground for rational doubt here in "Agnosticism."

11. The Principle of Indifference has recently received impressive

defense at the hands of George N. Schlesinger. See his book *The Intelligibility of Nature* (Aberdeen: Aberdeen University Press, 1985).

12. Terence Penelhum, *Religion and Rationality* (New York: Random House, 1971), 211–219.

12. RATIONALITY AND THE CHRISTIAN REVELATION

1. John Wisdom, *Paradox and Discovery*, (Oxford: Basil Blackwell, 1965), 19-20.

2. Grace Jantzen, "Incarnation and Epistemology," *Theology* 83 (May 1983), 171.

3. The challenge is addressed in chapter nine of *Understanding Identity Statements* (Aberdeen: Aberdeen University Press and Humanities Press, 1984), in "Divinity, Humanity, and Death," *Religious Studies* 19 (December 1983), 451–458, and in "Incarnational Anthropology," *Theology* 87 (September 1984), 344-350. It is explored in much greater detail in chapters one through six of *The Logic of God Incarnate* (Ithaca: Cornell University Press, 1986).

4. One contemporary theologian who has hinted repeatedly at the importance of this view is Brian Hebblethwaite. See for example his article "The Propriety of the Doctrine of the Incarnation as a Way of Interpreting Christ," *Scottish Journal of Theology* 33 (1980), 201–222.

5. Frances Young, "Can There Be Any Evidence," *Incarnation and Myth: The Debate Continued*, ed. Michael Goulder (Grand Rapids: Eerdmans, 1979), 62.

6. Brian Hebblethwaite, "Incarnation — The Essence of Christianity?" *Theology* 80 (1977).

7. Keith Ward, "Incarnation or Inspiration — A False Dichotomy?" *Theology* 80 (1977).

8. Grace Jantzen, "Incarnation and Epistemology," 173, 174.

9. See Richard Creel, "Can God Know That He is God?" *Religious Studies* 16 (June 1980), 195-201.